OUTRAGEOUS
FORTUNE

OUTRAGEOUS FORTUNE

Growing Up at Leeds Castle

ANTHONY RUSSELL

St. Martin's Press New York

www.stmartins.com

Design by Steven Seighman

Library of Congress Cataloging-in-Publication Data

Russell, Anthony, 1952–
    Outrageous fortune : growing up at Leeds Castle / Anthony Russell.—First edition.
        pages   cm
    ISBN 978-1-250-00601-1 (hardcover)
    ISBN 978-1-250-03137-2 (e-book)
    1. Russell, Anthony, 1952—Childhood and youth. 2. Leeds Castle (England) 3. Kent (England)—Social life and customs. 4. Nobility—Great Britain—History—20th century. 5. Baillie, Olive, 1899–1974. I. Title.
    DA664.L38R87 2013
    942.2'375—dc23
    [B]

                              2013016546

St. Martin's Press books may be purchased for educational, business, or promotional use. For information on bulk purchases, please contact Macmillan Corporate and Premium Sales Department at 1-800-221-7945, extension 5442, or write specialmarkets@macmillan.com.

First Edition: November 2013

10 9 8 7 6 5 4 3 2 1

For Catherine and Odo

CONTENTS

1. A View from the Pram   1
2. The Castle Way   14
3. Son of Sponge   31
4. The Launching of the Ducks   48
5. Hill House Days   71
6. On Vacation   81
7. Christmas and Crockett   90
8. Conversation Piece   114
9. Paradise Island   134
10. Boarding School   149
11. Record Roundabout   169
12. A Castle Way Letter   178
13. The Maiden's Tower   185
14. Terror at the Gallop   200
15. French Connection   213
16. Beatlemaniac   231

17. Stowe versus Home Front   237
18. Do What?   261
19. Heaven and Hell   278
20. The Unwary Beneficiary   291
21. The Man at the Gate   297

Acknowledgments   305

David Frost: *What was the most miserable thing about your childhood?*

Woody Allen: *Probably the fact that I was young. . . . If I could have been older at the time I think I could have carried it off more. . . .*

OUTRAGEOUS
FORTUNE

1.

A View from the Pram

My two grandmothers, Granny A (Christabel, Lady Ampthill) and Granny B (The Hon. Olive, Lady Baillie) were remarkably unlike each other in practically every way except one: They each owned a castle. Whereas Granny B's castle was rather large and had a moat and several thousand acres of park and farmland, Granny A's was rather small and consisted mainly of a tower with a wall around it. Granny B employed fifty people on a full-time basis to keep her estate running smoothly. Granny A had a cleaning lady come in from the local village, Kinvara, twice a week. This is not to say that Dunguaire, Granny A's castle, was in any way a lesser establishment than Leeds, Granny B's. Just different.

Both castles possessed, to a certain degree, the look and personality of their (at the time) owners. Dunguaire, situated at the mouth of Galway Bay on the west coast of Ireland, was very pretty in a rugged, highly individualistic way. There was an air of defiance accompanied by a discreet layer of vulnerability in how she dominated her low-lying promontory, as if daring the world to mock her smallness in lieu of revelling in her charm.

Leeds Castle, deep in the heart of Kent, southeast England, was so exquisite and romantic and medieval and imposing (Granny B had exquisite taste and was certainly imposing but was neither romantic nor medieval) that I never cease to marvel at my good fortune to have spent so much of my childhood within the confines of its warm embrace, wandering, exploring, bicycling and go-carting up and down the castle's mile-and-a-half-long front drive and three-quarter-mile-long park and back drives, which wended their way past woods and waterfalls, duck ponds and private golf course, a wood-garden, tennis court, grazing sheep, contented cows, horses, stables, garages, a petrol pump, the kitchen garden, greenhouses, laundry, an aviary, and the moat.

"Wonderful in manifold glories," wrote the historian of castles, Lord Conway, "are the great castle visions of Europe; Windsor from the Thames, Warwick or Ludlow from their riversides, Conway or Carnarvon from the sea, Amboise from the Loire, Aigues-Mortes from the lagoons, Carcassonne, Coucy, Falaise and Château Gaillard—beautiful as they are and crowned with praise, are not comparable in beauty with Leeds, beheld among the waters on an autumnal evening when the bracken is golden and there is a faint blue mist among the trees—the loveliest castle, as thus beheld, in the whole world."

The view from the pram, one of those handsome old shiny black models with giant wheels and a flying saucer–like compartment for me to lounge in, was equally sublime. From any angle, at any distance, the castle never failed to look anything other than awesome, swanky, huge, and gorgeous.

Growing up with Leeds as my second home, the other being my parents' well-staffed five-storey house on Egerton Terrace, in Knightsbridge, London, had the less than desirable effect of effortlessly rendering me more spoiled than a Buckingham Palace corgi before I understood the meaning of the word.

"Get out! Get out before I kick you out!" I yelled, aged five, at the visiting Princess Djordjadze, a flamboyant, five-times-married (two English aristocrats, Douglas Fairbanks Sr., Clark Gable, and her Prince Dimitri of Georgia) former chorus-line-dancer Englishwoman (born Edith Louisa Sylvia Hawkes), one morning when she was making her entrance through the castle front door at the precise moment that Nanny and I were going out for a walk. Having taken an instant dislike to her bouffant hair, lynx coat, yapping Chihuahua, and air of self-importance, I felt my exalted position as a junior castle grand poobah justified such an outburst. (I actually astonished myself with this spur-of-the-moment public display of vehemence because the word most frequently used to describe me in those days was "withdrawn.") This greeting passed immediately into castle folklore and provided endless amusement around my grandmother's afternoon canasta table (the card game was then much in vogue) when the Princess was far away.

One highborn guest, the Earl of Wilton, was asked by another, the Hon. Robin Warrender, at a castle dinner one evening in the 1960s, "Is there anywhere, do you think, grander to stay than here?" to which the Earl had apparently responded, "Windsor!"—referring to the Queen's 480,000-square-foot palace by the Thames in Berkshire. Under the circumstances it would have been difficult not to develop unworthy feelings of entitlement; after all, there was always someone to do everything for you. I never ran my bath, changed a bulb, cleaned my room, mowed a lawn, boiled an egg, washed up, fetched the newspapers, lit the fire, or helped at table. I was a catastrophically coddled boy brought up in monumental luxury, clueless as to where it might all be leading. Guidelines were never forthcoming from my parents or anyone else, in London or the country. Fortunately I had enough sense to refrain from passing on to others "news" concerning my "important" status in life. Due to my shyness, occasionally supplanted by fits of unusual boldness, I was in fact deeply inhibited, sometimes painfully so, in conveying my thoughts to most people on virtually any subject.

To this day I remain the slightly off-kilter product of my Leeds Castle childhood living. The power of its luxury brew (which came without any health and safety warnings on the side of the tin) went straight to my head as a child, and, despite the passage of time, a constant change of circumstances, and many years living in the United States, it has stayed forever warm in my mind.

I was born on May 10, 1952, four days after King Farouk of Egypt had himself pronounced a descendant of the prophet Muhammad and six months before Dwight Eisenhower was elected President of the United States of America. The importance of these developments escaped me at the time, but the killer smog that descended upon and tightly enveloped London between the fifth of December and the tenth did not. During those five horrible days the city came to a grinding halt; visibility was reduced to just a few feet, and old people, especially those with breathing problems, died in their thousands. The foul smoke, soot, and fog that seeped through every pore and crevice of our house on Egerton Terrace rendered it, and every other nook and cranny of England's capital, a very disagreeable place, and at six months of age I contracted asthma.

One of the great benefits of being at death's door as a baby is that one remains in blissful ignorance of one's impending demise. I have no recollection whatsoever of wheezing my way through 1953, and it wasn't until many years later that I learned how doctors of impeccable standing, in one hospital or another, had stood around muttering in hushed tones, "I doubt he'll make old bones." As it turned out, I was one of the lucky ones. Hundreds of babies and twelve thousand adults died as a direct result of the toxic darkness that suddenly and eerily appeared, and then, when the wind finally got up on the fifth and final day, dramatically departed, as in a horror film, but on this occasion, all too terrifyingly real.

At the earliest opportunity I was whisked off to the country, where the air was clean and I could breathe a little easier. By 1954 this is precisely what I was doing, my asthma having been so successfully treated that it went away for good. My early brush with mortality was then neatly filed away in the family archive of "things not discussed." Years later, when I was eight and about to go away to boarding school for the first time, my mother made a passing reference to my illness. "It really was touch and go . . . *so* unpleasant," she said, but I was not entirely sure for whom.

I learned about my illness purely by chance, over an easy-going conversation with my mother in our London drawing room before lunch, she with a glass of La Ina dry sherry, me a glass of Coca-Cola with ice cubes and lemon. The subject came up out of nowhere, for no apparent reason, "but everyone was simply marvellous," she was at pains to assure me. "We were all so *dreadfully* concerned." At least everyone had been concerned—to my mind the appropriate thing to be—so I decided to leave it at that.

And one day Nanny was there. This is my first distinct memory: I was two, and lying in my pram in stately comfort, propped up by puffy pillows and gazing up at—as it transpired—her, and behind her one of the ornately decorated windows of Harrods, London's grandest and most famous department store. It was the beginning of a beautiful relationship between Nanny and me. We would spend the greater part of the next five years—not to mention a substantial portion of the ten that followed—almost continually in each other's company. Of course I could not know this as my eyes roamed inquisitively over the passing shapes and objects that registered like ink splodges on a Pollock canvas. My white woolly bonnet and cardigan, knitted by Nanny with precision, kept me warm as toast despite being exposed to the elements on a slightly blustery spring day.

I decided very early on that everything about Nanny was perfect. She never made me eat soap if I was naughty or permitted my uneaten spinach from the night before to resurface at breakfast time, as my mother's ferocious nurse had reportedly done, occasionally even locking her in a cupboard until she promised to do as she'd been told.

My nanny's name was Irene Penney. I never met her parents or her sister, who lived in Birmingham. Though never fat, Nanny was a little dumpy, which to my mind perfectly offset her kind and comely face with its square jaw, straight mouth, and handsome nose. She had small blue eyes, topped off by daintily arched eyebrows and a full shock of white hair swept back off her high forehead. Her presence was utterly reassuring, her manner always calm, and she was a fount of vital information about all things, important and otherwise.

It was not until I was a teenager that I became aware of the awkward position of nannies in a household that had a number of staff. Since the nannies were neither quite family nor quite servant, there was often friction with the butlers, cooks, housekeepers, and housemaids, who felt they should not have to wait upon or be told what to do by a person whom they considered an employee like themselves. Irene Penney surely trod on many toes in the household over the years, but she did so only with my best interests at heart, and never with the intention of upsetting anyone.

As was the custom in families such as mine, Nanny did everything for me in terms of day-to-day care. Nannies performed the essential function of permitting parents to get on with their lives in a civilized way, unimpeded by the noise, nuisance, and constant demands of tiny tots. My parents paid the bills but otherwise resisted any urge to get too involved in nursery matters. That is not to say that my mother failed to climb the London or Leeds staircases to check on my progress or read to me from time to time. She did, and I came to enjoy her visits enormously. My father, though, kept his parenting on a strictly need-to-know, hush-hush footing, and did his level best to avoid actually setting foot in either nursery at all. When he finally did, he made me wish he hadn't.

My brothers, David and James, were five and four years older than I, respectively, which meant that by the time I was old enough to start enjoying their company they were away during weekdays at Hill House, the pre–prep school in Hans Place, not far from Harrods, where I also would be dispatched when I was five. I therefore saw them only first thing in the morning, and for a little while in the afternoon when they got home and the nursery decibels went up several notches. Our activities were seldom interrelated, as my bath, supper, and bedtimes were earlier than theirs, so I had to make the most of the snippets of time I had with them.

What I gathered was that David was the mild-mannered one with the brains, and James the mischievously disruptive one with the looks. I came to understand this as soon as words and conversation took on meaning and reports from school rounded out the picture. People called David "Sid" at Stowe, his public school, because he was gentle and nice and amusing like the famous working-class English comedian at the time, Sid James. That he also happened to come from the other end of the social spectrum from Sid James made the nickname doubly amusing. After one term at Aiglon College in Switzerland, boys were calling James "Lord Jim," I was told (often by him!), out of admiration for his good looks, manliness, and cool.

First at Hill House, and then at St Aubyn's, the prep school we all attended, near Brighton on the Sussex coast, David distinguished himself in the classroom, comported himself as an upright citizen, and wound up head boy, despite having never given more than passing consideration to shining at sports. James selected a different path, opting to give Prince Charles a severe working over in the corridors of Hill House, thereby establishing his reputation as a rebel, but finding little to inspire him in any classroom through which he passed. He did, however, take a strong liking to soccer, rugby, and cricket, and soon played all three well. This stood him in good stead when, due to his inability to pass exams in England, he was sent off to be educated first in Ireland and then in Switzerland, and discovered that good looks and sporting prowess (especially skiing) were noted, appreciated, and envied.

When we were together, my older brothers were generally solicitous towards me. In contrast, they were at battle stations with each other a great deal of the time, for reasons that escaped me beyond the obvious differing personalities. Regrettably they appeared to work overtime to find the other's weak spots—which, of course, they did.

Having Nanny and the children occupying the top two floors of what felt like an enormous London house was clearly ideal for a family like ours, where the modus operandi remained always, "Quiet please—grown-ups disinclined to be disturbed." A ghostlike hush hovered about my father's presence on those rare occasions when he actually came into my line of vision.

On one particular morning, with David already packed off to St Aubyns boarding school, a rumpus broke out in the London nursery, at the conclusion of which I was left with a highly disagreeable first impression of my father. I was sitting perched in my high chair, enjoying being three, attempting to go quietly and methodically about my business, but all around me pandemonium had erupted. I could no longer concentrate on spooning porridge into my mouth from my rabbit-festooned cereal bowl because James had taken it upon himself to start dancing around the breakfast table like a madman, laughing, pointing, and loudly exclaiming how funny the nursery maid Anne's varicose veins looked. Quite what brought on this sudden outburst I did not know. I was also totally unaware as to what varicose veins might be, but judging by my brother's extravagant behaviour there must be something about them that first provoked great mirth and, second, if the look on Anne's face was anything to go by, considerable anguish.

With the situation quickly deteriorating I started to succumb to a powerful sense of anguish myself. I was accustomed to a very deliberate, peaceful, and uncomplicated world. Outside interferences were rare, and until now, disturbing personal dramas (asthma aside) had been nonexistent. But now Anne, a tall, thin Canadian girl, about twenty years old with big eyes and long curly brown hair, was crying and getting very upset, standing in front of the cuckoo clock, which suddenly cuckooed to announce the time, further adding to the din.

Nanny was imploring James to stop, but the ineffectiveness of her words showed that she had little experience of situations such as this. I watched her kind, wrinkly face becoming taut with frustration. All thoughts of breakfast vanished as I stared at my brother, who wandered from the round table in the middle of the nursery back to his room to prepare for school, and then returned, never letting up, with Anne continuing to cry and looking lost and helpless. Finally Nanny started to leave the nursery, telling James, "I'm simply going to have to fetch your father." This sounded ominous. I had never seen my father on our floor. In fact, I had no distinct recollection of seeing him in any precise location.

With Nanny gone, my discomfort increased, but instead of contributing to the ruckus by bursting into tears myself or banging my cereal bowl with a spoon, I tried to block it out as if it had nothing to do with my world. But upon hearing the familiar floorboard squeak from just outside the bathroom on the half landing, I turned to see my father coming up the stairs, an aura of profound irritation emanating from his three-piece, navy blue pinstripe suit, and a stern, frighteningly stern, expression on his face. James was suddenly quiet as if struck dumb, and the only sound in the nursery was an intermittent gentle sob from Anne. Climbing the last few stairs, his left hand on the banister, my father entered the nursery and without so much as a by-your-leave (or a sympathetic offer of a hankie to Anne), he quietly instructed James to bend over the armchair adjacent to the storage cupboard by the left window, and started whacking away at my brother's bottom with his right hand, very hard.

I watched this whole affair in a state of extreme shock. I do not know how many whacks James received, but when it was all over he, too, was crying. When my father departed, he did so abruptly, without a word to anyone, leaving the four of us to try and recover as best we could from the unpleasantness of it all.

James went off to school in a sorry state, Anne cleared away breakfast and tidied up, and Nanny and I returned to our morning schedule of bathroom matters, a little music on the radio, and preparations to go out. She did not discuss with me the previous half hour, so I assumed she preferred not to.

I, therefore, was obliged to file the matter away in a new and unfamiliar category, one that for quite some time I referenced merely as "Bad."

This was the first occasion from which I could start to form an opinion about my father, and what an occasion it was! From a selfish standpoint I was peeved that he had failed even to acknowledge my presence. Undoubtedly he was concentrating on the task at hand, not a task he would have wished for and one he clearly would have wanted over and done with quickly. But all the same, I would have appreciated something from him, had needed something from him, right there and then, after sitting through such a nasty and really quite disturbing business. Sadly, frustratingly, I got nothing, not even a pat on the head; so I was left, feeling isolated, to ponder what I had just seen. I sought comfort by retreating into my shell during the whole affair, unaware as to what it all meant for the future and me. I never saw my father in the nursery again.

2.

THE CASTLE WAY

It was a bothersome affliction being a shy child because you always appeared to be taking two steps backward before the first, hesitant step forward. So whatever it was people might have been expecting of you, they tended to give up and move on (often with a quizzical expression and a raised eyebrow) long before you had worked up enough steam to say or do what you had originally intended. With people other than Nanny and my mother and brothers, it was frequently a struggle to present myself in a pleasing light, and on the occasions when I did succeed it was usually because I forced myself to.

I could be surrounded by a large number of people and still feel completely alone. Birthday parties were generally excruciating, including my own. I'd be sitting at the tea table or on my parents' drawing-room floor watching Popeye cartoons on a noisy home projector, mini revellers all around me howling like banshees, feeling as if I were on a desert island—in fact, wishing I were.

If I'd had my wits about me (which I tended not to because, after 1956, my wits became inexhaustibly tied up learning Lonnie Donegan, Cliff Richard, and later, Roy Orbison tunes on the nursery radio and David's record player) and had actually given some thought to my lacklustre social calendar, it might have dawned on me that the London/Leeds Castle bubble, inside which Nanny and I lived, acted as a powerful barrier against outsiders. Furthermore, it helped promote feelings of isolation that came and went during my childhood and that have never entirely gone away, despite my now being as happy as any man could legitimately wish to be.

At Leeds Castle the nursery was much larger than the one in London, but we conducted our lives there (or had them conducted) in much the same fashion, as an adjunct to those of the grown-ups. We were independent inasmuch as we were left to our own devices (with Nanny acting as supervisor in chief), but controlled by a framework of rules that included a flexible timetable as well as being seen no more than necessary, and heard somewhat less. There was a degree of stealth in how we comported ourselves, especially before noon; and a general understanding that our needs and wishes must always be governed—and duly accorded priority—by what I now call "the castle way."

The castle way was the all-encompassing, all-powerful, semi-feudal-system-meets-benevolent-dictatorship by which

Granny B ran the lives of all those who fell within her sphere of influence and control. That sphere included a select group of friends and advisers, my parents, my brothers, Nanny, me, assorted aunts and uncles, and, in some ways, the very air we breathed.

The castle way—or Granny B's way, generous to a fault but inclined towards imperiousness—permeated every aspect of our lives. Up to a point it governed what we should all be doing and when we should all be doing it, at any given time throughout the year. There may have been other upper-class matriarchal figures in postwar Britain lording it over their subjects in just such a fashion, but I was not aware of them and certainly never came remotely within their jurisdiction.

The structure of my existence revolved around the activities of my parents, and theirs, in turn, revolved around the weekly calendar of Granny B and "the court." The court was made up of close friends and immediate family who found it amusing to refer to themselves as though they were royal courtiers, most of them drawn from the higher ranks of society. If Granny B was amused by the unsubtle, gently mocking comparison of her domestic arrangements to the households of Queen Elizabeth and other monarchs, she hid it well. And I never saw anyone speak of "the court" to her face. Even my mother would only use the term with a wry smile attached.

Granny B and the court began each New Year with a three-month sojourn in the Bahamas; spent April, May, June, and part of July commuting between London and weekends at Leeds; shifted to the South of France for the summer and returned to the London/Leeds format for the autumn months and Christmas. Nothing about this programme—or, at least, the bits that affected me—struck me as anything other than normal at the time. It was what I knew. I spent my life with Nanny. I saw my mother and brothers every now and then, and periodically I had lively encounters with estate workers and Harrods doormen when out and about in the pram or going for a walk. By the time I was five I had still not been exposed to any useful indications—from inside or outside the London/Leeds Castle bubble—that my childhood was unusual. When I started making friends at Hill House, it came as a surprise to find that not everybody lived like me. In this instance the castle way never became my friend, let alone an ideal travelling companion, thanks to its preoccupation with keeping the real world at a pronounced arm's length from my own.

The castle way's feudal system—structured, top-down authority—was straightforward, and castle life was big, regulated, and formal. Granny B, as chatelaine and keeper of the purse strings, was the undisputed leader and ruler of the roost. She was ideally suited to this position thanks to her wealth and her personality, which bypassed gregariousness in favour of quiet authority and seductive style. Her manner was rigorously polite, her gaze unfaltering, her smile infrequent, her charm carefully rationed.

As in feudal times, she rested atop a layered hierarchy that included members of the court, her friends outside the court who came to the castle less frequently, and the family, which of course were the unpaid groups. Financial advisers, antique furniture and decorating consultants, personal staff, and estate workers comprised the paid groups. In the eleventh century the Normans, having bloodily subjugated Saxon England from top to bottom, established their layered hierarchy, which started with the king who ruled over the barons who ruled over the knights who ruled over the *villeins* who, despite being lowly workers with no landholding rights, were at least able to look down their noses at the serfs who dwelled at the bottom of the ladder of power with little chance of escaping their allotment in life. With a few perfunctory nods to the twentieth century, Granny B ran affairs at Leeds Castle along remarkably similar lines.

David Margesson was the court's undeclared ringmaster and Granny B's closest friend, adviser, and confidant. He rested in solitary splendour just beneath her in the Leeds Castle hierarchy—an unchallenged, viceregal position—and he helped her run the Leeds Castle estate with an astonishing lightness and deftness of touch. In feudal terms he was the most powerful baron.

David, or "Morg," as our family liked to call him, was a man of unparalleled wit, charm, erudition, and all-around impressiveness. Tall and always immaculately dressed, he had a face that seemed sculptured for posterity, and a speaking voice to match. As a teenager I did suspect, although it was never confirmed to me, that in his capacity as my grandmother's longest-standing male friend, his role, both in London and at

Leeds, could well have extended to one of an intimate, nocturnal nature. Granted their remarkable closeness, it would have been surprising had this not been the case.

Morg had won a Military Cross in World War I. He was elected to the House of Commons as a Conservative member of Parliament in 1922 and was government chief whip from 1931 until 1940. From 1940 to 1942 he was secretary of state for war under Winston Churchill. Created Viscount (Lord) Margesson of Rugby in 1942, he served in the House of Lords for twenty more years. As did the rest of the court, he went about his business in London during the week and came down to Leeds every weekend.

One of Morg's many gifts was making people feel special, no matter who they were or what their age, something I was happy to learn over a simple musical matter. It began with the first song I fell in love with on the radio, "The Happy Wanderer," by the Obernkirchen Children's Choir. Derek McCulloch, a famous BBC radio presenter better known as Uncle Mac, would play it often on his Saturday-morning *Children's Favourites* programme. Though the original 1953 hit was sung in German, by 1956 I'd heard it often enough in English, by other singers, to start learning it. Soon nobody in Egerton Terrace was safe from my persistent warbling, and I began to wonder if perhaps I might not brave the lion's den and attempt a "court" performance. The awkward question was, For whom? Although I was only five and had little experience of the grown-ups down at Leeds, my instincts told me that Morg was the one I would be most comfortable singing to. I asked my mother, who by that time was used to enduring my warbles in London—"How lovely, darling"—to arrange a show.

My performance was set for one morning, before lunch, outside the castle front doors. I presented myself at (high) noon, without Nanny, and waited for Morg. Soon he and my mother arrived, and after making themselves comfortable on the cushioned wicker chairs, with accompanying mutterings and mumbled asides, Morg looked up at me, as I remained standing, and smiled broadly. "My dear fella," he said, "what an honour you do me! A singer, I do declare. How about that!"

"Fire away, darling, if you're ready," my mother prompted, keenly aware that delay might bring on an unwanted dose of the collywobbles. I'd had the collywobbles since before leaving the nursery, but I knew this was a chance to shine—a rare opportunity, and one I had instigated myself. And besides, it was too late to call the whole thing off, so I started to sing: "I love to go a-wandering / Along the mountain track . . ." I completed four verses and two choruses, encouraged all the way by my audience's rapt attention—Morg even conducted with his right hand, index finger forward—and then stopped me before I forgot the words. "Oh my dear fella, marvellous, absolutely first-rate!" he thundered as he stood up and magically produced a half crown from behind my ear as a token of his appreciation. I was ecstatic and glowed with satisfaction. What a revelation to be paid to sing! But more than that, the fact that Morg had taken the time to listen, putting me at ease and entering into the spirit of the occasion, made me think that here was the man I wanted to be like when I grew up.

Next in the hierarchy, the number-two baron in feudal terms, came Geoffrey Lloyd. He was also tall and quite handsome, and though no one was able, or perhaps willing, to explain it, his nickname was Woody. Woody was less gregarious than Morg and had a slightly diffident manner but he, too, was a portrait of affability (with his peers) and possessed deep, wide-ranging knowledge. Throughout his life he remained a bachelor, and by the time I was twelve or thirteen I thought he probably was a "confirmed bachelor"—the always-affectionate euphemism for homosexuality my mother would use from time to time.

In the 1930s, when Leeds Castle became England's epicentre for spectacular weekend parties featuring royalty, aristocrats, leading politicians, newspaper barons, socialites, ambassadors, and Hollywood movie stars all eager to accept invitations, Woody and Morg were regarded as being foremost amongst Granny B's "admirers"—as lovers were delightfully called in those heady prewar days. Naturally that left her husband, the genial Adrian Baillie, with rather more on his plate to contend with than he might have liked, so it was perhaps fortunate that he had his political constituents in Scotland to occupy his time while "the Leeds set" got on with their high jinks, bedroom manouvres, drinking, gambling, and Cole Porter—the height of daring—on the gramophone. Mr. Porter came to the castle as well.

Both Morg and Woody were first introduced to Leeds Castle by Adrian Baillie, who was a fellow member of Parliament. Never could he have anticipated the inadvertent consequences of his action. He and Granny B were divorced in 1944, and he died of pneumonia in 1947.

Woody was elected Conservative MP for a Birmingham district in 1931. He was Prime Minister Stanley Baldwin's parliamentary private secretary. He had secret and specialized jobs during World War II, overseeing plans for setting the Channel on fire should the Nazis attempt an invasion. After the war he became governor of the BBC, minister of fuel and power, and minister of education. In 1974, the year Granny B died, he was created Baron Geoffrey-Lloyd of Broomfield, a village just up the road from Leeds Castle. As with Morg, Woody had his own quarters in the castle, and he, too, was a guest almost every weekend.

Woody had no time for children and made a point of ignoring them as much as decency permitted. On the rare occasions that David, James, and I joined him and Uncle Gawaine (Granny B and Adrian Baillie's son) for the morning nine holes of golf, we boys and the two older men hardly spoke to one another. I used to find that annoying, but my brothers assured me it was quite normal, so I gently fumed and got on with the game. Fortunately the course professional, Johnson, a Scot with an impenetrable accent and a golf swing from Mars, coached us and kept us focused while Woody and Gawaine sorted out the problems of the world during their round.

Granny B had given the go-ahead to build the golf course in 1931 not because she enjoyed playing—she would hardly have recognized one end of a golf club from the other—but because she felt that a vast expanse of beautifully laid-out trees and mowed grass, leading to an expansive sheet of water, with the castle as the focal point in the middle, would create as idyllic a country scene as could humanly be devised. She stipulated that no bunkers should be visible from the castle and that the skyline should not be interrupted by a flagpole on a green. The end result was a nine-hole course considered by many to be one of Britain's finest. Famous golfers such as Walter Hagen and Gene Sarazen came to play, and in the 1930s the American Ryder Cup team would make it their first port of call.

Woody's golf game was a catastrophe, and his swing was a mélange of uncoordinated movements more related to a jitterbug than to any known sporting endeavour. When standing over the ball preparing to strike, he made strange vocal noises, in two-note combinations, without regard for the musical sensibilities of his listeners. He wiggled his hips and banged the club on the ground several times. Often he'd look up at those standing about and guffaw before once more returning to the wiggle-and-bang routine. Finally he'd raise the club towards the sky and bring it down in a chopping motion, as though he were trying to slice off the back third of the tiny white ball instead of propelling it way into the distance in as straight a line as possible. Usually the ball skidded along the grass forty or fifty yards, and Woody would exclaim an emphatic "Bugger!" before handing his club to Johnson and resuming his singular hum.

Gawaine, on the other hand, a natural sportsman, swung his golf club like a man possessed. His driver had a head the size of a bulldozer, and his stance was so wide and aggressive it looked as though he were preparing to lay an egg rather than strike a golf ball. His preparation was short—a brief wiggle, and then he unleashed an immaculate, almighty, 180-degree swing that displayed the furies of hell and the power of a drag racer. The ball would soar on a trajectory to the heavens and, after its seemingly endless gravity-defying flight, plop back down to earth within easy chipping distance of the green. After a particularly good effort Gawaine liked to permit himself a self-congratulatory smile, which he would generously share with his audience.

My parents and other close family members, junior barons in feudal terms, came just below Woody in the castle hierarchy, followed by personal secretaries, Borrett (the butler), Cooper (the head carpenter and master builder), Mr. Money (the estate manager), lawyers, and an assortment of business advisers, all senior knights. The grandchildren might best be described as junior knights with promotion potential, while certain estate workers—Howard, the head gardener, Peter Taylor, the birdman—enjoyed permanent junior knight status.

Occupiers of the lowest ranks in the hierarchy, once downtrodden serfs and villeins, were now respected and admired workers, such as Dan and Charlie his cart horse, and Mr. Elves, the gruff, red-bearded electrician. Dan bore a striking resemblance to Popeye the Sailor Man, without the pipe. He could be spotted all over the estate loading his cart with unwanted rubbish and hauling it off to the furnace, which was tucked away in a far corner of the park, out of sight of the kitchen gardens and Mr. Elves's cottage. Charlie was gigantic, always moved in slow motion, and neither he nor Dan spoke more than strictly necessary.

A more formidable or magnificent butler than Borrett would be hard to imagine. From the top of his balding round head to the tip of his highly polished black lace-up shoes he personified all that a butler should be: intelligent, efficient, unflappable, and discreet. He had the complete trust of his employer and the absolute confidence of his staff. He was well liked, greatly respected, and he unhesitatingly returned the compliment to one and all. His manner was the same with me as it was with royalty; he called me "Master Anthony" until I was thirteen and "Mister Anthony" after that, a promotion that came as a blessed relief as it finally placed me on equal ground with my elder brothers.

When I went, without Nanny and the boys, to stay with Granny B in Nassau for the first time in April 1960, I had breakfast alone on the terrace every morning, served by Borrett, in his tailcoat, with the same grace and formality as if I had been the Duke of Edinburgh. He spoke to me kindly, though always with a sense of deference for my position as Lady Baillie's grandson. His politeness towards me taught me all I needed to know about how to treat others in differing circumstances from my own.

Cooper was very small and a man of few words (none of which came in my direction), but his set of skills was astonishingly broad. He could find and fix a worrisome leak, cure the ills of massive smoking chimneys, or mend a priceless Louis XIV desk. His knowledge of furniture was such that he would often advise Granny B on purchases she was considering, and when she was doing up her property in Nassau, he assembled, on-site, the delicate, prefabricated decorative work that Maison Jansen, then the most illustrious antique shop and decorating firm in France, headed by the equally illustrious interior designer Stéphane Boudin, had custom-built in Paris.

John Money had an air of grandeur about him that used to strike me as affected, but in the opinion of those who counted, his running of the estate office was both expertly and tactfully carried out. Despite his considerable bulk he walked in a delicate quickstep and held a cup of tea with his little finger crooked—which I took to be clear indications that, like quite a few of Granny B's friends, he was homosexual. His wardrobe consisted mainly of natty three-piece country suits, which he wore with considerable dash. When time permitted he was also an accomplished raconteur, and the story he once told me about the last great passion of Granny B's life, her collection of exotic birds, perfectly illustrated the grandmother I never had the opportunity to know at all well.

"It was the 1950s, the early days of rare-bird collecting and aviary building at the castle. Your grandmother and I took an early flight, one morning, to Düsseldorf, where we were met by three men who were rumoured to possess a large and important selection of parakeets. How they had come by these delightful creatures was not entirely clear, with Australian law being so strict on the export of their natural fauna. The men spoke no English, and your grandmother and I spoke no German, so our communications were severely limited. She, however, had no difficulty whatsoever, right from the word go, in making it quite clear that she wished to be driven in the slow lane, slowly. This request went down poorly.

"Upon our arrival at the converted mill in the small town of Haan, where the aviaries were located, we discovered that a treasure trove awaited us. Your grandmother wandered happily around telling me, 'I think, perhaps, we should have two of those, John, maybe four of those—oh look! Aren't those exquisite? We must have six of them.' And so it went on. All the while I was wondering if the Bank of England draft I had in my inside pocket—in those days, you know, buying things abroad was a highly complex undertaking—was not going to be hopelessly inadequate."

By this stage Mr. Money's voice, expressions, and gesticulations had become quite animated as he recalled the spirit of it all.

"When the time came for a price to be decided upon, Lady Baillie and I sat down at a table opposite the three Germans, who proceeded to discuss amongst themselves for a few moments before writing down a figure on a sheet of paper and passing it across the table to your grandmother. I nearly fainted when I saw what they'd written, but she calmly took a pen out of her Hermès crocodile handbag, drew a line through the sum indicated, divided it in half and, with a delicious little smile, told them, 'I shall pay you this.'

"Not used to dealing with people like Lady Baillie, the men slowly, reluctantly, agreed. So then it was off to the bank, where massive confusion ensued due to the fact that insufficient cash was on hand, resulting in the bank having to be temporarily closed while employees rushed out to remedy the situation.

"On the drive back to the airport your grandmother started feeling sick and announced she needed milk and a boiled egg. Instructing the driver to stop, she and I strode into a truckers' bar, where I did my best to mime what was required while she, never having been in such a place before, found herself entranced by the atmosphere and relishing the varied expressions of bemusement.

"Then at the airport there was a terrific ruckus because no customs papers had been procured, and the occupants of the many boxes were starting to make their presence keenly felt. The officials finally consented to let us on to the plane, but the birds, they said, had to fly freight.

"'I'm afraid that is out of the question,' Lady Baillie said.

"Somehow she managed to get through on the telephone to her close friend, and, of course, your cousin, Whitney Straight, the vice chairman of BOAC [British Overseas Airways Corporation] who immediately arranged for the front seats of the tourist section of the aircraft to be removed so we could fly home in the greatest comfort with our prized new purchases arrayed on the floor in front of us.

"Arriving, finally, at Lowndes House [Granny B's sumptuous London home], I naturally thought it must be time to catch the train back to Kent. But your grandmother had other ideas: 'It's been such a marvellous day, John,' she said. 'Let's go out and have dinner and see a film.'

"I didn't get to bed until the early hours of the morning, but I must say, seldom did I have as much fun as I did that day."

That was the grandmother I knew from afar. Strong willed, always in command, and able to get people to do the most extraordinary things for her as if they were absolutely normal—which often they were categorically not.

Although no one was expected to swear allegiance or provide fighting men—as in the days of William the Conqueror—to protect the castle and surrounding countryside should some desperate need arise, everyone was obliged to pay close attention to the castle way regulations and follow them with great dedication. In return Granny B provided luxury on a grand scale for family and friends, and a very comfortable living for her employees.

It was the most extraordinary, bizarre kind of merry-go-round. So many sophisticated adults, children, grandchildren, estate workers, financial advisers, personal secretaries, even airline staff and casino managers, ready and willing to do their honourable best to accommodate the wishes of one singularly rich, shy, sometimes charming, always fiercely determined woman.

3.

SON OF SPONGE

In contrast to Granny B (Lady Baillie), my mother's mother—whose American fortune made it possible for her to buy Leeds Castle and other grand properties, and to live a life of magnificent opulence—Granny A (Lady Ampthill), my father's mother, was dealt a different hand of cards, which she played throughout her life with a force and intelligence uniquely her own. Her son, my father, the 4th Baron Ampthill, a tall, unconventionally handsome (prominent nose, jutting chin), soft-spoken, funny man with dark, brooding eyes, a keen intelligence, and a mild temper, was born Geoffrey Dennis Erskine Russell in London in 1921 to parents of uncertain compatibility whose unwritten prenup (her insistence) declared there would be no sexual relations in the marriage. His father, John Hugo Russell, known as "Stilts" because of his great height (six foot six inches), himself heir to the Ampthill title at the time, had married the wild and free-spirited Christabel Hulme Hart, daughter of Lt. Col.

John Hart and Blanche Anstruther Erskine, anyway. What then happened was a pregnancy neither could explain. She was technically still a virgin, her hymen having only been partly perforated, and he said they had never had sex in the conventionally understood way. The result was a notorious divorce case—"the Case of the Virgin Birth"—which scandalized the nation and kept His/Her Majesty's Law Courts busy from 1922 until 1976. It was a battle over legitimacy, honour, and a title that came with no land, no country house, and no money. Crumpets! Nonetheless, it was a title with historical associations of note.

Lord Odo Russell, my father's great-grandfather, was the third son of Maj. Gen. Lord George William Russell (the Duke of Wellington's aide-de-camp both before and after the Battle of Waterloo) who was the second son of John Russell, 6th Duke of Bedford. George's brother, Lord John Russell, was twice prime minister of Great Britain, and John, who was created 1st Earl Russell, was the grandfather of Bertrand Russell, the renowned twentieth-century mathematician and philosopher.

Odo, whose eldest brother, Francis, became the 9th Duke of Bedford, was born in Florence in 1829 and educated at home by his mother, Elizabeth, niece of the Marquess of Hastings, governor-general of India (1813–23). His career in diplomacy included senior postings in Vienna, Paris, and Constantinople before he became England's unofficial representative at the Vatican for twelve years. His being on good terms with the Iron

Chancellor of the new German Empire, Otto von Bismarck, resulted in his appointment in 1871 as ambassador to Berlin, where he and Bismarck developed a remarkable friendship. For his efforts and consummate skill at maintaining honest relations with the hard-nosed, increasingly militaristic Germany—the reach of the British Empire was then approaching one-quarter of the earth's surface, provoking considerable hostility in some quarters—Odo was offered a peerage by Disraeli's Conservative administration in 1878, which he wanted to accept but was persuaded not to because of his family's powerful Whig associations. He therefore waited until Gladstone and his own party's return to office before being elevated to the title of Baron Ampthill in 1881. Acquiring a fortune, however, was never a motivating factor in Lord Odo's life, and in order to maintain a suitably lavish household while representing his country abroad, he was obliged to rely, from time to time, upon the largesse of his brother the duke.

John Russell, 1st Earl of Bedford, was a close adviser to Henry VII and Henry VIII (as was William Paget, 1st Baron Paget, my mother's ancestor). His descendants later became Dukes of Bedford, large-scale landowners—more than 86,000 acres, including Woburn Abbey in Bedfordshire and swaths of London around Covent Garden and the British Library now known as Bloomsbury—and one of England's leading Whig political dynasties. When the Whigs were known as the Country Party, one of their founders, Lord William Russell, was implicated in the Rye House Plot of 1683 to overthrow King Charles II. He was found guilty and executed the same year but he was later exonerated and his father, the 5th Earl of Bedford, became a privy councillor under William and Mary and, by way of recompense, was created 1st Duke of Bedford and Marquess of Tavistock in 1694.

It would have been no small thing to have been denied one's birthright with ancestors such as these.

"Injudicious use of a sponge" was the way Granny A became pregnant—allegedly—and I remained completely in the dark about this enterprising theory until Fred Hughes, Andy Warhol's charming and charismatic business manager, drunkenly roared "Sponge!" in my face one evening in 1976 while dining in New York with him and Andy at Elaine's. And I had to pretend I knew what he meant.

Three years before, in June 1973, David and I had been staying the weekend with my godmother Lady Buckhurst at Buckhurst Park, East Sussex (whose one-hundred-acre wood achieved legendary status in A. A. Milne's Winnie-the-Pooh books) when, at teatime, a call came through from our father, who was in London. He spoke with William (my godmother's son, the future Earl De La Warr and a close friend of David's) but apparently expressed no need to communicate directly with either of his sons. We were standing closer to the telephone than a matador to a bull's horns, but that, to my consternation, had no bearing on the matter. After a brief conversation William replaced the receiver and said, "Your father wishes to inform you that you have suffered a mild elevation!" What he meant by this announcement was that Stilts had died, and we were now the sons of the 4th Lord Ampthill and were therefore entitled to be addressed as "the Honourable David" or "the Honourable Anthony Russell."

A courtesy title—such as "the Honourable" if your father was a baron or viscount or "Lord" if your father was a marquess or duke—still possessed a modicum of pizzazz in 1960s and 1970s England. It adorned your chequebook and sometimes caused a flutter in a shopgirl's eyes or achieved a better table in a smart restaurant. For most Americans such recognition of titles was hard to take seriously. But "class" in Great Britain and "class" in America have always been two separate entities. In the former it bears no relation to money but rests squarely on the shoulders of your family tree. In the latter it is applied to wealth, and (aside from "classy" behaviour, often referring to exceptional manners) wealth alone. I enjoyed my "elevation," as I knew others were doing in similar circumstances. I brandished my chequebook adoringly about for a spell and remained blissfully unconcerned about the future status of my adornment.

But no sooner had the weighty news been properly digested than we found out that our father's much younger half brother, John, an accountant in the City, had himself laid claim to the Ampthill title as well. This, obviously, was the height of impertinence, since the whole question of my father's legitimacy had, as David once told me, been settled in the House of Lords forty-nine years before. Apparently not. John now claimed that the declaration of legitimacy my father and his mother had won when the "Virgin Birth" case was settled in their favour in the House of Lords in 1924 was not binding on the House of Lords in a peerage claim (someone claiming their title), and that it had been obtained by fraud and collusion. *Sacrebleu!* Whatever my father's faults, or Granny A's, fraud and collusion, I knew, were not among them.

If my asthma had featured prominently in the family archives of "things not discussed" the so-called Russell Baby Case was the absolute crown jewel of no comment. I never heard the affair being talked about in London, or at Leeds, by my parents or by anybody else when I was growing up. It seemed as if a blanket curfew had been imposed on words deemed unsuitable for public consumption, which, ironically, is exactly how King George V viewed the salacious revelations of my grandparents' 1920s divorce trials. "The pages of the most extravagant French novel would hesitate to describe what has now been placed at the disposal of every boy or girl reader of the daily newspapers," the king had lamented, carefully implicating only the French in the dastardly habit of writing in lewd language endless pages of love, lust, and fornication which, clearly, His Majesty had no time for.

The saga began in 1915 when Stilts, on leave from the navy, met my grandmother at a dance and fell in love. He was one of many dashing young officers who fell in love with the glamorous, fun-loving, and unstoppable Christabel Hart, who showed her fierce independence by working for the war effort at a factory lathe by day and dancing all night at parties and in nightclubs. She quickly forgot about Stilts, but he refused to give up the chase despite her prior warnings about the "proposal room" at the Savoy Hotel, where many suitors chose to vent their amorous intentions. My grandmother finally accepted Stilts's marriage proposal in 1917: "I thought it would be nice and peaceful not to be pestered by men asking me to marry them." After a brief hiccup in which she eloped to Gretna Green with Stilts's best friend, Gilbert "Flick" Bradley (an unconsummated, overnight affair), they were married in 1918.

Lord and Lady Ampthill, courtiers to King George and Queen Mary, were so appalled they refused to attend the wedding. They had wanted their son and heir to marry the Princess Royal, not some "fast" young woman who shaved under her arms, had been educated and had lived on the seamier side of Paris, and appeared to have no concept as to how to behave in a normal, civilized fashion. As if to underscore her unsuitability, when her husband lost his job, after the war, at Vickers in Victoria Street, a guns and ammunition company, Christabel opened a dress shop in Mayfair in order to pay the bills. The shop became a huge success, but if there was one thing still absolutely beyond the pale in those days, it was for a family with links to the monarchy to be "in trade." These, of course, were "their" rules, and my grandmother cared not a whit about anyone's rules but her own—which inevitably caused the establishment to groan into their teacups with undisguised opprobrium.

Despite living as man and wife under the same roof in a

small house in Chelsea, Granny A held fast to her prenup rules and insisted on separate bedrooms. Stilts went along with the arrangement ("Is this a man or a jelly?" my grandmother's lawyer, Patrick Hastings, was later to ask in court) and even went so far as to regularly bring her breakfast in bed, at which time she would regale him with news about whom she had seen the previous evening and whom she was going dancing with that night.

After three years of marriage to a force of nature beyond his understanding or ability to keep up with, Stilts moved in with his parents at Oakley House, their seventeenth-century manor in Bedfordshire. His fondness for dressing up in women's clothing had failed to impress upon his unimpressionable wife whatever needs he was endeavouring to impart, and it wasn't long before Lady Ampthill was pressing for an annulment. Nonetheless, risking his mother's anger, Stilts sent my grandmother flowers for her twenty-sixth birthday in June 1921.

Writing back to thank him, she suggested they have lunch, as she had some extraordinary news. Having first visited a clairvoyant and then a doctor for confirmation, she had discovered, she told him, that she was "five months gone." They both racked their brains for an occasion when "something might have happened," but the best Christabel could come up with was that a sleepwalking incident had concluded with lovemaking neither had been aware of.

In July 1922 my grandfather Ampthill's side of the family laid siege to my father's legitimacy and his mother's honour in a divorce which dominated headlines, titillated the nation, and caused conniptions in the royal family for years. The problem for my grandmother was that she had rendered herself the easiest of targets through her unusually flamboyant way of living. Stilts's lawyer, Sir John Simon, quoted from a letter Christabel had written to her friend Maud Acton, in which she claimed, "I have been so indiscreet all my life that he has enough evidence to divorce me about once a week." But her "indiscretions," as she would make abundantly clear during the two trials and two appeals, never included sleeping with any of the co-respondents (three were named, which surprised my grandmother, who had anticipated "rows").

Christabel Hart, whose father died leaving little money when she was fourteen, enjoyed every aspect of life to its fullest extent except sex, to which she had an aversion. She adored the company of men but infinitely preferred brushing down one of her hunters after a long day out chasing the fox to even contemplating the act of physical intimacy with a man. Both before and after her marriage to Stilts, she stayed the night with a number of different men, including two of the co-respondents in the first trial of summer 1922—Flick Bradley and Capt. Lionel Cross—but she never shared a bed nor had intercourse with any of them. Her proof lay in the examinations she underwent after discovering she was expecting a baby, by several eminent Harley Street gynaecologists, which revealed she was still, in medical terms, a virgin.

What got the papers, king, and country all in a lather were the intimate details produced in evidence during the first two trials, evidence that was available uncensored for the entire world to scrutinize and elaborate upon at its leisure. My grandmother's letters, some of which contained phrases such as, "I need hardly say your wife has a vast following of adoring young men. I've four in the Bucks Light Infantry. They are priceless and so naughty: so is wife!" did not help her cause. Christabel loved using the word "naughty." For her it was in tune with the absurdity of the whole sexual charade between a man and a woman. When Stilts was still serving in his submarine in 1919 and Christabel was in Switzerland with her mother, she wrote to him, "Darlingest old thing, I am so in love with a Dago young man. You'd have spotted him as my future fate the moment you set eyes on him . . . he is very slim and has lovely hands. Your very naughty wife, C." It was comments such as these, read out loud during the prosecution's opening statements in the first trial, that caused a lady juror to come over faint and ask to be excused.

Sir John Simon made my grandmother write down the names of all the men with whom she had stayed the night in a hotel. This she was obliged to do in silence in front of the whole court. Ultimately, though, it was the sex talk that pricked up all ears. In the early 1920s it was considered as raunchy as it gets. "Penetration" was not then a word used in polite society—indeed, any society—but it got tossed around in court (along with all its associated actions) like current-day footballers discussing a night out at a brothel.

On the weekend of December 18–19, 1920, Stilts and Granny A went to stay at Oakley House, where Stilts's mother, Lady Ampthill, in an effort to be encouraging, put them in the same bedroom. According to my grandmother, Stilts proceeded to force himself upon her (essentially to try to rape her—as he had apparently done on a previous occasion), but she refused him. She described what took place, in court, under oath, as "Hunnish scenes," and her testimony was simplicity itself: "He attempted to effect penetration but I would not allow it."

In the morning Christabel took a bath in the same water recently vacated by her husband, and it was this occasion which led some to speculate that she had made "injudicious use" of a sponge with which her husband had just "washed himself," thereby absorbing his sperm. Whatever the method of conception (and it will forever remain a mystery as to how far Stilts's penis had made progress the night before), my father was born October 15, 1921, and the doctors all agreed the ten-month pregnancy was possible.

The first trial was inconclusive on the paternity question, but in the second my grandmother was found guilty of adultery with an unknown man. The opposing legal team, this time headed by Sir Edward Marshall Hall, a barrister known for his grandstanding approach, had tried tricking her in court:

"I would die for my child," Christabel had said.

"You would lie for that child?" Marshall Hall asked.

"Die," she said.

"And you would lie for the child."

"Lying for a child is not necessary."

"You would do everything: you would die for it; you would lie for a child."

"No, that I would not."

"You would die for a child, but you would not lie for a child?"

"Exactly."

Marshall Hall did succeed, though, in tricking her into finding a resemblance between my father and pictures of children he hinted might be Stilts's but were not.

John Wells wrote in his book *The House of Lords*:

Whether it was the effect on him of Christabel's high-spirited performance in court or Marshall Hall's oratory, Mr Justice Hill clearly felt the need to influence the jury against her. He asked them to consider which was the stronger character: if Mrs Russell was bent on having her own way, she usually got it. Her letter about the rows of co-respondents suggested a frivolous attitude to adultery. He asked them to imagine her in the arms of a more persistent Hun than her husband: 'If the respondent gave herself to another man, is he likely to have stopped short of complete possession?' This, in view of the unanimous findings of all the doctors of her technical virginity, was scandalous misdirection.

My grandmother refused to accept being branded an adulteress, and she appealed to the High Court; but the appeal was dismissed. So in March 1924, having scraped together all

the funds she could, she took her case to the House of Lords—
the final appeal.

Everything turned on a judgement given in 1777 by the 1st
Earl of Mansfield, who had once dismissed charges against
a witch accused of walking upside down in the air stating that
anyone who'd seen her doing so was perfectly entitled to do
the same. He was a leading barrister and judge in the mid-
eighteenth century, and one of England's most respected lord
chief justices. In *Goodright v. Moss*, the best-known paternity
case of its day, he stated: "The law of England is clear that testimony of a father or mother cannot be admitted to bastardize
the issue born after marriage. . . . It is a rule founded on decency, morality, and policy, that they shall not be permitted to
say after marriage that they have had no connection."

The Law Lords agreed with Lord Mansfield, and two
months later my grandmother emerged victorious and my father was restored as the legitimate heir to the Ampthill title.
"I knew I would win eventually," she said. "Right always triumphs in the end."

The case saw the introduction into law of two new Acts,
the Legitimacy Act of 1924, and the Judicial Proceedings
(Regulation of Reports) Act of 1926, which restricted report-
ing of English divorce cases solely to the facts given in the
judgement and banned making public the actual evidence itself. King George was rumoured to have been pleased by that.

The Ampthills were now in poor financial shape after

spending a fortune on legal fees and private investigators, but my grandmother continued to do well with her dress business and was able to afford to give my father an excellent education at Cheam prep school (where the Duke of Edinburgh went) and the newly (1923) established Stowe School (where, in my day, Sir Richard Branson and Roger Hodgson of Supertramp fame went), previously a Georgian ducal palace one-sixth of a mile wide with six hundred rooms.

The reopening of the whole painful affair by John Russell in 1973 obliged my father once more to suffer the indignities associated with the horribly awkward "Russell Baby" saga and to resume battle-stations for his family title and his mother's honour, one last time. True to form, Christabel, aged seventy-eight, straightaway decided to take off for Australia and ride across part of the outback, leaving my father—all man, no hint of jelly—to handle the matter. So while Granny A was cutting out snakebites from her arm with a giant knife and driving a bus across Asia back to England without a driving licence or any form of insurance, my father went calmly and methodically about preparing the rebuttal to his half brother's tendentious claim.

In February 1976 the Committee for Privileges, a select committee of the House of Lords, heard the case. The Committee was made up of Lord Wilberforce, three law lords, and five lay members of the House. A spirited effort was made by John Russell's barrister, Harry Law, to introduce the old Lord

Ampthill's blood tests, but it was refused by the Committee, which agreed with Sir John Foster, my father's counsel, that admitting such records would be to put my father in "an Agatha Christie situation" (the tests could have been tampered with or mixed up in the laboratory). In April the Lords ruled, for a second time, in my father's favour, and he was confirmed beyond doubt as the 4th Baron Ampthill. As the icing on an ancient cake, my father was deemed by fair-minded observers to be the spitting image of the man who claimed not to be his father.

"If ever there was a family blessed by fortune, where the birth of a child was attended by an evil spirit bearing a baneful gift, liable to frustrate all the blessings, it was the Ampthill Russells," said Lord Simon of Glaisdale, one of the nine peers on the Committee. Lord Wilberforce concurred, insisting that it was time to close this chapter in our family's history.

My grandmother did not live long enough to hear, or witness, this final scene in her amazing life story. She died peacefully in a Galway hospital on February 16, 1976, aged eighty, close to the hunt country she had loved for so long. "I think it might be a good thing for the world to know that I have not one backward look that saddens or distresses me," she had said before departing for Australia. "I have loved every hour from one day old to seventy-eight." No more appropriate epitaph could there be.

———

On Tuesday, October 26, 1999, Britain's Labour Party, under the leadership of Tony Blair, passed the House of Lords Act and, in the words of Lord Strathclyde, the Conservative Party leader in the House of Lords, "took a knife and scored a giant gash across the face of history." Over seven hundred hereditary peers (the old aristocracy) were summarily banned from taking their seats and voting in the Upper House as they had done for seven hundred years. However, ninety-two of them were permitted to remain until the next round of "reform"—when the tumbrels could once again be summoned—and my father was one of those who received a vote of confidence from his fellow peers.

The amusing Harrow-educated (Eton & Harrow, Oxford & Cambridge, Tweedledum & Tweedledee) Marxist journalist Francis Wheen had a thing or two to say in *The Guardian* about titled grown-ups vying for space in their favourite, once entitled, institution: "the pathetic, hilarious spectacle of these lumbering beasts sleepwalking towards extinction would make a perfect sequel to Walking with Dinosaurs." Because all the hereditary peers had been asked to write a brief summary of the reasons why their fellow peers should vote for them, their natural inclination not to blow their own horns left them open to ridicule. "It would be as vainglorious to proclaim a personal manifesto," the Earl of Onslow wrote, "as it would be arrogant to list any achievement." Having no time for, nor wishing to give credence to, the scope of the aristocracy's contributions to Britain over a millennium, Wheen turned his attention to my father:

"He joined the Upper House in 1976 after a two-year battle with his younger half-brother—who pointed out that the marriage of Geoffrey's parents was unconsummated, as the baroness had revealed at the time of her divorce. She spent only one night in bed with her husband [not true] during which he engaged in Hunnish practices, otherwise known as masturbation . . . I fear he [my father] has missed a Unique Selling Point here. Of all the candidates in next week's election, Ampthill is the only one who can justly claim to have earned his seat in parliament by proving that his father was a wanker."

4.

The Launching of the Ducks

My mother, Susan Winn, grew up between Leeds Castle and Nostell Priory, where her father's family had lived for three hundred years and which is now the property of the National Trust. It is a testament to her wonderful character that with two such extraordinary places to call home she did not turn out to be remotely spoiled. She was a beautiful woman who dressed immaculately, but usually not in the latest fashions because she considered such things to be extravagant. She had refined manners (she never used coarse language) and odd habits. When something bad happened—for instance, some woman once crashed into our Mini as we were driving down Egerton Terrace when I was nine—all one would hear from her, even at her most strident, would be a heavily emphasized, "Oh, but how *maddening*!"

Some say it's an English trait to exaggerate in a downward direction. It is. Across the great class divide, when the wind howls and temperatures drop below zero it is "a little chilly outside." According to one of my uncles, obscenely frigid conditions were inevitably "a lovely day to be out!", especially if there were some pheasant, woodcock, or duck to be shot. I liked the way my mother shook hyperbole on its head. I tend to do the same.

Much to my father's amusement and annoyance, frequently in equal proportions, my mother hoarded newspapers and magazines and was often to be seen reading the *Daily Express* not just from the previous day but from the previous year. As time passed, her collection grew, and cupboards started to fill up with editions of *Tatler* and *Harper's Bazaar* from the 1940s. On the weekend drive down to the castle, suitcases and newspaper bundles fought for available space in the trunk of the Bentley R Type, a gift to my parents from Granny B. Later in life my mother frequently opted to wear eccentrically colourful ensembles and usually carried them off with style. Her dazzling, alluring forget-me-not blue eyes radiated warmth and kindness, and her personality, though given to moods, was generous and imbued with a contagious sense of fun. When discussing the American branch of the family she enjoyed referring to us as "the poor cousins," which amused and confused me greatly. If we were poor, living between a large house in Knightsbridge, London, and a fairy-tale castle in Kent, where, exactly, did that place everyone else?

———

What she meant was that in comparison with John Hay ("Jock") Whitney, Granny B's first cousin, who was U.S. ambassador to the Court of St James from 1957 to 1961 and founder of the world's first venture capitalist firm, J.H. Whitney & Co., we were poor. During the 1970s Jock was considered one of the world's richest men, with a fortune that would almost place him in Bill Gates territory in today's terms.

My father, who met my mother when he was invited by Granny B to a Leeds Castle weekend after the war, rose to be a Captain in the Irish Guards during World War II, was then General Manager of Fortnum & Mason for four years, Chairman of the New Providence Hotel in the Bahamas, a West End theatre impresario, a director of United Newspapers, Chairman of London's Emergency Helicopter Service, and for over thirty years a distinguished member of the House of Lords, becoming Chairman of Committees in 1992. None of the above produced an accumulation of wealth beyond what Jock Whitney might have paid his staff over the course of three or four years.

From the late nineteenth century on, the members of America's "aristocracy," the East Coast establishment, were businessmen and industrialists first and men of property second. In contrast, their British counterparts, with lands and often titles going back as far as a thousand years, rarely got the hang of the industrialist side of things, having grown accustomed to running their country from the comfortable perch of large country estates, imposing London mansions, and inherited seats in the House of Lords. When the wealth moved from the country to the city during the mid-nineteenth century Industrial Revolution, the landed upper classes, squeezed by higher and higher taxes following radical political change, had to adapt to making money in the newfangled way (work), and found themselves (to begin with) not very good at it.

William C. Whitney's sons grew the family fortune and wed appropriately. Harry Payne Whitney married Gertrude Vanderbilt, the great-granddaughter of Commodore Cornelius Vanderbilt, the second-richest man (after John D. Rockefeller) in U.S. history; she was a sculptor, an art patron, and the founder of the Whitney Museum. Their son, Cornelius Vanderbilt Whitney, continued the family tradition of inheriting vast sums of money and then making even more. He founded the Hudson Bay Mining and Smelting Co. Ltd. in Canada, and with his cousin Jock helped finance the film classic *Gone with the Wind* as well as backing the Technicolor Corporation. William Payne Whitney married Helen Hay, daughter of the U.S. secretary of state and former ambassador to Great Britain, John Hay. Payne inherited $63,000,000 (over a hundred billion in today's money) from his uncle, Oliver Hazard Payne, a Standard Oil magnate (today's equivalent might be an original Microsoft investor) who commissioned Stanford White to build his daughter and nephew a comfortable New York residence at 972 Fifth Avenue for their wedding present.

Payne's sister, Pauline, my great-grandmother, inherited her millions from her uncle and her father—less than the boys, but she wasn't one to grumble.

Great-grandmother Pauline married Almeric, the son of Lord Alfred Paget and the grandson of Henry Paget, Earl of Uxbridge, who commanded the British cavalry at the battle of Waterloo in 1815. The story goes that the earl, after one of the last cannonballs had been fired on that gory day, exclaimed to the Duke of Wellington, "By God, Sir, I've lost my leg!" to which the Iron Duke had apparently replied, "Good God, Sir, so you have!" When the surgeon was later sawing off what remained of the shattered limb in the nearby house of M. Hyacinthe Joseph-Marie Paris, Uxbridge is said to have commented with great stoicism, "The knives appear somewhat blunt!"

For his selfless contributions to the final victory over Napoleon, the Prince Regent created Henry Paget the 1st Marquess of Anglesey. Although it was offered, he refused a pension for the loss of his leg, which Monsieur Paris duly had buried in his garden, thereby establishing a shrine for visiting dignitaries and gawkers of a historical bent.

Almeric had emigrated to the United States in 1881 to seek his fortune. His first venture was a cattle ranch at Le Mars, Iowa, where he became acquainted with Teddy Roosevelt. Moving to New York, he met Pauline and worked with her uncle and father setting up the Dominion Coal Company and the Dominion Iron and Steel Company at Sydney, Nova Scotia. Their wedding was at Saint Thomas Church, on Fifth Avenue in New York City, with President Grover Cleveland in attendance. Granny B was born Olive Cecilia Paget in the United States in 1899.

Soon after, the family moved to England. Pauline Paget, who had always suffered from frail health, died after a brief illness in 1916, leaving my grandmother Olive, at seventeen, a rich woman in her own right. A year later she became the Honourable Olive, when her father was created 1st Baron Queenborough for having sponsored a battalion of volunteers during the war and establishing the Almeric Paget Military Massage Corps with clinics to treat wounded soldiers in hospitals throughout the United Kingdom.

In July 1919 Olive married the Hon. Charles Winn, second son of Lord St Oswald, who lived at Nostell Priory. They had two children, my aunt Pauline (born 1920) and my mother, Susan (born 1923), and lived in a large house on Hill Street, off Grosvenor Square in London, until they divorced in 1925. Because he later went to live in America with his third wife, Theo, I saw my grandfather fewer than a dozen times when I was growing up, but I am sure that my mother's warm personality, kindness, and sunny outlook on life came from him. I loved his expressive bushy eyebrows, handsome pinstriped suits, half-closed left eye (never explained beyond "from the war"), which frequently twitched involuntarily, and full-bore raspy chuckle. He would sit in my father's chair by the window in our London house, a glass of whisky in his hand, and talk with feeling and humour about our lives and what I took to be other vital matters. And then he would be gone, not to reappear for two or three years. I once spent half a day with him when he came to take me out from St Aubyns. Just he and I, going for a walk up in the rolling green hills known as the South Downs; having tea in a quaint old seventeenth-century teashop; shopping for sweets—enough sweets to fill half my locker when I got back to school! He had an easy generosity of spirit. I was always sorry to have to say good-bye to him.

Granny B married Arthur Wilson Filmer in 1926. He was a big-game hunter and a collector of fine antique furniture and tapestries. He also was the owner of East Sutton Park, near Maidstone, Kent, and he took my grandmother to see Leeds Castle, which had been vacant for two years, soon after their marriage. She straightaway spotted the potential in the somewhat derelict building, which had not seen repairs for almost a century. Not so William Randolph Hearst, who decided to look elsewhere for his *de rigueur* English castle—a weakness of American millionaires at the time—after his agent informed him that there were twenty bedrooms, one bathroom, and a crumbling ancient shell.

Granny B and her husband were thus able to buy Leeds in 1926 for the then-gigantic sum of $874,000. The Wilson Filmers parted company soon after the purchase was completed, and in 1931 my grandmother (retaining ownership of the castle) married Sir Adrian Baillie, 5th Baronet of Polkemmet, a Scottish businessman, sportsman, and member of Parliament. Her full name therefore became the Honourable Olive, Lady Baillie, but it was simply as Lady Baillie that she became known. Granny B was the last private owner of Leeds Castle, the eleven-hundred-year-old former stronghold of Saxon kings and Norman knights, which she lovingly restored, lavishly decorated, and exquisitely maintained, transforming it into a unique and magnificent twentieth-century country home.

I was lucky with lineage. Money, and lots of it, appeared to grow on trees, especially those which adorned the Leeds Castle parkland. Ancestors with glowing titles and extraordinary accomplishments filled the history books, but there would be consequences for being handed everything of a material nature on a plate, with no clear indication of what one might be expected to do with such good fortune.

The castle's three long drives led to the gatehouse, which for eight hundred years had guarded the entrance to the two small islands upon which sat the castle and the Maiden's Tower. Inside the gatehouse were a squash court, golf clubs, bicycles, and two go-carts. There was a large storage area for the estate workers' tools and gardening equipment facing a small house where the gatekeepers, Mr. and Mrs. Jenkin, lived. And there was a gun room where shotguns and cartridges were kept locked up and made ready by the gamekeepers, George Riggel and his son, Peter, for pheasant-shooting Saturdays. The circular croquet lawn, lying reverently before the statuesque castle facade, and the swimming pool, tucked away behind a tall neatly trimmed hedge, adjacent to the Maiden's Tower, rounded out the array of outdoor activities and visual majesty.

In the milieu of aesthetics, taste, and the international beau monde, Granny B's undertakings at Leeds Castle became renowned and a byword for matchless taste. On a lesser-known and smaller scale, her homes in London and Nassau enjoyed similar degrees of recognition. For more than thirty years, she worked closely with Stéphane Boudin, who became a close friend and went on to be hailed, by many, as the finest decorator of his time. James Archer Abbott, curator of the Evergreen Museum & Library at Johns Hopkins University, wrote in his impressive history of the Jansen firm: "As a result of her [Lady Baillie's] association with Jansen, she became the iconic tastemaker of pre–World War II England." Granny B might have huffed and puffed a bit at such an accolade, perhaps out of false modesty, but I suspect it would have pleased her greatly.

About Granny A I had mixed feelings. Her domineering personality could one day whisk me along on a magic carpet ride, but on another give me a drastic case of the heebie-jeebies. I seldom saw her because she was always travelling or foxhunting or both, but when she did enter my life she blew in like a hurricane, engulfing the household for however long she was around in a blitzkrieg of nonstop activity. Walks, games, come here, go there, do this, do that. It took everyone at least a week to recover after she left—even Nanny, who would have her job explained to her in the minutest detail, daily. Granny A was a terror but she loved us, and this was her way of expressing it. "After all, my darlings," she would say. "You don't get to see me that often."

In keeping with her whirlwind character, Granny A was always a dashing dresser, and the day she took me, aged six, to my very first film at a cinema on Oxford Street, was no exception. She wore a hat, veil, scarf, jacket, flowing skirt, and high boots, all flung together with a superlative eye for cut and colour. Everything she did seemed to be done at breakneck speed; her thinking, riding, talking, driving, cooking, arranging—all were conducted so crisply and rapidly that anyone within striking distance had to concentrate ferociously on keeping up or be prepared to be left trailing in her formidable wake.

The film was called *Tonka* (aka *A Horse Named Comanche*) and, to my initial delight, she insisted on taking the bus ("Much more economical and so much more fun"), another first for me. Of course she also insisted on sitting up top, at the front, so she could energetically tell me—and the entire upstairs section of the bus—all about everything we were witnessing from our vantage point, including the personal faults in half the population's general appearance, the unsatisfactory skills of our bus driver ("Much too jerky, he should know better!"), and how filthy all the buildings looked ("Something really *must* be done"). Every time I found myself looking the other way when she was speaking, she would grab my leg and vigorously shake it: "Pay attention when I'm talking to you." After being instructed "Sit up straight," "Don't touch the handrails, they're full of germs," "Straighten your tie, it's unbecoming on a young man to appear slovenly," I was feeling a little the worse for wear by the time we arrived at Oxford Street, and I noticed some fellow passengers giving Granny A peculiar looks as we made our way off the bus.

I have no idea why this particular film was selected for my introduction to the joys of big-screen entertainment. Perhaps the equestrian subject matter seemed appropriate for a small boy, but it may have been due to Granny A's obsession with horses and hunting. Once comfortably ensconced in our seats, however, I found myself sitting through a one-hour buildup to the Battle of the Little Big Horn (I, of course, possessed little knowledge or understanding beyond Indians bad, U.S. cavalry good). After that I was obliged to endure the nightmarish sight of countless horses being slaughtered by streams of arrows. To make matters worse, the doomed soldiers then used the wounded animals as cover before being annihilated themselves. I emerged from the spectacle sobbing like a lunatic and had to be comforted by Granny A over tea and buns around the corner.

"There, my darling, try not to get yourself all wound up. It's only the cinema."

"But it looks awfully real. Did it actually happen?"

"Well, historically speaking, yes. . . ."

This was almost too much to bear, but on the bus ride home she was sympathetic to my feelings and calmed me down by insisting that the horses were not hurt in the making of the film. Even though she was generally more restrained than on our outward-bound journey, I still wondered how anyone could have such supreme self-confidence and jaw-dropping disregard for what others might be thinking about her.

Granny B, by way of contrast, conducted herself and her affairs with great deliberation and thoroughness. If she needed to talk to someone during castle weekends, including a member of the family, an "audience" would be set up by Borrett with precise timings as to when it would begin, and end. "Audiences" were almost always held in Granny's boudoir, her private sitting room, adjacent to her bedroom.

All her finances were scrupulously attended to, from the largest sums down to the smallest. If a guest at one of her houses expected to get away with surreptitious and extravagant use of the telephone provided in each bedroom, Borrett would discreetly place an itemized bill there before their departure. Anything so rash as nonpayment curtailed future invitations. Once, the immensely sophisticated Johnny Galliher, a New Yorker with a wicked sense of humour and, so the story goes, a frighteningly large cock, failed to pay. Only because he was such a good friend and prized cardplaying member of the court was this isolated incident allowed to be swept under the rug—though not forgotten.

Granny B was generous with her friends, her family, and especially with those in her employ, but she refused to be taken for a ride and skillfully chose the people who worked for her. Cash was her preferred method of payment for purchases, whether in person or by a member of her staff. From time to time stories filtered through as to how this worked.

One day Lily, her London housekeeper and dog walker, was dispatched to Christie's to collect a pair of gorgeous porcelain ho-ho birds destined to end up on brackets in the drawing room at the castle. She arrived at the very grand West End auctioneers clutching a loosely tied and rather grubby-looking brown paper bag. "I've come to collect some birds!" she announced at the reception desk. Once her identity had been established, and the objects in question located, she handed over the bag, which contained several thousand pounds in cash.

Each of my grandmothers was a law unto herself, and unto all those who came into her orbit. I always thought my mother's feelings towards Granny A—especially when an upcoming visit triggered the red-alert systems in our London household—hovered uneasily between dread and resignation. She would get noticeably agitated as arrival day loomed, and the rest of us took our cue from her, except my father, whose bond with his mother appeared to be so strong that little could upset their equilibrium. When I was little, one of the best things about Granny A's visits was that she would always come up to the nursery and spend a lot of time with me playing games and reading stories. I particularly enjoyed "bing" (her word). I would sit on her lap as she bounced me vigorously up and down, holding my hands, laughing and singing and generally making the most foolish of noises. Suddenly she would part her knees, I would fall to the floor with a tremendous thump, yelling, "Again, again!" and we would repeat the manoeuvre at least a dozen times. "Enchanting," Granny A once described me in a postcard to my mother, which now comes as a surprise, because I always thought she regarded me as a young chap rather in need of some straightening out.

Granny B did not play games with me. In fact she very seldom saw me, even though most weekends we were both in, or around, the castle. She ruled her roost with an imperial touch, keeping a watchful eye over the efficiency of her operations and the well-being of her friends, employees, and family. Fraternizing with the grandchildren was not her forte. Indeed, I never had what might be called a proper conversation with her.

My first participation in a full-fledged castle way event turned out to be both pleasurable and mildly disheartening. The joyous prospect of finally being allowed, at the age of six, to join Granny B and the court in observing one of the weekend's most keenly anticipated ceremonies was muddied by my being treated like the invisible man from start to finish.

It was a glorious afternoon. The sun bathed the magnificent castle and its equally ravishing moat and parkland in a glow of spring perfection. Not a single cloud was visible. The daffodils that lined the outer edges of the moat danced merrily in the occasional breeze. The black swans and their families whistled and crooned with gusto. The pike rested dreamily in the shallow water. The smell of recently mowed lawn permeated the air like a delicate aroma from the kitchen of a master chef. The ranks of lush woodland stood firmly to attention behind the commanding and majestic cedars. It was a scene of consummate beauty and tranquillity.

I, on the other hand, was in a state of feverish excitement now that Nanny and I had been given permission to join the highly select group invited to accompany my grandmother to the launching of the ducks.

Granny B had always struck me as looking very old, very distinguished, and more than a little fierce. Everyone would say she was a wonderful person, albeit eccentric. That may well have been true, but I never got to know her because the only times I was in her company were when I watched her play croquet and when I was allowed down from the nursery for tea with the grown-ups. These occasions were so fraught with ritual that leaping off the castle battlements always seemed preferable to making inept attempts at conversation with people who appeared indifferent. No amount of shyness, however, was going to prevent me from witnessing the launching of the ducks. I'd had my lunch, and my rest, and at three o'clock on the dot Nanny and I positioned ourselves right outside the castle doors on the very comfortable chairs from which guests liked to watch the croquet, or have a snooze, the one often leading to the other.

I was surprised to see Granny's huge black Mercedes 600—a gift from Gawaine, who was in the motorcar business and was also an accomplished racing driver—and Brewer, her chauffeur, waiting. The duck ceremonies took place only half a mile or so down the front drive, and I had assumed we'd all be walking. But there were more cars behind Granny's, including the dark green van I knew belonged to Peter, the birdman, so clearly a convoy was going to be the order of the day. It wasn't long before I heard voices coming from the library and the *clomp-clomp* of shoes on the stone floor in the entrance hall. I wondered who would speak to me and what they'd say.

The door opened, and there was my grandmother, looking very old, very distinguished, and more than a little fierce. She was holding on tightly with one hand to the arm of Peter, the birdman, and smoking a cigarette through a long ivory holder with the other. I wasn't sure if she'd seen me because her glasses made it quite hard to tell if she was looking at you or not. After a pause I heard her say, "Anthony, darling, why don't you and Nanny come with me?"

Granny B's voice was deep, husky, and mesmerizing. It seemed to travel through space and time, which is exactly what I did upon hearing it. I found myself between Nanny and Brewer in the front of the large black car, and immediately felt carsick from the smell of leather. Fortunately, my mother's smiling face suddenly appeared at the window, so Nanny wound it down and let in some air.

"Everything all right, darling?" she asked me, puffing on a cigarette and adjusting her scarf at the same time.

"Fine thanks," I replied, this being one of my longer speeches of the day.

"I'm going to walk down and join you at the ducks," she

announced, as if the ducks were very grand people who lived down the road and were expecting us all for tea. Off she strode with her purposeful gait and all round air of charm and civility, leaving Brewer, Nanny, and me to talk amongst ourselves like old friends, which I suppose is exactly what we were. I heard a *tap-tap-tap* on the back window, and as Granny wound it down there was Johnny, the young head footman, looking very handsome in a dark suit and tie: "Everyone is ready, m'lady."

"Thank you, Johnny. All right, Brewer."

With that brief exchange completed, Brewer started the engine and we were off. At a snail's pace, Granny B not being fond of speed. Funnily enough, the unstoppable Borrett, who actually won a medal in World War II for running an officers' mess with distinction, was also known about the estate as Fangio, after the famous Argentine racing driver, because of his fondness for driving around at frightening speeds, usually in second gear.

As we eased our way around the croquet lawn towards the gatehouse, I saw we were being followed by two more large cars, a silver Rolls-Royce and a blue Facel Vega—the weekend's favoured guests, no doubt. Peter's green van had gone on ahead, leaving in a cloud of smoke. It was then that I noticed a curious feeling of importance creeping up on me. For the most part, children at the castle tended to get overlooked in the grand scheme of things, but there I was, ensconced in the great Mercedes 600 with Nanny, Granny B, and Morg, on my way to the launching of the ducks and feeling almost elated.

The convoy wound its elegant way down the little tree-shaded hill, across the stream, past the giant rhododendron bush in full bloom on our left, with the tennis court, pavilion, and wood-garden beyond. My gaze drifted to the right as we drove up the small incline, and I marvelled anew at this magnificent view of the castle. Slowly on for a couple of hundred yards, bisecting the first hole of golf, and we had arrived.

A large pond sat on either side of the drive, each covered with an array of ducks, geese, and assorted flying beasts. We parked beneath the tall beech trees to the left. Nanny and I climbed out while Brewer hurried round to get Granny's wheelchair out of the trunk and help her out of the car. Morg was laughing, and after making a joke about the long journey we'd all just undertaken, he asked me: "Might we have another concert soon, my dear fella?"

"Absolutely. I know 'Puttin on the Style' by Lonnie Donegan pretty well now."

"Well, that sounds like a fine plan! Off we go now. Let's not keep those ducks waiting."

I pondered briefly if Granny B really needed the wheelchair—after all, she happily played croquet for an hour or two, using just a shooting stick for the occasional rest—but I took it that she merely preferred to oversee the ceremony in maximum comfort. The chair also allowed her to cover her legs with a large rug: Despite the warm weather my grandmother often felt the cold.

As the group gathered, I noticed many familiar court faces were present and correct. Lady Huntley, plumpish, tweedy, and, for the most part, rather delightful. Her thinning red hair sat very flat and left something to be desired. She wore excessive makeup, had a beak for a nose and eyebrows that looked painted on. She drove the Rolls-Royce, which may have been her sign of assertiveness. She was chatting with Colonel Anson (Ret.), also known as "Bottle," a moniker readily explained by his corpulence and voluptuous red nose. Whenever I saw him Bottle was genial, and everyone said he was brilliant at golf. Guysy-Wee (Capt. Guy Lambert) was also there, a little stooped and frail. He was the oldest member of the court and possibly the sweetest natured. His clothes were always exquisite, his manners a dream, and he played croquet and backgammon with grace and consummate skill, something I discovered after another six or seven years had gone by and he was kind enough to play with me.

The homosexual contingent, the ever-revolving door of well-heeled, international sophisticated wits and card players, was represented by Johnny Galliher and Bert Whitley. I used to enjoy observing the mannerisms and walk of these two gentlemen, with the exaggerated thrust of the hip and grandiose use of hand gestures, usually accompanied by a wrist cocked backward at forty-five degrees. Bert, I heard later from unimpeachable sources, liked to wear red trousers and a navy cashmere smoking jacket when he dined *alfresco* with friends in Beaulieu, near Cap-Ferrat, in the South of France, where he kept a small pied-à-terre.

Mickey Renshaw, a social gadfly of ill-defined occupation, very tall, thin, and outré in manner and dress (far more so than Johnny and Bert), hovered next to Granny B. I always thought he slithered rather than walked, which helped explain the venom in what passed for his sense of humour. After Granny B's death, when the castle had become a foundation, he and my mother were discussing "the old dump"—as she liked to call it—in the library before lunch. My mother referred to Leeds as "her home," which Mickey Renshaw, unapologetically, almost with zeal, corrected to "Your *ex*-home, Susie, darling," in his deep-voiced exaggerated drawl, giving offense and causing hurt at the same time.

Rounding out the group were the Duchess of Roxburghe, dark-haired, compact, and well turned out in an unobtrusive way, who appeared to be *gentille* without any overwhelming evidence one way or the other, and the Hon. Mrs. Robin Warrender, a small, charming, and very pretty lady whose two lovely daughters, Carolyn (my age) and Annabel (three years younger), were my best friends in the world.

As we made our way along the little pathway to the special launch area, my mother, bursting with energy after her vigorous walk, caught up with Nanny and me. "How was the drive, darling?" she asked, removing her gloves and smoothing her coat.

"A bit *long*," I replied, borrowing Morg's joke, "but okay."

Just up ahead, parked close to the water's edge, I saw Peter the birdman's green van. Its back doors were open, and there were lots of big cardboard boxes stacked up, all of them with holes in the side. Peter, a tall handsome man who never failed to look anything other than furious (perhaps he was merely serious) was talking to two young men standing beside him and pointing to the boxes. All three were wearing corduroy trousers and gumboots.

Then I spotted the funniest thing. I must have played around that area a hundred times, but I had never seen it before. In all its glory, sloping gently down from the grassy bank into the water, was a six-foot-long and two-foot-wide wooden plank. I grabbed Nanny's hand, struggling to control an onslaught of the giggles. A launching pad, of course, I thought to myself. You don't just toss a duck into the water and cry, *"Bon voyage!"* Indeed you do not. Especially not Granny B.

Morg had positioned Granny's chair at the uppermost tip of the launchpad, and one of Peter's boys handed her what looked like a clipboard with a pencil attached.

"Now, have you got them all in the correct order?" I heard her ask Peter.

My mother took my hand and guided me to an exalted position just to Granny B's left, giving me an uninterrupted view of everything that was about to take place.

As the last of what looked like about ten boxes was laid out on the grass, Peter began opening the first. It wasn't sealed or fastened, so it was a matter of seconds before it was open. With both hands spread wide, he leaned in and lifted out into the afternoon sunshine the first quintessentially well-bred duck.

Amidst a smattering of applause, Peter brought the duck over to Granny B and held it close for her inspection. With her glasses delicately perched on the end of her nose, Granny studied the duck with the intensity of an art historian who has just been introduced to a newly discovered work by an Old Master. Checking a little marker attached to the duck's right leg, she proclaimed, "Ah yes, George is a most handsome fellow. And what a fine beak!"

Good heavens, I said to myself, they have names! Granny has actually given the ducks names. Astonishing! Granny continued her conversation with George for a few moments, then she said with a flourish, "Right ho, Peter. Let's see him go."

Very gently and with great decorum, Peter placed George at the top of the launchpad, and without further ado George started to waddle, with as much elegance as he could muster, down the ramp as Granny B, having changed from her short-range to her long-range glasses, leaned forward in her chair, straining to appreciate every nuance of the performance.

George entered the water and reacted with a flurry of wing flapping and frantic footwork, immediately followed by an exhibition of the most serene paddling imaginable, especially by a duck who has just been introduced to a new habitat, albeit a very beautiful one. As George ambled around his new domain, our gathering responded with the polite enthusiasm of a Wimbledon crowd on Ladies' Day. A few clapped; I heard Guysy-Wee gruffly mumble "Fine show" a few times; Morg hummed a brief "Trumpet Voluntary" before being overtaken by hiccups. I grinned at Nanny and awaited the next stage.

Granny was still making notes when Peter appeared with

duck number two, and then the whole extraordinary procedure was repeated. Nine ducks were launched that afternoon: George, Jane, Rupert, Sally, Horace, Fred, Bill, Margaret, and Ted.

When it was all over, the assembled company seemed to agree it had been a sensational display. My personal impressions were not sought by Granny B or any of the court members present—not even Morg—which, at least, upheld a level of consistency for the afternoon and, happily, failed to put a dent in my enjoyment of the show.

If Granny B were alive today, and the taxman, in his infinite wisdom, had been persuaded to leave her fortune intact, I can imagine BBC television crews periodically being invited down to the castle to record such stimulating "reality" spectaculars as the launching of the ducks for the benefit and bemusement of invited observers and television viewers across the land. Quite what they would make of it all I can only surmise; the hushed tone, the pomp and circumstance, the regal chatelaine and her watchful attendants, the subdued humour, the rather strange intensity—all for nine baby ducks who had received no warning about what to expect from their formidable *grande patronne.*

5.

HILL HOUSE DAYS

I was ill prepared for school when I first started at Hill House, aged five. Between the hours of 8:30 a.m. and 3:00 p.m., my formerly self-contained, well-ordered, calm, and exquisitely comfortable nursery existence was suddenly transformed into an unexpected series of embarrassing yet unavoidable encounters over which I had no say or control.

Arithmetic caused my head to spin and my brain to rattle because never before had I been obliged to display my foolishness so nakedly and in front of so many. Fortunately I developed an ability to play cricket quite well, which placed me in good stead with both my teachers and fellow pupils. Similarly, by then I was listening to music on the radio with an almost obsessional happiness, and found I could pick up a tune and sing along with it after just a couple of listens. Together with life lessons from Robin Hood, Davy Crockett, and William Tell, my favourite television heroes, these new skill sets became my defence against being completely alienated from my peers by the castle way.

During my Hill House days, I started to love my mother as much as I learned to be wary of my father, who remained, to this small person, both distant and unapproachable. She became my periodic glamorous companion and teacher of certain things beyond Nanny's purview. I'd been expecting Chapman, our London butler, to drive me from Egerton Terrace to Hill House for my first day of school, because I knew my mother's morning routine began when Agnes, the housekeeper and Chapman's wife, brought her breakfast in bed at 10:00 a.m., long after I was scheduled to be at my desk. But to my astonishment she was up and ready at 8:00 a.m., looking as beautiful and well turned out as ever, fussing over her handbag and preparing to "bundle me" into the Bentley.

It was an eight-minute drive to Hans Place, a pretty Victorian square where Hill House sat at one corner and Harrods was a cricket-ball throw away. When we arrived, she parked close by the school and we walked, hand in hand, up to the entrance, mounted the steps, and entered the main hall, which was packed with parents dropping their children off for the new term. A fearful discomfort gripped me from head to toe in a flash. I felt as if I was being forced to participate in a ghastly social experiment that I wanted curtailed immediately, so that I could be driven back home to Nanny and the comforts of the nursery. Then a woman of terrifying appearance, dragon eyes and eagle nose, wearing a tweed suit and with lacquered hair, came up to us and announced: "I am Mrs. Townend, the headmaster's wife." I was struck dumb. The grown-ups proceeded to have a brief conversation, after which Mrs. Townend took my hand and firmly led me away to the classroom across the hall to begin my education.

My mother would pick me up from Hill House at least twice a week and either walk me home or, better by far, take me to Harrods. The fourth-floor toy department and the second-floor record department now reigned supreme in my firmament, mystical in their ability to enthral me with the vastness of their rooms and the luxury of their appointments. The most wondrous toys were displayed with panache, including a shiny pedal motorcar temptingly available for testing on the floor. Hundreds of the greatest records were placed in perfectly proportioned wooden racks, just low enough for me to flip through until my fingers ached or I was told it was time to go. There were delightful little booths where one could listen to a single, or part of an LP, before deciding whether to buy it. My mother rarely bought me toys or records on the spot because she thought I should wait for the special occasions when they could be presented as a surprise.

We frequently visited "Women and Children's Wear" (I can still hear the uniformed elevator operators now), which gave me a chance secretly to admire the mannequins wearing nothing but naughty underwear in some instances and what appeared to be glamorous costumes in others.

The ground-floor food hall was always a sight to behold. Wood panelling, tiled floors, and endless counters filled with the best meat, poultry, game, and fish, tended by men in blue-striped trousers, white aprons, and flat-top hats. On shelves and tables, countertops and stands, foods from all over the world were laid out with style and finesse. Most of them were yet to become part of my diet, but they all looked enticing in this exotic locale.

Whenever my mother wanted to purchase something in Harrods, she would hand over a small, dark green plastic card. I soon found out that such a card was the same as money at this most regal of shopping establishments. Once a month a bill arrived for all the goods she had bought, and all she (or Miss Bird, her secretary) then had to do was send them back a cheque. A Harrods card, I gathered, was a "must" for all who frequented the place, and possessing one was a clear indication of one's social standing. Although American Express and Bank Americard (later called Visa) were introducing credit cards around this time, it was years before the Harrods account became superfluous and multiple credit cards leaped from every self-respecting wallet.

At Leeds, my mother played tennis with me and took me out on the golf course, showing me the rudiments of a golf swing, which I quickly picked up because she was a good teacher and had a good swing herself. She never played, claiming she didn't really enjoy it, but I wondered if the castle way was placing too many other demands on her time. Audiences, card games, weekend guests, Monsieur Boudin visits, local dignitaries stopping by, sometimes the vicar for sherry, always "the birds"—all were time-consuming activities that could never be put on hold.

"Anthony settled very well to school life and he has made good progress in all subjects." So began my first end-of-term report, which ended with, "He is a happy form member." It was written on one page.

"Well done, darling," my mother said.

She, Nanny, and I were in the castle nursery, seated at the big round table in the middle as I devoured bangers and mash for supper. Evening sunlight filled the room, casting light and shadow over gloomy portraits of gloomy people. With only five minutes remaining until *Robin Hood* was on television, I wasn't sure the time was right to begin a discussion about the powerful inaccuracy of what I had just heard.

"Are you sure that's my report?" I asked.

"Of course, darling. Whose do you think it is?"

"Hard to say, really."

I was not nearly as happy in my first term as the report maintained. For example, I objected to the headmaster's habit of raising one's shorts to smack one hard on the thigh when he thought one deserved punishment. Nanny's approach to wayward behaviour—"Come now, dear, I'd rather you didn't do that"—felt more in keeping with castle way standards. Lunches at school were most awkward, all of us crammed onto benches and given unpleasant tinned Spam and Russian salad (mostly diced vegetables in a mayonnaise dressing). I'd performed adequately in the classroom but hadn't been able to come out of my shell in a convincing manner. Only the excursions to the Duke of York's playing fields on the King's Road, ten minutes' walk from Hill House, to learn cricket three times a week, brought joy. The columned magnificence of the military barracks which loomed above us as we played, the wide, flat expanse of perfectly mowed grass, and the comings and goings of soldiers, jeeps, and sometimes artillery added lustre to the already eye-popping surroundings, and gave a temporary lift to my spirit.

There was little opportunity to discuss my new favourite activity when I got home. Chapman was a cricket fan but I hardly ever spoke with him or with his wife, Agnes, because they were either too busy or didn't want to talk to me. Unfortunately neither Nanny nor my mother had the remotest interest in sports. That left my brothers, my father, and Miss Preston, the cook.

Miss Preston lived in the basement, in her bed-sitting room, and in between cooking assignments sat by her mantelpiece, coughed, and pondered her dizzying array of bizarre ornaments: porcelain animals and lockets, ceramic mugs with pictures of the Queen and Brighton Pier, even a miniature Eiffel Tower, all picked up during her holidays at English seaside resorts. Though I was seldom to be found in her lair I never saw her without a cigarette dangling from her enormous, heavily rouged lips, even when she was rolling pastry, slicing vegetables, or cracking eggs into a mixing bowl. She was a large lady with huge eyes, puffy cheeks, and puffier arms. Her legs were always wrapped in bandages to protect her varicose veins, and, in the house, she wore floppy open slippers and a hairnet, or bath cap, over her unkempt halo of frizzy white hair. Her voice was deep and resonant and hoarse from smoking. I loved her cooking, especially her toad in the hole (sausages in batter) and chocolate mousse, the texture of which was a household legend for its ability to house a number of upright spoons without any form of manual support.

Though never overtly unkind, Molly Preston wore a stern expression most of the time. It later dawned on me that her downstairs life was a lonely one, not alleviated by the less than congenial relations she enjoyed with Reg and Agnes Chapman, whose base of operations was just down the corridor. Alas, Miss P had no interest in cricket. Her main interest was listening to the radio because it meant she didn't have to keep getting up to bang on her tiny black-and-white television set when the screen went fuzzy and made annoying, distracting farting sounds.

My father and I never talked about cricket or anything else, even on the rare occasions we were in the same room. After the nursery incident, when he'd smacked James and I'd been a high-chair witness, it was a couple of years before I was prodded by my mother into occasionally stopping by his bathroom to say hello as he made his morning preparations for the office. I think he found it as difficult communicating with me as I did with him. Having been abandoned—in fact disowned—by his own father seemed to have left a mark on his ability to establish a meaningful father-son relationship. The combination of work, a full social calendar, and the comfortable expectations of the castle way suited my father to a T, keeping him heavily occupied and generally removed from the company of his three sons.

As he lay in his bath and doused his hair with Geo. F. Trumper's gentlemanly hair products, I would gaze at the posters of his theatrical productions that lined the walls. One in particular, featuring Cliff Richard in *Expresso Bongo*, with Cliff adopting a balletic pose, always caught my eye. It turned out to be from the movie of a musical that had been produced at the Saville Theatre, managed by my father! As much as I might have liked to hear about the seemingly glamorous life of a West End theatre producer, an awkward silence usually prevailed.

When it came to cricket, my father took the utmost pleasure in informing all those within earshot that when he was at Stowe, the remarkable founding headmaster, J. F. Roxburgh, had called him in to his study one day to make a personal request: "Geoffrey," the beautifully mannered and always immaculately dressed headmaster had begun, "I do hope you won't take this amiss, but I was wondering if perhaps you wouldn't mind taking leave of your endeavours on the cricket field because it has come to all our attention that your skills in the game are rather limited and you might well find yourself better employed elsewhere." My father was simply delighted. Not having to play cricket, or any other game, was the ideal situation, and he remained forever more uninterested in sports.

At least my brothers were cricket fans, so I wasn't flying solo at home. It would have been churlish to grumble, and I didn't.

I continued with my bangers and mash, mentioning between mouthfuls, "I suppose for a first term it wasn't all that bad." Nanny, of course, knew otherwise, but in her kind and thoughtful way she selected the course that best served my rather complex comfort levels, and said nothing.

"I'll be off, darling," my mother said gently. "I know you don't want to miss *Robin Hood* on the box, do you now?" I was so startled by the fact that my mother knew about my favourite television programme being about to start that I found myself staring at her as if seeing her for the first time as another important ally deep inside the bubble. It should have been obvious.

By the 1960 Lent term I had three times received headmaster's reports along the following lines: "He has far more ability than he is displaying at present. . . . He has not been concentrating well, not making much effort. . . . He seems interested in history but is very diffident about joining in oral lessons and discussions . . . in fact his whole approach to life seems to be lacking in self-confidence, which inevitably affects his schoolwork. . . . He is at his happiest and most relaxed when painting or drawing, at which he is most gifted." These were accurate assessments, but nobody spoke to me about them or suggested straightforward guidelines for improvement. I imagine my parents read these reports and then retired them to a filing cabinet to gather dust in peace and quiet. In the meantime the castle way and I were given free rein to continue on our merry way.

———

"Russell, am I disturbing you?" my Latin teacher enquired one frigid February morning during my last term at Hill House. I was sitting, as was my custom, slumped at my desk in the back row of the classroom, staring at the blackboard with a totally blank expression. The room was wide, painted white, with a hardwood floor, and its bay windows looked out over the circle of handsome red-brick Victorian buildings of Hans Place, with a tree-lined garden in the centre. There were four rows of individual desks, worn and scratched, each with an attached bench and a top which opened to house pens, crayons, and exercise books. I had never liked this room, whose floor always smelled of polish—a school smell. I felt the other boys often sensed my habitual discomfort, which alienated me further.

"Er . . . no sir."

"What a relief! For a moment I thought we'd lost you."

"Yes sir."

"So we did lose you?"

"I don't think so."

"You might find it extremely helpful, Russell, if you made an effort to concentrate more."

"Yes sir."

"Good. I look forward to seeing you follow through on that."

I detested being told what to do by strangers, especially gruesome, grotty schoolmasters. Only Nanny was allowed to tell me what to do. Or that was the way I saw it.

6.

ON VACATION

When I was four—one year before I went to Hill House—the castle way and family holidays conducted a joint summer experiment. For two weeks Granny B, the court, assorted aunts, uncles, cousins, and friends, my parents, David, James, Nanny, and I assembled on Venice's fabled Lido Beach and waited to see what would happen.

My grandmother and the court booked into the five-star Excelsior, while the rest of us stayed at the family-friendly Quattro Fontane, a stone's throw away. The Excelsior contingent then disappeared off the face of the map, leaving the children (and nannies) to bucket-and-spade their way through the long, hot, sandy days, and the parents to endure the associated hullabaloo, fortifying themselves with a steady stream of Bloody Marys every day at noon. At lunchtime children and nannies retired to the pretty garden of the Quattro Fontane for spaghetti, while the grown-ups took a well-deserved break, joining the court at the Excelsior, a local trattoria, or the villa of a friendly count.

Granny B evidently saw a bleak future in three-generational groupings at foreign hotels, because the experiment was not repeated. For her it was misery not having a full complement of personal staff to attend to her daily important needs. I spotted her twice on the beach, sitting under a parasol puffing away through a long cigarette holder, accompanied by Morg (who wore the largest swimming trunks I'd ever seen on any man, and who swam with the children whenever he could), but that concluded her holiday outreach.

The castle way was not to be trifled with. Granny B's summers would henceforward be centred around a villa in the South of France, where she could set herself up, with her castle staff, in the comfort and style she was accustomed to, and conduct her affairs as she pleased. Should grandchildren or young cousins need to be put up for a few nights, every effort would be made to meet the request, so long as card-table pairings, dinner-table settings, visits to and from local grandees, afternoon siestas, staff rotations, and a host of other vital considerations were not in any way disrupted.

Much to my surprise (I was unaware that they'd enjoyed the experiment), my parents took David, James, Nanny, and me back to the Quattro Fontane the following year, this time accompanied by their close friends, the Hon. Robin and Mrs. Warrender. Granny B rented the fabled Château Saint-Jean in Saint-Jean-Cap-Ferrat that summer while she searched for a nearby villa more to her taste. Enjoying the close companionship of my brothers and my two lovely cousins Sandra and Paget for a whole fortnight (the one and only time) made this second, court-free, taste of Lido glamour rather a special affair for me.

There were three highlights of the initial Venice excursion, all eye-openers for their stark newness after four years cloistered in a brace of nurseries. First, the sights and sounds of Victoria Station: its thirty-metre-high glass ceiling and iron beams; the noise and energy of the platforms with travellers and porters hustling and bustling about; the smoke of the steam engines—which bore a striking resemblance to the pictures I was so familiar with but were a lot dirtier—and the powerful whistle blasts that echoed like a chorus of ill-tempered parakeets through the station as trains prepared for departure to destinations unknown. And all this was a mere run-up to the exhilarating overnight sleeper to Venice.

Then there were the water-taxi rides up and down the canals and across the waterways of the lagoon. By day I was awed by the grace and beauty of the palazzos, churches, bridges, and gondolas. By night, as we raced past an enormous American warship, anchored so close to land that the gorgeously lit tower of the Doge's Palace appeared to form a part of her structure, I sensed with strange delight the piquant aromas of salt water, sewage, and fine cuisine wafting up into the starry sky.

Last there was the occasion when Auntie Pops, my mother's equally striking but less forgiving older sister (mother of Sandra and Paget), shouted at me ferociously when I walked in on her stark naked as she was changing in her beach cabana. "Get out!" she cried (subconsciously prepping me for my upcoming encounter with Princess Djordjadze in the castle hallway), startling me with her vehemence. Get out I did, closing the curtain behind me, blushing furiously but still quite taken with my first official sighting of the adult female form in all its glory and abundance. I had grown accustomed to splashing and playing with ducks in the large nursery bath at Leeds with Carolyn and Annabel, but this was a gratifying new format.

Granny B needed the court on hand during the winter months in Nassau and the summer in the South of France. Those who resisted making themselves available on the dates assigned to them did so in the knowledge that they would be incurring the chatelaine's displeasure—not something to be taken lightly.

Realistically, the castle way and family holidays never had much chance of seeing eye to eye. The former required constant adherence to established guidelines from sophisticated adults, with the bare minimum of interference (if any) from the young. The latter required intermittent adherence to intangible guidelines from sophisticated adults, with the emphasis on giving (for limited spells) small amounts of pleasure to the young.

My next two summers were therefore spent away from family with Nanny, Nanny Warrender (English nannies used to take the name of the family), Carolyn, and Annabel in an idyllic little town called Bembridge on the east coast of the Isle of Wight. We stayed in the prettiest street, lined on both sides with clean, delicate-looking, almost identical Victorian houses, most of which were used during the summer months as bed-and-breakfasts for families such as ours. The Warrenders were four houses down from us because we could not find a house for us all to be together. The beach was just a few minutes' walk from our respective B and Bs, and there was a newsagent on the corner for picking up sweets and magazines. It was calm, it was peaceful, it was bliss.

We would meet up with the Warrenders at the gate of our B and B at ten thirty or a quarter to eleven. The five of us would then set off for the beach, the girls and I leading the way once we became familiar with the route. We three had our buckets and spades to carry, and our nannies brought up the rear, laden down with towels and changes of clothing. Our morning activities were confined to splashing in the frothy water after the waves had broken, seeing who could be the boldest by venturing just that little bit further out before the inevitable warning to be careful from one barefoot nanny or the other (neither of whom was ever far behind). Periodically we chose to play in the wet sand, energetically digging, building up, and slapping into shape our constructions, the three of us nattering away like the three musketeers until it was time to go and change for lunch.

The Bembridge beach facilities clearly were never intended to resemble those of the Lido, and our changing cabin was a far cry from the Italian cabanas. Such matters, though, were far from my mind. The three of us loved being together, and indeed plans had already been laid for us to get married, with only one small detail to be worked out: Was I to marry Carolyn or Annabel? On the walks back to our respective B and Bs, marital discussions would resume exactly where they had left off.

"I'm older and therefore I should get to choose, and I think I will marry Anthony," Carolyn told Annabel, her mellifluous voice firm, her sharp features focused.

"But I'll be so unhappy, and you mustn't make me unhappy!" Annabel responded, and I agreed that this was a very important point.

"Look," I proposed. "Can I marry Carolyn first, then you after?"

"But how long will I have to wait?" Annabel asked. "It's not at all fair."

"I could marry you first," I said undiplomatically.

"No, you won't. You'll marry me first. Please don't be silly." Carolyn put her foot down forcefully, which left me wondering if we'd ever resolve this intractable problem.

We'd been walking down the alleyway, away from the beach, a wall on one side facing a tall hedge, and were almost at the corner where the newsagent sat. We turned onto our street and in front of the shop I asked Nanny if I could go inside to have a look at the new "trash-mags," the World War II comic adventure magazines all the boys I knew, especially my brothers, were reading, collecting, and swapping like maniacs. I had recently become a devotee myself and had brought a small selection with me to Bembridge.

The Warrender girls declined the opportunity to join me for a browse, so we said our farewells for that day, placing all wedding plans on hold until the morning. Inside the shop I quickly located the swivel stand upon which hung racks of brand new trash-mags. While I began my search I watched Nanny wander off to the other side of the store, where the grown-ups' magazines and postcards were located. The shopkeeper, an elderly lady dressed in a worn floppy cardigan, was partially obscured from view by the stand, and as I flipped through one or two of the best-looking trash-mags, whose covers all featured pictures of fierce-looking soldiers, English and German, firing machine guns, hurling grenades, and generally appearing heroic, a hitherto unimaginable thought crept into my mind. I could easily slip one of the quite small magazines inside my shirt. Nobody would see me. Nanny, surely, would not notice the difference between the magazines I already had and a new one? With so many of them lined up six inches from my nose, I wanted a new one, wanted it badly, and it would be easy. I didn't have any money on me, so what should I do? Ask Nanny, do nothing, or take it—steal it?

I needed to act fast because I knew Nanny would soon finish her transaction and the shopkeeper would start to wonder about me. I opened my two top buttons, slipped a trash-mag down the front of my shirt, did up the buttons, and arranged my arms, still holding my trusty bucket and spade in front of me, as the vicar would do when standing in front of the altar at St Nicholas's Church in Leeds village.

Instantly I felt my neck grow warm and my heartbeat go into overdrive. My scalp began tingling, and my skin was turning puce, but instead of putting the magazine back I glanced once more in the direction of the shopkeeper and with as much sangfroid as I could muster, wandered out onto the street, hoping that Nanny would soon follow.

She did, enquiring kindly, "Did you have fun looking at your magazines, dear?"

"Yes, thank you," I said, my eyes glued to the pavement as if searching for a fallen coin, desperate not to have my perfidy uncovered. I dared not look behind me as we strolled back to our B and B for fear that the old lady from the shop would suddenly appear and demand retribution for my heinous act.

It wasn't until we were back in our room and Nanny had ventured down the corridor to the bathroom that I was able to take my illicit cargo from its hiding place and slip it into my drawer with the other trash-mags, an act that brought blessed relief from the immediate fear of being caught. Still, it did not dispel the grim possibility that Nanny would somehow recognize that I had all of a sudden acquired an addition to my reading material and ask me how that might have come to pass. She never did, but the tainted trash-mag remained out of sight until long after we had gone back home.

A new quandary presented itself. Having now firmly established my credentials as a bold and fearless thief, should

I do it again? Robin Hood stole from the rich to give to the poor. But I was stealing from the poor to give to . . . the rich? Of course I was not rich myself; otherwise my need to sing for a half crown or patiently await an annual Christmas record or book token would not have been so acute. But the bubble in which I existed bred a mind-set that followed me everywhere. It told me I was richer (without needing any actual money) and better than the rest, and that I could have everything I wanted. I assumed that my great good fortune would remain sacrosanct and unchallenged forever, without my having to do a thing. These were perilous thoughts for a child on the cusp of being sent off to boarding school for the next ten years. They were also thoughts I kept entirely to myself, and so nobody— not my brothers, not Nanny, not my school friends, and certainly not my parents—was given the opportunity to dispel them or knock some sense into my head.

Soon after the Bembridge robbery I found myself in need of money for a 45 rpm record. I rifled through Nanny's bag and found a crumpled ten-shilling note. I stole it. Briefly. The horror of doing such a thing to my favourite person in the world racked me with guilt (another dreadful new sensation) and raised, once again, the fear of being caught doing something horrendously bad. I quickly, secretively, put the money back, believing that my honour had been restored.

7.

Christmas and Crockett

Nothing, absolutely nothing, ever came close to matching the raw physical excitement I felt as the Bentley was being loaded and the final preparations being made for the one-and-a-half-hour drive from our house in London down to the Kent countryside for Christmas at the castle. I never mentioned this to anybody because when I was seven, it didn't feel like the right thing to do, but for me it was all-consuming and breathtaking in its power.

So intense was my focus on the pleasures to come that for once it did not bother me that the clock had sailed past the allotted three o'clock hour of departure. There we were, Nanny and I, ready for hours, days, sitting in the study with its dark brown carpet, dark green sofa, and French antique side tables and desk, where my mother paid the bills and attended to household matters with Miss Bird (whose face looked a lot like an American eagle's), and where my father liked to watch the news on television after dinner.

At ten past five my mother was yet to finish her cup of China tea and digestive biscuit. I was still contemplating how Nanny was always able to remain totally unflappable whatever the circumstance, an especially desirable character trait given her constant exposure to the idiosyncrasies of our family life.

All of a sudden the study door was filled, or at least partly occupied, by Chapman's diminutive yet dignified presence. His head was egg shaped, his thinning hair combed straight back, and his expression imperturbable at all times. He wore a tailcoat and striped trousers, removing the coat only when he was in his pantry polishing silver, or relaxing with Agnes over a cup of tea in their sitting room, which looked out over the walled, herbaceous-bordered back garden.

Agnes had wiry red hair, hollow cheeks, and a forceful gaze emphasized by her large and powerful spectacles. When she was cleaning the house, pushing, pulling, and twisting her heavy, noisy machinery with utter disregard for the safety of the skirting boards, she looked like a hornet with a Hoover, hell-bent on completing the task before moving on to the next.

"Your mother is ready," Chapman informed us and discreetly withdrew. My mother was in the hallway, immaculate in a headscarf and warm coat, making a final inspection of her handbag, which as usual looked enormously full. "All right, Nanny," she said, snapping the bag shut with great authority and popping an Altoid extra-strong peppermint into her mouth. "Let's bundle him in."

It had already snowed lightly in London, but the castle and grounds, we'd been told, were covered top to toe with thick, beautiful snow. And it was very cold. A perfect start to the festivities as far as I was concerned. If my mother felt the same way, she kept it to herself, mentioning only something about driving becoming hazardous, but Nanny and I were confident our passage would be a smooth one, and it was. Despite the blackness of night, the bright lights, and slushy roads, our spirits were high as, just before seven o'clock, we turned off the main A20 road, passed through the gates of the front drive, and entered the castle grounds.

I immediately felt the familiar rush of excitement and anticipation that struck me each time we arrived at the castle gates, only this time it was stronger, more palpable.

No description of Leeds's transcendent beauty has, to me, ever sounded adequate, nor the effect such beauty had on those fortunate enough to have known it, and known it well.

I opened the window and leaned out. The air, cold and crisp, smelt like Christmas. Despite the darkness I could see the snow all around us, a ghostly white.

"Darling, would you mind, before we all freeze?" my mother said.

I wound the window back up as we went over the top of the first small hill, our big tyres making *crunch-crunch* sounds in the snow just as my cereal used to do at breakfast. Then we started going downhill, way down, with woods all around and Granny B's duckery over to our right. Then sharply up a steep hill, over the top, round a bend, to the most thrilling moment of the journey.

Off in the distance I saw the castle lights twinkling, the outline of the Gloriette (the site of the original Norman keep), the battlements and the bell tower barely visible in the pale moonlight. A wondrous sight. For this child it was, and will always remain, a moment of pure heaven.

As we made our way up the drive I remained in my private rapture, my nose glued to the window, my breath fogging it up, necessitating a rapid clearing with the palm of my hand. Much too soon the castle went out of sight as we descended again, up and round the last hill, through the gatehouse, around the croquet lawn, and we'd arrived.

Before I knew it there were people everywhere, opening doors, rushing around. "Good evening, Madam," once. "Good evening, Madam," twice. Borrett stood in the open doorway directing operations like the Duke of Wellington at the Battle of Waterloo. "Good evening, Nanny. Good evening, Master Anthony," he said with the same formality as if he were addressing the Queen of Sheba. "I hope you had a pleasant drive."

Unable to restrain myself, I pushed past everybody to get a first look at the Christmas decorations. In direct contrast to the grand formality of the castle's usual appearance, Granny B insisted on pulling out all the stops and transforming the whole feel of Leeds over Christmas. Holy Moses! I thought, looking up at the hall ceiling, where giant multicoloured paper streamers hung in perfect arcs from all four corners, meeting in the centre at a huge forest green paper bell. Through to the left in the main hall I admired more streamers, more bells, more colour, and the glorious sensation of Christmas all around.

Nanny took my hand and, as she guided me under the Gothic archway, up the great stone staircase over which three massive sixteenth-century Flemish hunting tapestries, of wild animals and exotic foliage woven in gorgeous greens and gold, loomed large, I heard my mother telling me she'd be up soon to "tuck me in." My day was drawing to a close, and all further activities were to be put on hold until the morning.

"When will David and James be here?" I asked Nanny from the bath, thinking how much livelier the nursery became when my older brothers were around.

"Your father's driving them down in the morning," she informed me. "I expect they'll be here in time for lunch. Now hurry up, please, because Vincent is on his way up with supper."

I liked Vincent more than most of the other footmen, whose names I would often forget. He arrived in an elevator, which I found amusing. He would deposit the food on a large tray in our little pantry, and Nanny would then bring it to us in the playroom. Later he'd come back and remove all the debris.

My mother tucked me in so tightly that after a goodnight kiss and the lights were turned out it took a few kicks and wriggles to free up some breathing space. Then I drifted off into a sleep filled with exotic snowmen and reindeers at the gallop.

Nanny and I were up, dressed, and had eaten breakfast by eight. For a long time after that I became wholly occupied staring out of the tall windows, feasting my eyes on the glorious sight of the golf course and parkland covered in snow. The lordly cedars off in the distance, graceful through the ages, their presence so dignified, so reassuring; and closer in, the triangular red flag on the ninth green flapping away merrily like a clown's foot at the circus. How many nurseries in England, spacious enough for a family of four to inhabit, could there possibly be with views to equal this? It soon dawned on me that no ducks or geese were to be spotted on the moat. "Nanny, look!" I cried. "The moat is completely frozen!"

"My goodness, so it is," she said, peering through her glasses with one arm around me, a look of wonderment on her face equal to my own. We wrapped ourselves up like South Pole explorers and set off for a walk. Quietly. We knew the drill. Not seen, not heard until the castle and its guests had fully awoken, breakfasted, read papers, dressed, and left their rooms. I preferred it that way. Bumping into the wrong people unexpectedly could set off unwanted alarm bells and was best avoided if possible.

We walked for over two hours, building and demolishing snowmen with casual abandon. In the stable yard, perched atop the hill which overlooked the castle island where the horses used to be kept but were no longer because nobody ever rode, we bumped into Mrs. Brewer. She was the wife of Granny B's chauffeur, a compact, well-turned-out lady for whom I had a soft spot, especially when she invited me into her cottage for some of her scrumptious homemade scones.

Strolling through the kitchen garden in all its immaculately cropped, incessantly formal and, now, snow-covered splendour, we encountered Mr. Elves, the electrician (whose son, Johnny, was head footman), as always wearing rumpled corduroys and a worn tweed jacket, today with a heavy sweater underneath.

"Morning, Happy Christmas!" he said from beneath his peaked cap, beady eyes courteous but wary, enormous red beard camouflaging his round, ruddy-cheeked face and obscuring all further expression.

"Good morning, Mr. Elves," Nanny and I said in unison, "Happy Christmas! What a lovely day."

"That it is."

"See you at the party later," Nanny added.

The annual staff Christmas party was, for me, a combination of thumbs-up (home territory and Granny's present) and thumbs-down (another social event with too many unfamiliar faces to contend with). A large number of estate workers, most of whom I knew, and their children, most of whom I did not, gathered in the ground-floor rooms of the Gloriette for tea and entertainment, followed by a mad frenzy of balloon popping and Christmas gift distributing to the children by Granny B (who enjoyed this annual opportunity to greet in person her employees' children and exchange a few words), assisted by Morg and John Money, the estate manager. I knew I was supposed to be enjoying myself on these occasions but I seldom did.

The Gloriette was first constructed in stone by Robert de Crèvecoeur in the twelfth century when Henry I was king of England. The ground-floor ceilings were high and beamed, and Granny had the floors, once stone, laid in the finest ebony when she began the massive reconstruction work in the 1920s. The seventy-five-foot-long room where the staff party took place had been King Edward I's banqueting hall, but Granny used to call it the saloon because before World War II she and her guests spent some serious partying time there, dancing to music piped in from hidden gramophones, drinking, gossiping, enjoying films, and, in one of the adjacent rooms, gambling with riverboat fervour. At this time the saloon walls were covered in deep red velvet and adorned by tapestries including *Narcissus,* which later went to the Museum of Fine Arts Boston. A mighty sixteenth-century stone fireplace with carved figures, lions, and grotesque heads, brought over from a French château, looked down over silk Eastern carpets and across to the bay window, which dated from the rebuilding work undertaken by Sir Henry Guilford for King Henry VIII in 1517. There was also a Steinway concert grand piano in the event some maestro happened to be present, which was often the case.

The prewar guest list at Leeds Castle was always kept as quiet as possible because Granny B was a private person who greatly disliked publicity. In this she was ably assisted by her friendship with the major newspaper proprietors of the day, who were happy to trade weekend invitations for maximum discretion on castle matters. But a scrutiny of the visitors' book, kept in the library during the 1950s and 1960s and available for family and guests to peruse, revealed the ink signatures of people ranging from Edward, Prince of Wales (later Duke of Windsor), and Wallis Simpson, Prince George and Princess Marina of Greece, Queen Marie of Romania, and Alfonso XIII of Spain, to ambassadors, government ministers, an assortment of well-bred landowners and gentry, film stars such as Douglas Fairbanks Jr., Charlie Chaplin, Errol Flynn, David Niven, and Gertrude Lawrence, even Nazi Germany's ambassador to Great Britain, Joachim von Ribbentrop. In those days the gathering storm in Europe looked as if it might not draw in the British Isles, but still one wonders what he and Britain's foreign secretary, Anthony Eden, might have discussed over the port and cigars.

A friendly man but one of few words, Mr. Elves soon went on his way, as did Nanny and I. We arrived back in the nursery without having seen another soul, and I wondered where on earth everybody was. When David and James eventually arrived, storming into the nursery dressed in corduroy trousers and pullovers, I briefly contemplated their superior outfits to my uninspiring khaki shorts and school woolly before we all set off for the party.

It was a journey which took us down the main stairs, under an arch, past the Yellow drawing room where the grown-ups played cards after dinner, past the gentlemen's washroom, down more stairs, past the kitchens and Borrett's pantry, an area we hardly ever visited, down the long, narrow, tiled corridor that connected the new castle (eighteenth century) with the old (twelfth century) and, finally, to the Gloriette, where the tea-room looked as if everybody had arrived and the party was in full swing.

Ladies in black dresses and white aprons rushed about carrying tea, jugs of milk, lemonade, and orange squash, and serving cakes, biscuits, sandwiches, and scones. There were probably a hundred people nattering away, happy and seemingly full of Christmas spirit.

Nanny and I managed to squeeze ourselves in somewhere while David and James went off in search of the rowdier element. I did not recognize the people around us, although Nanny gave me the impression she did, so as she chatted and sipped tea I did my best to make myself agreeable to the pretty girls seated on either side of me, an effort that strained my resources to the limit and produced no positive results to speak of. Perhaps this was because my castle status induced shyness on their part, thus rounding out the troika. Whatever the reason, I opted to make a strategic withdrawal as soon as politeness allowed in order to have a quick, private inspection of the tree.

As always, it stood by the bay window rising up from floor to ceiling, emitting a sensational sweet smell of pine, and was garlanded with tinsel, coloured lights, and enough sweets and chocolates to sink a battleship. Underneath, neatly arranged and beautifully wrapped, were presents for all the children.

As the former saloon began filling up, happy faces appeared wearing paper hats in all the colours of the rainbow, blowing whistles, and bearing other strange objects found in the Christmas crackers. Then Granny made her stately way into the room, accompanied by my mother, and everyone made a lot of fuss over them. Morg followed and made a lot of fuss over everyone else. No other members of the court made an appearance. Nanny eased her way through the crowd towards me, selecting, to John Money's annoyance, one of the large, ochre-coloured cushions (made from Breton sailcloth and found on the cane chairs outside the castle front door in summer) for me to sit on, in front of my mother's chair. He felt this was stuff and nonsense, me being silly, not participating on equal terms with the other children, and Nanny pushing her weight around. I just thought she was being kind.

Slowly but surely we were all in place; castle grown-ups in armchairs against the wall, close by the tree; children on cushions from in front of the stage to three-quarters of the way back; and the estate parents, some standing, some sitting on folding chairs, lined up along the back wall. For a brief moment the noise of chatting stopped as the curtain swept back to reveal a very funny-looking man in black tailcoat and top hat who bounced onto the stage bellowing, "Good evening, Ladies and Gentlemen!" several times before proceeding to pull a large number of handkerchiefs from both his ears.

I enjoyed that. For half an hour he regaled us with tricks and stories, sometimes asking for assistance from someone in the audience. I dreaded his asking me, but fortunately I escaped his attention, and as the final rabbit was gamely plucked from the ever-faithful hat, we all waved and said farewell. Time, now, for the presents.

Granny and Morg stood up, their commanding presence drawing all eyes. One by one John Money passed Morg the gifts and he, revelling in the situation, glanced at the card and whispered the name in Granny's ear. She then called out the names in her deep, husky, and mesmerizing voice, each time being assailed by a happy shout of "Me!" and "Over here!" When it was my turn she lowered her voice a little because I was sitting right in front of her.

It was large. "Darling Anthony," the label said, "Happy Christmas and much love, Granny." I tore away some of the paper and saw exactly what I had been hoping for. I felt a surge of excitement. It had been top of my list. I tore off more paper. *Yes!* Fantastic! A Davy Crockett outfit! Concentrating hard on the decimation of paper and ribbon, I almost forgot my manners. "Thank you, Granny," I said. She smiled at me, as did my mother. They could tell they'd picked a winner with this one.

I grabbed Nanny's hand and told her I was going upstairs to put my costume on. Oblivious to the pandemonium all around, balloons popping, babies crying, adults getting ready to leave, and children begging to stay with fierce intensity, I rushed back up to the nursery. I opened the box on my bed and took out the heavy buckskin jacket and long pants. The moccasins. The powder horn and strap. The leather belt and holster, the double-barreled pistol and hunting knife. And the hat. The big fur hat with a tail.

When dressed, I went over to the mirror on Nanny's dressing table. It looked great. It felt great. King of the castle. King of the wild frontier.

It was time to hang up my stocking. Nanny had found for me a long, thick woollen sock that we hung over one of the bedknobs. I wondered which fireplace Santa Claus would come down.

Indeed, considering his remarkably heavy load, I wondered if he might not consider putting tradition aside and come in through the front door. Mildly frustrated at my inability to assist Mr. Claus with his complicated travel arrangements, I turned out the light and tried to go to sleep. I could just hear Nanny and the boys watching television next door. Perhaps if I stayed awake Santa wouldn't come. Help! What was he going to bring? . . . An orange for the bottom of the stocking, surely . . . and lots of toys . . .

James had a stocking just like mine, and it seemed logical that David would too, although being in his separate bedroom meant waiting until the morning for comparisons. Strangely, Nanny's stocking was a lot smaller than ours, which mystified me a bit. Why did Father Christmas bring fewer gifts for Nanny? I should have asked her, but never got round to it.

When I awoke it was totally dark. My big toe had come into contact with something hard. Wary of making a noise, I gently prodded and explored with both feet, coming rapidly to the conclusion that Santa Claus had paid his call and left behind a full and weighty stocking as evidence of his endeavours. With reluctance I waited patiently for a while, but as my eyes adjusted to the dark, and what was lying across my feet became visible (as well as the sleeping figures of Nanny and James), curiosity got the better of me and I reached down. Christmas Day had begun, and not a moment too soon.

By the time James's head popped up, accompanied by a "Bloody hell, what time is it?" I was able to read Nanny's clock and inform him that it was just past six o'clock. I had already been hard at play for about an hour, but such was my diligence in maintaining minimal noise I had succeeded in opening only three small parcels, two of which remained a mystery as to what they were, or what they did, the third being a very smart pair of slippers. Small pieces of wrapping paper were strewn across my entire bed.

By six thirty the lights were on, we were all up, and Nanny was making tea. While David and James nattered and squabbled over their presents in the playroom, I went to work on an Airfix model Spitfire fighter plane, with one-third of my sock still remaining.

Breakfast over and dressed in full Crockett regalia (chest, accordingly, a little pumped up), I awaited zero hour, nine thirty—the only day of the year we were allowed to invade our parents' bedroom quarters so early—with outward calm and inner turmoil. I had recently been introduced to the music of Cliff Richard and the Shadows. That was as deeply significant as my introduction to cricket. So intense was my enthusiasm that, having saved enough tokens and pocket money to buy, and become intimately acquainted with, their long-playing record, I had concluded that I must have a guitar just like the one they played. On the back-cover sleeve-notes of the record there was a description of the instruments Hank, Bruce, and Jet favoured, and so onto my Christmas list, under the Davy Crockett outfit but above a new cricket bat, pads, and ball, went "One Fender Stratocaster, red, with tremolo arm." To make things sound a little more authentic, I put the word out that I'd had a few guitar lessons at Hill House and was well on my way to achieving a modicum of skill. Curiously, my claims were not greeted with the ridicule which they deserved.

Christmas Day was, in fact, practically the only day of the year we invaded our parents' bedroom quarters at all. At nine thirty on the dot, the three of us left the confines of the nursery and trooped down the corridor, past the long seventeenth-century oak refectory table, above which hung another fine Flemish verdure tapestry, under the arch, past the housekeeper, Mrs. Walsh's linen closet, and past Lady Huntley's bedroom.

Knocking loudly, we entered the inner sanctum. Cupboards right and left, designed by Monsieur Boudin and hand built by his craftsmen. Father's bedroom to the left, mother's to the right, marbled bathroom straight ahead. A sumptuous and very comfortable set of rooms with plenty of space to swing a few cats. We knocked again on our mother's door.

"Come in," she said, loud and clear.

There she was, neat and tidy, not a hair out of place, pink cardigan around her shoulders, sitting up in her antique four-poster bed having breakfast off a tray and glancing through a newspaper.

"Happy Christmas," everyone said all at the same time, followed by a flurry of kisses and more "Happy Christmases."

During the greetings, our father had entered the bedroom wearing a fine-looking pair of striped pyjamas, to be greeted by another chorus of "Happy Christmas." Eyes darted about the room in an effort to locate the presents. Our mother directed traffic from the bed, telling us in which direction to head. I experienced what can only be described as the onset of grave disappointment as I noticed that my pile of gifts contained nothing large enough to house a guitar. I inspected the labels: Mummy, Daddy; Mummy and Daddy; Godmother Anne; Godmother Margaret. And two envelopes: Godfather Francis, and Godfather G. All present and correct. No guitar. Too bad, on with the show. D and J had bought Daddy a tie, which seemed to give him great pleasure.

"Ah! My dear sirs," he said, smiling broadly. "A tie. How delightful. Many thanks!"

All three of us had boxes which contained the different parts of a motor-racing game called Scalextric. It looked incredible. I was just opening one of my envelopes when I noticed my mother bringing something out of the corner cupboard. My heart took a leap. Could this be it? It looked like a giant violin case.

"Here you are, darling," she said in a tone which, had I been older, I might have described as verging on the conspiratorial. "It's not quite what you asked for, but we hope you like it." I felt everyone was looking at me, and I wished they wouldn't. The paper had bells all over it. Perhaps "Jingle Bells" wasn't so hard to play. The case was soft, in dark brown with a zipper. The guitar didn't look at all like a Fender Stratocaster. It was non-electric and had strings like a tennis racquet. I was still pleased but had no idea what to do next. I was caught out in a fib. What on earth had I been thinking? I hadn't been thinking. I had been dreaming, salivating, imagining a glorious red Fender Stratocaster slung over my neck, my fingers miraculously finding the positions on the frets to make the desired sounds ring out loud and true, and all without the benefit of an amplifier which I didn't even know was needed for an electric guitar.

I toyed with the instrument a bit, holding it in a manner which I thought appeared exceedingly professional, knowing my face was turning the colour of a red letterbox. I gave my mother a hasty kiss and said thank you, explaining I was a bit rusty and in need of a little practice.

Fortunately it was time to get ready for church. Nobody but me seemed at all put out by my acute discomfort. We tidied up and carried what we could back to the nursery. Before changing into church apparel I hid the guitar under my bed.

Outside the front of the castle a spectacular array of motorcars sat waiting. Bentleys, Rolls-Royces, an Aston Martin, and Granny's huge black Mercedes-Benz directly in front of the door, all with their engines running to warm them up. Borrett, Brewer, and other chauffeurs had brought the cars down from the garages and were in the process of brushing off the snow and ice in preparation for the ceremonial ride to church.

The mere two occasions during the year, Christmas and Easter, that Granny and the court attended St Nicholas, our very pretty village church built around the same time as the original stone castle, revealed a certain lack of religious fervour in the castle way. By way of recompense, those two visits, at 11:00 a.m. sharp for all attendees, did succeed in maintaining a connection with those who lived and worked on the estate, the villagers, and church workers. For many of them it was a rare opportunity actually to see Granny B in the flesh, and sometimes to speak with her. It was also a semi-formal spectacle which, in our 1950s English countryside, gave voice to a unique form of affection for one's locale and the continuity of a way of life that was better understood and better appreciated then than it is today.

As we waited in the hall, I got to see some of the grown-ups who had come for Christmas—briefly evaluating their potential with regard to the well-established and all-important precedent of distributing, during the prelunch adult beverage period, Christmas Day cash hand-outs to the young.

Lady Huntley and the Duchess of Roxburghe: only C+ on the generosity scale; Bert Whitley and Johnny Galliher: full of fun and each a sure B+; Guysy-Wee, Bottle, and bridge champion Reg Shurey, commonly known as the Old Faithfuls: fluctuating B's if I remembered correctly. Then there was Princess Djordjadze, my brief, but lively, hallway encounter with whom, two years previously, I hoped was forgotten. Granny B and Morg were not down yet, and Woody and Uncle Gawaine never went to church.

Granny B's father, Almeric, the first (and last) Lord Queenborough, had had three daughters—Audrey, Enid, and Cicili—with his second wife, Edith Miller, another American woman, whom he married in 1921. My mother, therefore, had three aunts approximately her own age, one of whom, Cicili, lived with her husband, Capt. Robert Evans, and their family, at Squerryes Lodge, a handsome seventeenth-century manor house in Westerham, about forty-five minutes' drive from Leeds. Bobby and Cicili were towering, strong-willed, no-nonsense types; they were kind, good natured, amusing, and were stalwart family members. Uncle Bobby ran the castle shoot and Aunt Cicili seemed capable of running everything else. They came to the castle, and we went to see them in Westerham, often.

Audrey and Enid lived abroad and were infrequent castle guests, but every now and then Audrey turned up with her husband, Cdr. Peter Lucy, formerly a Royal Navy submarine man, who had an Aston Martin and a yacht generously provided by her. He was quite dashing and, for the most part, agreeable company. His reputation, which preceded him at all times, was that of an accomplished swordsman. Indeed there was a rumour that he enjoyed displaying his expertise with the wife of another family member while that other family member practised his own lovemaking skills with a petite and pretty family friend.

Uncle Bobby, Aunt Cicili, Uncle Peter, and Aunt Audrey had driven over from Westerham, so after we'd all piled into the motor cars and the stately procession had begun to wind its way slowly up through the park, I felt the outlook for the day's take looked favourable.

By one o'clock the library was throbbing with animated chit-chat and tinkling ice cubes. It was one of my favourite rooms in the castle, with its tall bookshelves chock-full of leather-bound books, celestial globes perched atop; cosy sofas everywhere; oak table in the centre strewn with more books, including the visitors', and a pair of handsome lamps; the backgammon table at which Guysy-Wee was kind enough to play with me sometimes; and the hidden bar tucked away in one corner. Nanny and I had boldly positioned ourselves in one of the window banquettes, enabling us to see and be seen without actually having to participate. As executive decisions go, it could not have turned out better. Everybody stopped by with a little something, and their individual methods of disguising the inherent vulgarity in handing out cash proved irresistible theatre.

Lady Huntley sidled up in the manner of a French prostitute attempting a pick-up, her hands behind her back and a come-hither expression on her face. Murmuring "Happy Christmas," she turned and leaned backwards, wiggling a pound note between her fingers.

"Thanks, Lady H," I cooed, as she meandered off looking to all intents and purposes as if a rejection had just taken place.

Woody strode up and manfully shook my hand, dispensing the two pounds from his palm into mine with the precision of a robot and the secrecy of a spy.

The princess stopped and looked at me in much the same way I imagined she looked at the accidents on her carpet left by her Chihuahua.

"Which one are you?" she enquired (clearly she had forgotten being forcefully instructed by me to leave the premises) in a throaty mid-Atlantic drawl.

"This is Anthony," Nanny replied for me. Personally I felt like ignoring the woman, but as she started to shuffle some envelopes, I forced myself to remain neutral. She found mine, dropped it in my lap, and moved away with a flourish. Although her perfume lingered rather longer than I would have wished, inside the envelope was a record token for two pounds. An LP and a single. I made a mental note to try and modify my opinion of the princess.

The Old Faithfuls slipped one-pound notes into my shirt pocket with ease and charm, as if they were repaying an outstanding debt. They all stayed for a moment to find out what I'd been up to, which struck me as polite. Morg came over and sat with me for a moment. When he produced a five-pound note from behind my ear, it merely confirmed my growing belief that here was a substantial man whose words and deeds I should emulate if remotely possible.

Borrett announced lunch and opened the double doors to the dining room, where a children's table had been set up in the giant bay window. The pair of late-eighteenth-century Louis XVI Aubusson pastoral tapestries, set in panels, continued their vigilant watch over the long William IV mahogany dining table laid in customary fashion for the grown-ups, with French china and silverware, Baccarat crystal glasses, and lilies of the valley in the centre. A precise replica of the Gloriette's floor-to-ceiling Christmas tree, decorated for adult consumption, stood in regal splendour in the smaller bay window behind Granny B's chair at the head of the table. The morning's activities gave every impression of having turned out well. Despite the disappointment of no Fender Stratocaster, it would have been churlish in the extreme to think otherwise.

As friends and family assembled, footmen in dark suits and ties flew in all directions, assisting ladies with their chairs before dispensing magnums of chilled vintage champagne. Then Borrett, in tails and striped trousers, went around the table serving foie gras de Strasbourg that Woody had brought down, as he always did at Christmas, from Fortnum & Mason, London's grandest food hall. Because of the tallness of the pot and the firmness of the foie gras, Borrett was obliged to struggle just a little to maintain a dignified posture as each guest attempted to extract the correct portion size of the famed delicacy with a silver serving spoon and fork.

Our table was not invited to try the foie gras, perhaps because no one thought we'd like it. Nanny, David, James, and I, joined by our cousins John and Michael (and Nanny Evans), munched away on chipolata sausages wrapped in bacon and baby triangles of toast as we awaited the arrival of the Christmas turkey.

Finally, with great fanfare, Borrett strode into the room carrying the enormous bird on an oval silver platter, presented it for Granny's inspection, and immediately took it back to the kitchens for carving. Returning with three footmen in tow, Borrett served the thinly sliced turkey as the footmen offered an array of vegetables, all from silver dishes, including roast potatoes, Brussels sprouts and chestnuts, parsnips and swede, stuffing, bread sauce, and hot gravy.

We, at the children's table, were served with the same splendid formality. After the grown-ups' glasses had been refilled for the umpteenth time with more champagne, or claret for those who preferred red wine, and our glasses of water, fruit juice, or Coca-Cola had been topped up, Christmas lunch entered that stage of conviviality so often the hallmark of this day.

Only the arrival of Borrett and a flaming Christmas pudding, as large as a football and stuffed full of sixpences, could adequately crown the occasion. At the time my fondness for this sticky mess of suet, sultanas, raisins, currants, brown sugar, and many other ingredients was limited to a search for the silver coins and a quick sampling of the brandy butter.

When she felt the time was right, Granny B stood, followed by everyone else, and led the ladies out of the dining room, through the library, the main hall, and the inner hall, to the drawing room for coffee, leaving the men to their port, politics, and cigars. This was the cue for the children to retire to the nursery for a rest.

Christmas at Leeds displayed the castle way at its best. The hierarchy softened noticeably, and special consideration was given to all, by all. Time off for the staff included a festive banquet in their own dining room, and Granny B's oft-beleaguered card-table companions enjoyed the benefit of eased regulation.

Even I, during these few glorious days, found myself treated as something other than a mere annoyance. This forever sealed in my imagination the otherworldliness of the whole thing.

8.

CONVERSATION PIECE

By the age of seven I had, quite knowingly, begun to develop different conversational styles based on a number of specific influences. As I was so unsure of myself, it made exquisite sense to me to base my words and phrases on people whose words and phrases reeked of worldliness, brainpower, and panache.

As I was not in a position to speak directly with Robin Hood, William Tell, or Davy Crockett—television heroes who set shining examples for my confused young mind through their upright behaviour, decency, and strength—all three were obliged to remain rather more in the realm of motivational speakers than act as direct aides to my linguistic advancement. This left the field open to Nanny, my father, and Morg (whose combined expertise in the art of conversation I considered to be nothing short of matchless) to beef up whatever talking skills I may have attained up to that point.

I was, of course, very seldom in my father's company, and even less Morg's, which made it vital to pay attention whenever I was. Morg's expressions of uplifting humour came trippingly off his tongue, and even when he swore after a bad croquet shot ("God rot it!"), he made it sound like a friendly aside and not an expression of anger. It would have been ideal if Morg had had the time or inclination to be my mentor as well as a man I looked up to. Life lessons conveyed in his inimitable way might well have worked wonders in correcting my more wayward inclinations, but unfortunately "mentoring" was not a recognized word, or activity, in the castle way system. It would have interrupted the ebb and flow of the mentor's normal daily functions and, probably, disturbed the chatelaine's calm. As a result, despite having a number of brilliant and important individuals close to my sphere of operations, I was not able to benefit much from their wisdom.

My father spoke at all times with quiet authority, just like his mother, and could also be very funny, but often at some poor innocent soul's expense. Later, that poor innocent soul too often turned out to be my mother. Both Morg and my father always gave me the impression of possessing enormous vocabularies and the ability to string words together better than anyone else I came into contact with at the time.

Nanny, my constant companion, kept it simple and to the point. She never was at a loss for well-spoken words, and I suspect her fondness for BBC radio, which in the 1950s insisted that the English language was a thing of beauty and should be spoken as elegantly and formally as possible, played its part in keeping her standards high.

It is conceivable that some A. A. Milne descriptive passages and even some tried-and-true cricketing metaphors wormed their way into my youthful subconscious, but that is conjecture at best.

It was four thirty in the afternoon on a cold Saturday at the beginning of January. David and James had gone to stay with friends for the weekend, so I had Nanny all to myself in the castle nursery.

Word had filtered through the system that the grown-ups were expecting me down for tea that day. Not being convinced that this was cause for celebration, I was about to go in search of Nanny's advice when she walked into the room carrying a large bundle of knitting. I stopped my rummaging through the bottom drawers of the tall oak cabinet where I kept some of my toys and turned to face her:

"Nanny, do I have to go down for tea?"

"I would think so, dear. They are expecting you."

Nanny sat at her worktable in between the windows and arranged her knitting. "Is there something bothering you? You look rather worried."

"Well, the last time I had tea in the drawing room nobody talked to me. Hardly anyone."

Nanny peered at me over her needle and thread and

eds Castle, Kent, England. (Courtesy of the Leeds Castle Foundation)

The Daily Mirror

NET SALE NEARLY TWICE THAT OF ANY OTHER DAILY PICTURE NEWSPAPER

No. 5,834. | Registered at the G.P.O. as a Newspaper. | FRIDAY, JULY 14, 1922 | One Penny.

THE BABY IN THE RUSSELL CASE: NEW PICTURE

An exclusive portrait of Mrs. Russell and the baby whose parentage is disputed.

The Hon. John Russell leaving court with his mother, Lady Ampthill.

Miss Maud Acton said Mrs. Russell treated her husband almost with dislike.

The Hon. Mrs. Russell leaving her house for the Law Courts yesterday.

Lord Ampthill (right), father of the Hon. John Russell, leaving court with Mr. Bayford, K.C., one of his son's four counsel.

Remarkable evidence in the case in which the Hon. John Hugo Russell denies that he is the father of his wife's baby was given at the continued hearing yesterday, when Miss Maud Acton, who said for eight years she was an intimate friend of Mrs. Russell, de-

scribed letters from her. One of these contained the passage: "I have been so indiscreet that he has enough evidence to divorce me about once a week." Once, said Miss Acton, Mrs. Russell told her: "When I do have a child it shan't be his" (her husband's).

The Daily Mirror covers the famous Russell baby case, 1922.

Lady Baillie (Granny B) at Leeds Castle with her German shepherd, Elsa, 1960s. (Courtesy of the Leeds Castle Foundation)

In 1948, Lady Baillie commissioned the French artist Etienne Drian to paint a "conversation piece" to be hung in the drawing room. The portrait features the author's mother, Susan (left), Lady Baillie (center), and the author's aunt Pauline (right). (Courtesy of the Leeds Castle Foundation)

Lady Ampthill, Granny A, in full flight with the Limerick Hunt, Ireland. (Photo by Frank H. Meads, courtesy of Jim Meads)

Dunguaire, Granny A's castle, Ireland, 1963. (Photo courtesy of the author)

Author's parents, the Hon. Geoffrey and Mrs. Russell, Leeds Castle, c. 1940s. (Photo courtesy of the author)

Nanny Penney at Leeds Castle, c. 1958. (Photo courtesy of the author)

Outside 24 Egerton Terrace, London: James (left), David (centre), author (right), 1952. (Photo courtesy of the author)

ıthor having tea with Carolyn Warrender, Leeds Castle, 1956. (Photo courtesy of
e author)

Morg, the author's mother, the author (front left), James, Lido Beach, Venice, 1957. Photo taken at Hotel Excelsior, Venice Lido, Italy. (www.hotelexcelsiorvenezia.com)

Drinks at the Excelsior Hotel, Lido Beach, Venice. Left to right: The Hon. Mrs. Robin Warrender, author's father, author's aunt Pauline, author's mother, The Hon. Robin Warrender, 1957. Photo taken at Hotel Excelsior, Venice Lido, Italy. (www.hotelexcelsiorvenezia.com)

Author with Annabel Warrender, Bembridge, Isle of Wight, 1959. (Photo courtesy of the author)

A portion of the court relaxes after tea. Left to right: Morg, David, Colonel Anson, James, Captain Lambert, Reg Shurey, c. 1959. (Photo courtesy of the author)

Author at riding school, Bearsted, Kent, c. 1961. (Photo courtesy of the author)

Author with sister, Vanessa, in go-cart outside castle, 1960. (Photo courtesy of the author)

Author (with guitar) and siblings in the Maiden's Tower "playroom." (Photo courtesy of the author)

Author, the Silver Bugler, St Aubyns, The March Past, 1964. (Photo courtesy of the author)

The author's parents off to a Buckingham Palace event, c. 1965.
(Photo courtesy of the author)

The author rehearses with his band at Stowe, 1968. (Photo courtesy of the author)

Author on the croquet lawn, Leeds Castle, 1972. (Photo courtesy of the author)

Author's mother presents the "key to the castle" to Queen Elizabeth with Pauline Vanessa, 1981. (Courtesy of the Leeds Castle Foundation)

e swimming pool, Leeds Castle. (Courtesy of the Leeds Castle Foundation)

The drawing room, Leeds Castle. (Courtesy of the Leeds Castle Foundation)

Lady Baillie's bedroom, Leeds Castle. (Courtesy of the Leeds Castle Foundation)

responded thoughtfully, "They probably didn't want to up-set you."

"Upset me?"

"Yes. By forcing you to talk when you didn't want to."

"Forcing me?"

"Yes. You see, if someone talks to you, that means you have to say something back. Maybe they think you prefer not to be put in that position."

"Sounds a bit odd."

"Yes. I don't know why they might think that. We all know you talk very well. Extremely well. In fact, I think you have an outstanding vocabulary."

"Vocabulary?"

"Words, dear. You know a lot of words."

"Ah!"

This came as a surprise to me, but Nanny ignored that and went on,

"I wouldn't worry about it."

"What, my vocab-u-lary?"

"Oh no, this tea business. Who's going to talk to you and who's not. Why not approach it as a learning situation? Think about it. Here you have gathered all these intelligent, worldly, and important people, and they're talking to each other about high-level things. You never know what interesting informa-tion you might pick up if you keep your ears open."

"Is Granny B important?"

"Why yes, dear, she's very important. She takes care of lots of people, gives them jobs and houses to live in. And she's your mother's mother. That makes her very important."

"What sort of high-level things should I be listening out for?"

"Oh, I don't know . . . current affairs, history, all sorts of things."

"I still wish they'd talk to me more."

Nanny's face lit up with sudden inspiration. "Why not try talking to them first? That should put a cat among the pigeons."

"Do what?"

"Make them take notice. Acknowledge your being amongst them. A representative of the nation's youth in their midst, alive and well and dying to contribute."

"That doesn't make an awful lot of sense."

"*Mmm*, perhaps my last cup of tea was a little strong."

"So you think I should go down to tea?"

"Why not? It makes Fortnum & Mason look really quite a simple affair. And besides, now you have a strategy. It will make all the difference."

Now it was my turn to be inspired. "I think I'll wear my Davy Crockett pistol."

"Good thinking," Nanny concluded. "Always be prepared!"

I reopened my investigation of the bottom drawers and soon found the splendid double-barreled pistol in its leather holster. I stood up and tied it round my waist, thinking back to the staff Christmas party when I'd been given the Crockett outfit by Granny. I checked the clock on the mantelpiece. Five to five. It was time to go.

"Nanny, why don't you come with me?"

"No dear, it's not my place."

"I know it's not your place. It's Granny B's! But that doesn't mean you can't come down to tea with me."

"No dear, that's not what I meant. What I meant is that it wouldn't be right for me to come down with you, unless I was specifically invited."

That sounded beyond the pale. "But you're Nanny! Why do you need to be invited?"

"Well dear, it's complicated, I know. But it's a bit like you'd never see Mr. Borrett sitting down to tea with your grandmother and her guests. Both of us, you see, work in the house. Well . . . not unless specifically invited, of course."

"All this inviting!"

"Off you go now," Nanny told me. "You wouldn't want to be late. And remember, it's *William Tell* on television tonight. Seven o'clock. You'd better have your bath before."

"Gosh, thanks. I can't believe I'd forgotten. I'll see you in a little while."

"Very good."

Curiously, at no point during my childhood did it ever cross my mind (so concentrated had it been on manufacturing acute levels of self-importance, artfully encouraged by the opulence of my surroundings) that I, too, was, and always had been, as much in need of an invitation to castle way ceremonies and functions as both Nanny and Borrett.

I left the playroom and strolled down the short corridor, past the giant rocking horse and a bevy of family portraits—why did we need so much family representation in the nursery?—and raised the iron handle on the heavy door which led to the landing. Closing the door behind me, I set off down the staircase. I loved the wide, solid stone stairs; you really felt you were in a castle as you raced up and down.

Passing under the central Gothic arch, I made a right turn, paying little heed to the pair of handsome sixteenth-century Flemish *feuilles de choux* tapestries (so-called because of the mass of cabbage-like leaves hosting rabbits, a lioness chasing a lion, and plenty of exotic birds dotted around the wild foliage) that faced each other across the inner hall, and stood before the double doors to the drawing room.

I listened for a moment, trying to pick out any familiar voices. I dreaded this "making an entrance" business when everyone in the room turned to look at you and did their best to come up with something nice to say.

I heard only my mother's voice and Borrett's firm reply, "Yes, Madam. I would say so, Madam." I paused, marshalling my courage, then cautiously turned the handle and went in.

My eyes were drawn immediately to the massive and beautiful Italian marble chimneypiece and the roaring, crackling log fire which lent the wood-panelled room a sensational warmth and glow. In front of the fireplace, providing additional protection (together with the fireguard) for the eighteenth-century English armorial carpet, and the ring around the tea table of George II walnut balloon-backed chairs, from wayward sparks, was a late-seventeenth-century Chinese coromandel wood screen.

My mother was seated on the far sofa smoking a cigarette and glancing through a daily paper. Behind her stood an eight-foot-tall lacquered Chinese screen depicting people and pots, gardens and birds, and further back, to the left, was the lofty and imposing bay window where my mother, Granny B, and Auntie Pops had had their portrait painted in 1947 by Étienne Drian. Since it was dark outside, the elaborate French silk curtains had been drawn. In front of the bay window sat a handsome Louis XV desk, and close by, next to the double doors leading to the Yellow drawing room, was a splendid mahogany gramophone, grander by far in appearance than the small contraption in David's London bedroom.

In the centre of the room was a round table covered with a white linen tablecloth, and in the centre of the table was a large silver teapot mounted on silver legs. It was so high it partly obscured my mother's face. Around the table were cups and saucers in fine china, silver spoons and knives, rolled knobs of butter, and a selection of homemade jams in individual silver dishes, a plate full of scones, a chocolate cake, and a sponge cake, both of them fresh from the pantry. The tea napkins were hand-embroidered linen with budgerigars around the edge.

To my right was another sofa, facing and identical to the

one my mother was sitting on. In front of me were the backs of two Louis XV fauteuils. Opposite the fireplace were two smaller bay windows, also with their curtains drawn, and on a table between them sat a spectacular Chinese mantel clock. Just beyond, in the corner, was the card table and four more balloon-backed chairs, the setting for Granny's daily (when in residence) canasta marathons, a card game with which I was not, as yet, familiar.

There were lamps on covered round tables each side of the fireplace and on the Louis XV desk. There were also three mid-sixteenth-century iron standing lamps with curvy tops and downward facing shades. They could be moved around which, of course, everybody did when the scene shifted from tea, to cards, to after-dinner cards, conversation, and so on. By each sofa was a black lacquered Chinese side table, with flowers and ashtray on each, and all around the room was an array of eighteenth- and early-nineteenth-century Chinese porcelain, figurines, and biscuit ware.

Subdued grandeur was the drawing room's tone. I was feeling mightily subdued myself, at five o'clock on the dot, with only my mother and I present and correct.

"Hello, Mummy." I walked over, taking the fireplace route around the tea table, and gave her a kiss.

"Hello, darling," she replied, putting her paper down and folding it neatly. "Heavens above, you've come down fully armed! Are we expecting trouble?"

"Sort of. Anyway, I thought I'd be prepared."

"What a good idea," said my mother. "You never know

what might happen over tea. Shall we ask Borrett for a glass of milk when he returns?"

"Yes, please."

I sat down next to her on the sofa. "What's in the paper?" I asked.

"I was just reading about your friend Mr. Richard. Apparently his latest tune is near the top of the hit parade."

"Yes, I know. 'Travellin' Light,' it's called. I've never met Cliff, Mummy."

"Of course you haven't. What a curious idea."

"So why did you call him my friend?"

"Because you like his music and talk about him a lot. That makes him sort of like a friend."

"Do you think so?"

"Don't you? Well, never mind. Did you have a good walk? I'm sorry I couldn't come. Granny needed me to make up a four at canasta. I think Lady H dropped out for some reason."

"I took my bicycle, and we went up to the woods above Mr. Elves's house. It was fun."

"Did you bump into anybody on your travels?"

"Actually, I bumped into a tree. But the bike's fine."

"You didn't hurt yourself?"

"Oh no. We saw the peacocks outside the laundry."

"Oh yes, extraordinarily colourful, aren't they?"

"Ugly! And sometimes they make dreadful noises."

Up until this point my reluctant descent into grown-up territory had gone smoothly. All the usual navigational hazards involving unwanted encounters in distant corners of the castle had been avoided, and for a brief while I was able to enjoy my mother's company in peace and luxuriate in the sumptuousness of the drawing room, set in all its panoply for tea.

Then, all of a sudden, pandemonium erupted. Voices came from the hall and from the corridor leading to the kitchens. Footsteps were coming from all directions. The three sets of doors—the main, the ones to the kitchens and pantry, and the ones behind the Chinese screen leading to the Yellow drawing room—were opened simultaneously and what looked like the whole company of the Apostles entered the room.

Granny B came first, filling the drawing room with her understated yet forceful presence, accompanied by Uncle Gawaine, Morg, Bottle, and Lady H. As they made their way in, my mother and I stood. Borrett, accompanied by Johnny and Vincent, the footmen on duty that day, waltzed in, carrying plates of wafer-thin sandwiches, biscuits, napkins, and sundry items without which the conducting of the tea ceremony would be quite unthinkable.

From the Yellow drawing room came Lord and Lady Wilton, not my idea of fun. He was pompous, potbellied, spoiled, and aloof, and he walked and talked like a caricature of an aristocrat from centuries past. She was nice looking and well dressed but, like him, had no time for me. With them were the Honourable Robin and Mrs. Warrender, and my father, all of them chatting away earnestly and clearly eager for tea.

No sooner had I started to think that that must be it than through the main doors came Reg Shurey and Guysy-Wee, the Old Faithfuls, muttering away cheerfully to each other, their country outfits a portrait of no-fuss refinement. Mr. Shurey wore a three-piece earth-brown Donegal tweed suit and sober tie, and Guysy-Wee wore a blue-grey houndstooth tweed jacket, grey flannel trousers, and sober tie. Woody brought up the rear, dog whip clasped in both hands behind his back (which I never saw him use for any purpose other than to gently slap his leg when out walking) wearing his customary green tweed single-breasted suit, and sober tie.

At this juncture I had no idea what to do next. Should I go and give Granny a kiss or remain rooted to the spot and hope for some kind of greeting from someone before the ground swallowed me up? Forcing myself to remain calm, the answer came when Granny said to my mother, "Susy, darling, come and sit by me," and then, noticing me, "Ant, darling, how are you?" Before I had time to reply or venture a move towards her, she continued talking to my mother: "I need to talk to you about Nassau."

Wearing her customary *tailleur* Chanel and small amount of exquisite jewellery, Granny walked to her regular chair, the one with its back to the fireplace, while everybody else made beelines for their regular positions.

"Hello, Granny!" I wasn't sure if she'd seen me, but Nanny's words had emboldened me, and I was determined not to let her down.

"Hello, darling. How are you?"

Not realizing she'd enquired after my health twice in less than one minute, she proffered her cheek for a kiss; then, after I'd given her one, she sat down without waiting for a reply. It seemed my presence was going to be of vital importance to the gathering. I girded my wits about me to make the best of the situation. My mother sat on Granny's right, and Morg took the chair to her left.

"My dear fella," he addressed me. "What do you call that fine-looking piece of weaponry you carry about your waist?"

Thank God for Morg, I thought. He could rescue any situation.

"Glute," I blurted out for no reason whatsoever. The word had arrived in my head as if planted there by a Dalek.

Apparently Morg found this extremely amusing.

"Glute, you say! Bless my soul, what an excellent name!" He chuckled loudly and passed me the sandwich plate.

Guysy-Wee and Reg Shurey sat on the sofa to my left. Gawaine, Mrs. Warrender, and Lord Wilton made up the group at the round table. Lady H and Colonel Anson sat on the sofa to my right, and my father and Mr. Warrender sat at the card table in the corner, deep in conversation.

For the next few minutes Borrett, Johnny, and Vincent passed around teacups, saucers, spoons, and napkins. Then Borrett poured tea from the silver pot with one hand, using a silver strainer to collect the leaves with the other. Johnny offered milk and sugar cubes from a silver salver. Vincent took round plates and offered scones. When Borrett had finished pouring tea (for the first time), he offered sandwiches and napkins, and when Johnny had finished serving milk and sugar, he took round the chocolate and sponge cakes. Not wishing to interrupt this finely tuned performance, I decided to be bold and slip down to the pantry and get myself a large glass of milk. I encountered Johnny in the pantry, there for the same purpose as myself, to top up on milk. We walked back to the drawing room together, chatting.

Resuming my position by the fireplace, I noticed that a plate of plain white bread, cut into triangles with the crust removed, had been placed on a small side table next to Guysy-Wee, who stood up, took two pieces of bread, and headed in my direction.

"What was that name you gave your pistol?" he asked me.

"Glute," I told him.

"Yes, how about that! Well, Glute," he said, "why don't you and I make some toast together?"

Upon which he removed two three-foot-long poles with forked ends from little hooks by the side of the fireplace—I'd never noticed them before—skewered a piece of bread onto each fork and handed one to me. "Best toast in the world," he said as he stuck his prong not into the flames but close to them, in order not to burn the bread. I copied Guysy-Wee, and to my absolute delight he proved to be one hundred per-cent correct. It was the best toast ever. I smothered mine with butter and jam and demolished it with a flourish.

I could tell our activities had not gone unnoticed. As Guysy-Wee resumed his seat, Lady H sidled up to claim his abandoned toasting prong, and together we set about making some more serious toast.

"Glute, you say?"

"That's right."

"Well, Glute, I happen to be extremely partial to a slice of toast at teatime myself."

Judging by Lady H's girth, this comment came as no surprise. Pleased to be engaged in activity and conversation with a person I did not find at all intimidating, I went to pick up the bread plate and brought it closer to the fire.

"Were you playing truant this afternoon, Lady Huntley? I had to speak quietly, conspiratorially, because Granny was close by. But with the fire and everybody talking, I saw no danger.

"Truant?" Lady H seemed taken a back.

"Avoiding Granny's card game."

Lady H regarded me with a quizzical, Sherlock Holmes—type look. I noticed her toast starting to burn. "Watch out! Your toast's burning!"

"Drat!" She discarded her burnt morsel and affixed a fresh slice. "Are you checking up on me, good sir? Are you with security?"

"Granny's Gestapo, at your service, ma'am."

"Oh dear. It looks as if I could be in a spot of trouble here!"

"Don't worry, Lady H. I know you're a good sort. I'll protect your reputation."

"My reputation?" At this Lady H looked genuinely concerned.

"Oh yes. As a loyal and dedicated supporter of castle law

number one—always be available for cards with Granny unless you're tremendously sick, or some other really good reason prevents you."

"Yes. Quite so."

Lady H and I were making our third piece of toast at this point. Four neatly toasted triangles sat on the bread plate; the bread was no more. "Perhaps," she said, "we should move this important discussion over to the sofa where we can be more comfortable?"

"As you say, my dear Glute," she continued once comfortably seated, "I would be the last person—heaven help me—to break castle law number one. This afternoon I was, indeed, struck down by a most virulent headache and was obliged to retire to my bedroom, take two aspirin, and lie down for a while. Fortunately, your mother was willing and able to take my place at the table."

"Funny how important some things are, Lady H."

"Isn't it just?" said Lady Huntley, and we left it at that.

Once again Borrett and Johnny materialized from nowhere for another round of tea pouring, scone dispensing, and other vital duties. Clearly, they were taking every conceivable precaution against anybody feeling the tiniest pang of hunger before dinner. Personally, I felt as stuffed as the proverbial Christmas turkey, but I did marvel at the intake capacity of the grown-ups, returning as they would in only three hours' time to the dining room for a four-course dinner.

My mother turned and spoke to me. "Darling, be an angel

and see if your father or Mr. Warrender would like a sandwich or a piece of cake, would you?" She handed me two plates, which I carried over to the card table in the corner. It did not seem likely that Borrett had overlooked this area, but there was no point in causing a stir.

"My dear sir, how enormously kind," my father said as I offered the sandwich and cake, "we were beginning to fade away over here." He took a sandwich, and I offered the plates to Mr. Warrender.

"I won't, thank you so much." No wonder Mr. W remained so thin.

"My dear sir," my father went on, "is everything all right? I see you've been passing the time of day with Her Ladyship."

"Everything's fine, thanks. She's a really good egg."

"Indeed she is."

I sensed that my father and Mr. W would prefer to continue their own conversation rather than engage in idle banter with me, so I moved away. Judging by the speed with which they picked up where they had so recently left off, I considered my decision to have been prudent.

I put the plates down on a side table instead of returning them to centre stage because, by now, I was starting to feel like going back upstairs. I thought if I did nothing for just a few more moments, I could maybe slip away without anyone noticing.

Granny, my mother, and Morg were still sitting together, drinking their tea and talking. Gawaine and the Old Faithfuls had left, and Lady H was chatting with Bottle on the other sofa. I felt a familiar twinge of indecision: To speak or not to speak? Granny decided for me.

"Anthony, darling, come over and have a chat with us, won't you? Borrett, bring a chair up for Master Anthony, please," she said, her throaty voice infused with a lifetime of asking with polite authority.

I had not noticed that Borrett was still in attendance. What remarkable discretion. But now, instead of heading back to the nursery for my bath and *William Tell*, I had to cope with what might turn into a full-fledged "audience" with Granny.

I sat between her and my mother, a little back from the table because that is where Borrett had positioned my chair, but I had a clear view of Morg, who started to hum loudly as he polished his glasses with a spotted silk handkerchief, winking at me as he did so. The round table was littered with debris from tea—crumbs, tea stains, scrunched-up napkins, empty cups, and full ashtrays.

"Darling, your mother seems to think you might be bored, might not have enough to do, but my view is you're old enough now to think for yourself, and be sensible. I'm talking about Nassau. I was wondering if during your Easter holiday you might like to come and join us for a couple of weeks?"

No sooner had Granny's words sunk in than my brain went into crisis mode, as I attempted to determine if the pros outweighed the cons in this frankly awkward decision. Apparently noticing my hesitation, Granny peered at me disconcertingly through her tortoiseshell spectacles.

The crux of the matter came quickly to me. "Can Nanny come?"

"Your mother and I think it's a very good idea for Nanny to come too," said Granny, removing her finished cigarette from its ivory holder and stubbing it out in her highly individual way. This entailed a combination of left-and-right sideways motions, followed by a few circular twists, culminating in the crushing of the stub by pressing down gently until the half fold extinguished the last dribble of smoke, thereby transforming a ritual that most people conducted with a simple two or three precision stabs into a ladylike performance of high style.

"Excellent," I said. "Thank you very much."

"All right, darling," said my mother. "Off you go now. I'll be up to see you in just a little while."

"How did it go?" Nanny enquired.

"It could have been a lot worse. Guess what? We've been invited to Nassau."

"That's nice."

"I wasn't sure."

"Let's not worry about it now, dear. Get a move on, if you don't mind. Your bath is running, and *William Tell* starts in half an hour."

"You know what, Nanny?"

"No, my dear, tell me."

"You were right."

"Right about what, dear?"

"About talking to them first. I did it. I talked to them first and put a cat inside their pigeons, just like you said. It took some courage, but after a bit things didn't go at all badly."

9.

PARADISE ISLAND

It was April 1960. I was close to being eight years old, and was off to boarding school in May. Overnight, fifty thousand French francs had become worth five hundred for reasons not entirely clear. I was surprised I even found out that because nobody ever told me anything. There was, never, for instance, any illuminating talk at Hill House referencing the struggle of others to put bread on the table, and it was only when my mother popped up to the nursery one day and discovered some uneaten spinach on my plate that I heard about "the starving children of China." This really confused me because I had no clue as to why the children of China should be starving.

Adding insult to my multiple layers of ignorance, a serious flaw had arisen in my travel arrangements for joining Granny B in Nassau: Nanny was no longer coming, and not even she could explain to me why. Quite why David and James were not invited was also a mystery. Perhaps the house was full, or they had to go back to school before me, or had they simply made other plans? Nanny had been my constant companion and guide since I could remember, and this would be the first time my mother had sole charge of me, at least in theory, for fourteen days in a row. I was venturing into new territory here, and all I could do was hope that our growing closeness would continue to blossom in what I had been told was a tropical paradise.

My relationship with my mother had always been closer than either of us recognized, perhaps because we were so similar in many ways. We shared sweet-natured exteriors which we hoped covered our shyness and insecurities from prying eyes, but we knew reality spoke otherwise. She had grown up with a dominating mother and sister, neither of whom had shown much in the way of tenderness or support for her delicate nature. We also shared determination and a degree of fortitude, she in the face of sometimes withering scorn coming from people who should have been ashamed of themselves for picking on her for not possessing whatever self-inflated intellectual standards they had granted their ungentlemanly selves. I wanted to wring their necks, but my strengths lay elsewhere at the time, and verbal confrontation with grown-ups was not one of them.

We did not talk about these things because it didn't occur to either of us to do so. Emotional outpourings worked fine on television and in novels, and from our perspective it was best left that way. Even as a nation we had never been comfortable wearing our hearts on our sleeves until, as Melanie Phillips wrote in her London *Spectator* blog, the onset of Diana Derangement Syndrome, "a mass epidemic of which broke out in Britain upon the death of Princess Diana when it was revealed to be the defining disorder of contemporary British society. The main characteristics of DDS are the replacement of reason, intelligence, stoicism, self-restraint and responsibility by credulousness, emotional incontinence, sentimentality, irresponsibility and self-obsession." I'm glad that in 1960 we still had a way to go before collectively turning into mush.

A BOAC Boeing 707 flew my parents and me to Nassau in just over eight hours. I had heard about, and seen pictures of, these beautiful aeroplanes with their sleek lines and four powerful jet engines, and I had been revved up to the maximum in anticipation. Not one iota of disappointment came my way. Every aspect of the journey was a revelation, though the adrenaline rush of accelerating rapidly down a runway for the first time and then lifting off into the cloudy blue sky at some fantastic speed was sensational. I looked out through the window, down at the stunning spectacle of London stretching for miles in every direction. It looked almost like a map brought to life, without any boundaries, free to shrink or grow as time or population dictated.

My mother and I had a whale of a time on the flight, chatting, playing gin rummy, and reading before eventually having a snooze. My father buried his nose in newspapers and magazines for most of the trip, and we exchanged only a few words.

Nassau airport was warm and humid and full of black people, whom I'd rarely seen before. Most, including the immigration and customs officers, wore loose short-sleeved shirts, and light cotton trousers. But the policemen looked as smart as the Household Cavalry at Trooping the Colour. They wore white tunics, black trousers with a red stripe down the side, black belts, black boots, and some topped it off with a white pith helmet. They could have been Royal Marines in tropical uniform. I wondered if that was actually how they felt, as the Bahamas were then still a British territory.

We arrived at the dock after a thirty-minute taxi ride, during which I spent most of my time attempting to decipher what the driver had been saying to my parents, so different was his way of talking to the one with which I was familiar. I found myself surrounded by elegant buildings and a sea of colour; hundreds of black ladies, some of considerable girth, who sat on stools and steps and wobbly wicker chairs, weaving and sewing baskets and tropical clothing of multiple shapes and sizes. They were all dressed in rainbow patterns of flowing cotton prints and talked endlessly and excitedly to themselves and each other.

And there, finally, was the sea, a dazzling turquoise, casually lapping at the stone steps leading down to Granny's boat the *Canard,* a slightly decrepit and weatherbeaten motorboat whose sole function was to ferry guests to and from Harbourside, her house on Paradise Island, and the mainland. A former Royal

Navy petty officer was the boat's captain. His strong hands easily transferred our suitcases from shore to vessel, and then we were off for the short ride across the bay.

When Granny B had bought her house in 1950—at the time, not a single standing house but an enclave of buildings—the long, narrow strip of "paradise" was called Hog Island because it had formerly been inhabited primarily by semiwild pigs. Now, this lush tropical habitat, having been bought by a rich American called Huntington Hartford (heir to the A&P supermarket fortune) in 1959 and appropriately renamed by him "Paradise Island," contained just a handful of private houses, all with large gardens, nestling along the western half. Hunt, as he was called, turned out to be a man with grandiose development plans, plans which, over time, would destroy the natural beauty and tranquillity of the island forever. But in 1960 they were of course just plans, which Hartford felt no need to divulge to people like us. The last thing he would have wanted was to incur the wrath of Lady Baillie, who might have opted to use her influence with friends in high places to try and stop him in his tracks.

Stéphane Boudin, one of the world's most famous interior designers following his work at the Château de Laeken, near Brussels, for King Leopold III of Belgium; Ditchley Park in Oxfordshire, for the British MP Ronald Tree and his American wife, Nancy; 24 boulevard Suchet in Paris, for the Duke and Duchess of Windsor; and, of course, Leeds Castle for

Granny B, had been closely involved in the reconstruction and decorating of Harbourside. As we approached the island, the first example of his handiwork could be seen, a stone landing stage of simple elegance, with a miniature pagoda at the tip. Borrett, Johnny, and two black footmen were waiting to greet us and take the luggage to our rooms. It was just like arriving at Leeds.

My fortnight in Nassau was saturated with a surfeit of castle way dynamics and dampened by spectacular amounts of rain but nonetheless instructive and periodically fun. Armed with some good books (Dennis Wheatley novels featuring my new hero, Gregory Sallust, a debonair, wickedly cool, and brave Nazi-fighting agent) I was never at a loss for something to do. Because there was no possibility of retreating to a nursery, I was exposed to the court and its ways as never before. Entertainment value aside, this provided useful opportunities to work on my underdeveloped drawing-room skills.

At Harbourside I took my breakfast alone each day at nine o'clock, on the sun-dappled outdoor terrace, brought to me with impeccable dignity by Borrett, who always enquired, "And what can I get you this morning, Master Anthony?" Having recently acquired a taste for bacon and eggs at breakfast (thanks to Miss Preston's insistence) I was thrilled to be introduced in Nassau to American bacon in all its crispy magnificence. It made English bacon seem limp and thoroughly uninteresting by comparison.

"Scrambled eggs, bacon, and sausage, please, Mr. Borrett."

"Very good, Master Anthony."

In an effort to be accommodating, my mother was always the first grown-up to surface, usually around eleven. We walked through the garden in our swimming outfits, she with a pink terry towelling bag full of beach accoutrements and puffing away on a du Maurier cigarette through a white holder called an Aquafilter. Once at the covered beach-bar and sitting area, she would deposit her things on a favourite chaise longue, apply sun products to her face and body, asking for my assistance with the exposed areas of her back. She then covered me with the same products before replacing them neatly in her bag.

I would fetch my swimming goggles and a beach towel from a cupboard, and off to the sea we'd go. Day after day we'd repeat the same procedure (even when it rained we'd potter about in the water for a while), never seeing anyone until the houseguests started to assemble around noon. My mother told me that Hunt had a house a little way down the beach, and someone called Sam Clapp (it would be a few years before we learned more about what he was getting up to) had one a short walk in the opposite direction. It wasn't until our second week that Hunt chose to show his smiling face, accompanied by two rather attractive and talkative women, for drinks before lunch, thereby breaking the spell, for me, of spoiled privacy.

———

There was a couple staying at Harbourside I'd never met before called George and Lydia Gregory. Both were short, owlish, and tended to stay out of the sun. I hoped their conversation sparkled around Granny B as they conducted their afternoon and evening bridge and canasta sessions, because with me it was desultory and dull. Johnny Galliher was staying, down from New York like the Gregorys and Auntie Pops; Woody and Morg, naturally, were there; Mickey Renshaw was there, and Grace Dudley, a tall, attractive, and gregarious woman (widow of the Earl of Dudley) came over frequently from her house on the mainland for lunches, dinners, and cards.

One evening the whole house party put on long dresses and dinner jackets to go and dine with the prime minister, Lynden Pindling, in Government House. It was said that by setting herself up so comprehensively on Paradise Island, Granny B had helped a great deal to establish the island's reputation in international circles and to bring like-minded investors to Nassau. No one in Granny's circle, least of all she, could have known exactly what type of investors were headed her way.

I had supper on a tray in the dining room by myself.

I ate lunch with the grown-ups on the terrace, always sitting next to my mother, and on rainy days we moved to the dining room where the table extended to fit us all. There was crazy white trelliswork all over the dark green walls with circular mirrors in the middle. The floor was grass matting, and there was a giant porcelain swan on the sideboard. This was a fun room and had an unusual atmosphere. One lunch I sat next to Johnny G, who was as kind and funny as Mickey Renshaw was not.

"Are you enjoying your stay?" Johnny Galliher asked, his thin, handsome face, creased, tight cheeked, cocked a bit to the left and peering downward.

"Very much, thank you. And are you?"

"Oh, it's divine here. You know your grandmother entertains like no one else and, believe me, I know."

"Do you know a lot of swish people?"

"Oh my goodness, do I!"

"But what is so special about her?"

"Well, I think probably it's her attention to detail. Nothing is overlooked, so the end result is always as perfect as it could possibly be. And that applies to everything she does, from the decorating of her houses to taking the best care of not only her guests but also the people who work for her."

I thought about mentioning that Granny hardly ever talked to me, but decided against it as she was sitting four chairs down. Also, I knew how silly it was to grumble. Elegantly breaking the silence, Johnny G continued, "Your mother tells me you're off to boarding school in May. Are you looking forward to it?"

"I think so. Hill House is going to double in size in May, and I've never really liked being there."

"And boarding school will be better?"

"I don't know, but we'll play proper cricket every day during my first term, and James will be there for that one term too."

"My! I wish you all the best."

"Thank you, Mr. G. I look forward to telling you about it at Leeds."

As it happened, I never did tell him about it at Leeds because of castle way restraints; and by the time we became friends in late-seventies New York ("My, haven't *you* come out of your shell—and some!" he informed me as I found myself enthusiastically participating in the city's frothing and foaming ebullience), it quite slipped both our minds to spend time catching up on the pros and cons of English boarding school.

My mother took me with her to the town that afternoon because she needed to stock up on cigarettes, Aquafilters, and Squibb Angle toothbrushes, which she always brought back to England in the belief that they worked better than any other kind. Bay Street looked splendid with its single-storey row of shops on each side and raised sidewalks like a Wild West town. By now I had become used to seeing mainly black people wherever we went, many of whom struck me as possessing far more jovial personalities than a majority of the people I came into contact with back home. But still I wondered why my parents had not told me anything about Nassau and its population before we'd left.

For my last night I was allowed to join the grown-ups for a dinner party on the mainland. Carl and Bubbles Holmes were our hosts, and very charming they were. He wore dark red trousers, a blue jacket, and had a freckly, sun-tanned face; she, with her dress billowing and white hair in a bouffant, resembled a sophisticated version of Miss Preston; but she treated my grandmother like royalty and entertained in the same gracious manner. The house had warmth and was well staffed, and the evening was no more stressful than any other of its kind.

Increased familiarity with the court and its ways helped broaden my understanding of castle way protocol. Although, in Nassau everyone around Granny appeared to be relaxed, at ease, and enjoying themselves, there was always the implicit understanding that her wishes must be at the forefront of each day's activities. As at Leeds, her mouthpiece was the ever-present and unflappable Borrett, ably and loyally assisted by his staff. Morning, noon, and night, he would appear to make announcements, "Her Ladyship wishes you to do so-and-so" or "Her Ladyship is in conference with so-and-so, and therefore lunch will be delayed by half an hour." Sometimes Borrett was given the unenviable task of changing the after-noon four at the card table, which entailed a whisper in the ear of the relevant guest or guests (usually during the lunch-time cocktail hour), who may then have had to cancel or re-schedule other plans for that afternoon.

Unfortunately a single unpleasant incident almost ruined the whole trip for me. One day, before lunch, I discovered Mickey

Renshaw's venom, purporting to be humour, to be even more pronounced than I had previously suspected. Whenever I'd found myself within hearing range of his conversation I would notice a distinct preference by him to focus his agile mind on destroying as many reputations as possible with a stream of hypercamp critiques and *bons mots*. Worse, I thought, was how Woody and my father, instead of registering even mild disapproval when the nastiness was directed at my mother, guffawed gently into their cocktails, Cheshire-cat grins spread wide.

My mother and Mr. Renshaw, together with Auntie Pops, Woody, and my father, were sitting at the beach bar almost in a circle, out of the sun, drinks in their hands, and I was perched on a bar stool, nursing my Coca-Cola, observing. The conversation was centred on the presidential campaign in the United States, and, in particular, on the chances of the young, handsome Democrat, Senator Kennedy, winning his party's nomination.

"I think Senator Kennedy is likely to win" was Woody's view. "Because now television is playing such a prominent role in political campaigns, his looks and charisma will bolster his obvious intelligence. His being Catholic will, of course, upset many, but perhaps not enough to stand in his way."

"Woody's right," Auntie Pops said with authority. "My friends in New York and Long Island are gung-ho for Kennedy, as am I. There's nothing wish-washy about him at all, which stands in marked contrast to the drift of late from Eisenhower."

"Susy, darling," Mickey Renshaw then addressed my mother in his heavily Noël Coward–influenced diction. "You like reading the newspapers, what do you think?"

My mother seemed to know where this line of questioning was headed, and it did not please her at all. "Really, Mickey, you do like to put me on the spot," she said.

"Indeed not, darling girl, but I'd like to think you are *au fait* with what is going on."

"I think Susy's still wading through last year's crop of papers, or possibly the year before that," my father said, his voice heavy with sarcasm.

"My, what a hoot! Which article are you reading at the moment?" Mr. Renshaw went on.

Woody and my father were now displaying signs of being distinctly amused at my mother's discomfort, and not trying to hide it. She gamely attempted to ignore the slight.

"If you must know, I think Mr. Kennedy seems quite charming and capable, and so does Mr. Humphrey." She looked embarrassed and sounded indignant. "And, Mickey, you are starting to make me cross."

At this Woody, my father, and Auntie Pops almost laughed out loud.

"Ahhh." Mr. Renshaw stretched out the word, opening his eyes wide as if greatly enlightened. "And Mr. Nixon. Do you find him charming and capable, or, perhaps just charming, or merely capable?" This was like Hamlet toying with Polonius, but Mr. Renshaw was not feigning madness with his

"Words, words, words." He was enjoying causing my mother distress.

"I feel Mr. Nixon may be untrustworthy. There's something about him—his expression—but what do I know?"

"That is what we're trying to determine."

"Mickey, that is so rude," said my mother. "And now I really am cross." To my astonishment nobody appeared to think there was anything unusual or ill-mannered about this exchange. I was soon to learn that making fun of my mother was an all-too-frequent court indulgence. It pained her, and it infuriated me to witness it.

"Come, come, Susy, you know the last thing I'd ever do is try to upset you deliberately." This blatant untruth only served to heighten the company's amusement.

"Well, that is precisely what you are doing, and I'd like you to stop," my mother said, clearly in a state. I was mortified on my mother's behalf by this spectacle and breathed a sigh of relief when Morg wandered up from the beach, dripping water, instantly helping to dissipate the cloud of acrimony that hovered in the air: "Ho ho, what's going on I'd like to know." I felt sure he knew. The conversation changed course, and the previous few minutes were seemingly forgotten—not, of course, by my mother, and not by me.

After my mother, who occupied my time heroically, Morg and Borrett were unquestionably the two best items on the

Paradise Island menu. They upheld castle way regulations with ease and a sense of proportion, Morg through his commanding presence and sense of humour, Borrett through his mastery of organization and dignified service. I felt fortunate to have been granted the opportunity, at last, to observe these impressive men from a highly advantageous position, and hoped that one day some of their style and communication skills might rub off on me.

10.

BOARDING SCHOOL

Silent and graceful as a panther in a tailcoat, Chapman entered the dining room, his egg-shaped face devoid of expression save total concentration on the silver serving dish he carried perched in the palm of his right hand, upon which eight breaded and sautéed lamb chops were carefully displayed. He served my mother first, who sat at the head of the table in my father's absence. Then he went around the table, serving James, who was sitting across from me, Nanny at the opposite end from my mother, and, finally, me. Before leaving the dining room he rearranged slightly the spoon and fork, which I had returned to the dish correctly, side by side at an angle of sixty-five degrees, but which appeared to him to be a degree or two off. He returned a moment later, this time with a silver dish full of green beans and roast potatoes, and repeated the procedure. The entire ceremony was conducted, bizarrely, in an awkward silence, made worse by the tinkling of silver on silver as, one by one, we picked up and replaced the serving spoon and fork to the accompaniment of Chapman's gentle wheezing, an aggravation brought on by his fondness for cigarette smoking and a weak respiratory system.

Finally, after my mother had picked up her knife and fork and we had all followed suit, James decided to wade in with, "Blimey! These chops have been cooked in enough lard to sink an aircraft carrier!" Not being familiar with the term "lard" disqualified me from either laughing or commenting, but my mother said, "Darling! Do please watch what you say."

"Sorry, but it's true."

Nothing stopped James from pursuing his chosen path, and on this occasion it turned out to be Miss Preston's method of preparing what everybody present knew was one of my favourite main courses. But I was unable to eat. My tummy felt as if it had been tied in knots by a sailor of merciless cunning. My grey flannel suit was a whole size too big. It felt cumbersome and foolish, and both the matching light grey shirt and trousers itched horribly. My striped school tie already had a gravy stain on the bottom, which no amount of water and rubbing with my napkin showed any signs of wiping away. I was languishing in the doldrums of "off to boarding school for the first time blues"—and there was still pudding to come.

Boarding schools in England in the 1950s still retained some remnants of the ferocious discipline for which, over the centuries, they had become notorious. Beatings, bullying, and buggery continued to flourish in many of the top ones with famous names, but—as I was to learn over the next few years—St Aubyns and Stowe were relatively mild adherents to the old-fashioned ways of preparing young gentlemen for the rigours of running an Empire.

James was clearly of no mind to allow going back to school to interfere with his enjoyment of lunch. Amidst the gentle clinking of cutlery on plate, well-mannered chewing, and periodic use of their napkins, he and my mother chatted away, a cheeky grin never far from his face, until their chops were devoured, their vegetables gone, and the pantry bell was rung to let Chapman know we were ready for pudding. When the chocolate mousse arrived, I almost gagged after a tiny taste. James was kind enough to notice the depths to which I had plummeted and said, "There's nothing to worry about. Really. Besides, I'll be there to take care of you."

This helped a little. Once back in the nursery Nanny and I had about half an hour until it was time to leave for the station. We both realized the significance of what was taking place. For nearly eight years, we had spent the greater part of our lives almost exclusively in each other's company and had become much more than just a child and his Nanny. In my eyes she was part of the family, an intimate part, a best friend, and I loved her in precisely that way. Now the time had come for her to stop taking care of me and for me to start learning how to take care of myself.

We said little as she fussed over last-minute things, brushing imaginary fluff off my new grey flannel suit, miraculously removing the stain from my tie with a few rubs of something liquid and evil smelling, and checking through the small suitcase I would take with me on the train (the school trunk having been sent on ahead many days in advance to allow the school matrons plenty of time to arrange their charges' clothes) just as she'd already done two or three times that morning. We knew we were going to miss each other more than words could say.

"Good-bye, my darling one. I hope all goes well for you. I'll look forward to seeing you at half term." Nanny gave me a nice squelchy kiss.

"Bye, Nanny. I won't forget to write." I kissed her, too, and, holding back the tears, went back down to where my mother and James awaited.

Victoria Station lost its charm with the school train lurking on platform thirteen. We walked down the side of the station accompanied by a porter who wheeled our suitcases on his trolley. I noticed with mounting trepidation the ever-increasing number of boys dressed in grey, all headed in the same direction, surrounded by assorted family members and their dogs.

My godfather Colonel G, whose son, John, was a St Aubyns pupil, came up, put a firm hand on my shoulder, and asked, "Now then, godson, are you looking forward to boarding school?" An unfortunate question to which there was only one answer. "Very much," I replied, my eyes wandering over the mêlée of parents and boys (most of whom appeared unbearably cheerful) conducting their farewell ceremonies. I spotted a man dressed in an immaculate Prince of Wales check suit heading our way. He immediately reminded me of Colonel Townend, the headmaster of Hill House, natural authority in every step and gesture.

"How are you, Susan?" he said with a broad smile and a handshake. "I'm absolutely delighted to welcome Anthony to St Aubyns." He turned to me and offered his hand, which I shook a little hesitantly.

"I am very fond of both your brothers," he informed me, his voice gruff but kind, "and David was a most exceptional head boy. I know you will do very well. My name is Gervis, and I am the headmaster. You may call me Mr. Gervis, or sir, but avoid both at the same time because we're not in the military!"

Addressing my mother again, he said, "Susan, may I take Anthony to his seat and introduce him to some other new boys? He can step out again for a last good-bye."

Lugging my case I followed him onto the train, noticing his ramrod-straight bearing and the spring in his step. He then gave me an exceedingly friendly minute of his undivided attention. I liked him well enough, although I suspected that might not always be the case. He told me Soames and Steel would be sitting with me on the journey, but since they were currently nowhere to be seen, introductions had to wait. James came aboard and parked himself by me as he had promised to do, and with only a few moments left before departure, we returned to the platform to kiss our mother good-bye.

"Good-bye, darling, and don't worry, you're going to be

fine. James will take care of you, and I'll be down in three or four weeks to see you both." The whistle blew, we returned to our seats, sliding open the top window and jockeying for position with other boys, eager for one last look, one last wave. There was a small jolt, and the train moved forward.

"Bye!" A high-pitched, powerful chorus resonated up and down the carriages.

"Bye!" Frantic waves, kisses from the platform blown.

"Bye!" Into a long bend, and they were gone.

Miss Pentland, the head matron, an Amazonian woman with a hooked nose and intimidating presence, had turned out the lights at seven o'clock on the dot. It seemed like ages ago but the luminous hands on my Bulova watch told me it had been only half an hour. Before closing the door she'd issued a stern warning against talking, which struck me as a strange rule for all us new boys spending our first night away from home.

I lay on my back, staring up at the high, barn-like ceiling with its pointed roof and white beams, concentrating, rather oddly, not on how miserable and lonely I was but on the remarkable comfort of my bed. Despite looking like some relic from a medieval torture chamber with its iron bed-head and surround, vicious springs, and five-inch-wide, rock-hard mattress, it turned out to be infinitely more comfortable than anything I had ever slept on in my life. Thinking back over the afternoon, I realized that ever since the train had pulled out of the station, even with James sitting beside me most of the way and two-thirds of the school being in close proximity, I had felt alone. More alone than ever before.

Strangely, it had not bothered me unduly. I often retreated into my shell when awkward situations presented themselves. I found it a pleasant-enough place to be, and circumstances always controlled the length of stay. It could be just a few moments, sometimes longer. I knew it was going to be difficult with so many strangers and so many rules. Shyness didn't help; people often mistook it for lack of interest or even arrogance.

I heard sniffles coming from one or two beds, but still no one spoke. I reminded myself how smart and determined I could be, or thought I was; there would probably be a lot of chances to put this theory to the test in the months to come. Having James close by was a major plus. I wanted to be like him: strong, handsome, self-confident. It had been a good idea asking my parents if I could leave Hill House early, so that my brother's last term at St Aubyns would be my first. And it was the summer term, which meant we played cricket: another plus.

I thought of our older brother, David, who was now a small fry again. I wondered what that was like. After being the biggest cheese here he was back to being a squirt, or whatever the junior boys were called at Stowe. I suspected he would be fine; he was clever, easygoing, and could be very funny. He was probably quite popular already.

I yawned and looked at my watch again—almost eight thirty. Nanny would have turned my light out about fifteen minutes ago and would be running her bath. She liked to have a nice hot bath after I was tucked up for the night, put on her night clothes and dressing gown, and then listen to her radio while doing a spot of knitting or maybe reading a little bit. I hoped she'd be all right without me to keep her company. It felt horrible, the idea of not seeing her for . . . how long? . . . six weeks until half term?

"Hey, Russell," a whispered voice broke the silence, seemingly from the bed directly across from mine. It took me a few moments to readjust back to my current surroundings.

"Yes," I whispered back.

"You're still awake."

"Yes. I was thinking." I hoped no one was listening. "I can't go to sleep."

It was Steel. We'd been sitting opposite each other on the train and together on the bus. "I can't either."

"No talking!" a voice snapped from down the dormitory, startling me and putting an end to all talk. Authority, it appeared, had spoken. Silence returned.

Was I imagining things or was somebody always trying to tell me what to do? Nanny told me what to do, of course, but it was always in such a nice way that it never seemed as if she was bossing me around. My mother too. But the rest . . . It was different talking in the dark. From the safety and comfort of your bed you could say what you meant. You could say things that in the cold light of day were so much harder to say. Not that Steel and I had spoken much. But we'd spoken and nobody else had. I was glad.

In the coming days I worked out what I believed to be the essential rules of the game: First, pay close attention to the television programmes *Robin Hood, Davy Crockett,* and *William Tell,* trying to the best of your ability to adopt the courage, chivalry, and manners exemplified by these small-screen heroes. These men are always unfailingly polite, even to their adversaries who wish to do them great harm.

Second, never rat on any older boy who has clearly failed to study such heroes, and decides you need to be taught a lesson you had not, up to that point, been aware you needed to learn. The bloody nose and lost pride quickly heal, and, if you inform the headmaster it was a speeding cricket ball that did the damage, you are likely to gain a small but ever-increasing amount of grudging respect.

Before the completion of my first fortnight I was obliged to put these rules into practice. I was standing in the doorway to my first-form classroom five minutes into morning break, contemplating just how bad I was at algebra, when I felt a powerful arm go around my neck and somebody drag me into the empty room. I dropped the books I'd been holding and was immediately engaged in a fierce struggle. My assailant was slightly bigger and stronger than me, but I did my best not to give an inch.

From the outset, it was a most peculiar fight. There were no punches thrown, no kicks, no elbowing. It was mainly an arm-wrestling contest, with neck holds and aggressive tie pulling thrown in for good measure. After perhaps two minutes Mr. Gervis materialized suddenly in the doorway, and the hostilities came abruptly to a halt.

"What the devil's going on here? Who started this?" he demanded, this time not sounding quite so kind. I was now able to recognize my attacker as we stood facing each other, huffing and puffing from our exertions like four-minute milers: His name was King. A red-cheeked, brutish-looking fellow, he was one term ahead of me, and we'd hardly spoken before this engagement, so I was utterly in the dark as to what provoked the attack. We both said nothing but continued to glare at each other in a combative fashion, waiting to get our breath back. It seemed obvious that Mr. Gervis would have to punish both of us, or neither. He swiftly chose the latter.

"Don't let me catch you two at this again," he said, his stern expression full of menace and a clear indication that "next time" would mean deep trouble—deep trouble being the cane, or, as Mr. Gervis liked to say, "the stick." Alone with King again, the wretched fellow congratulated me for not telling tales, and we parted almost amicably.

Sports Day, the precursor to the half-term break, came not a moment too soon. I won the new-boys' eighty-yard sprint, and James picked up a whole collection of cups. My father declined to participate in the fathers' race ("But my dear sir," he later explained, "a snail runs faster than I do. If I'd been competing we'd all still be waiting for the race to end!"), which disappointed me though I enjoyed his reason. I took part in my first March-Past, a military-style ceremony, like Trooping the Colour, in which the school, and school band, paid tribute to the St Aubyns boys who had lost their lives in World Wars I and II. The dignified and moving sounding of the "Last Post" in front of the small memorial by the cricket pavilion, with the colours (the Union Jack and the flag of Saint George) lowered and the massed ranks of parents and visitors gathered closely around, brought a lump to my throat. I wondered if I might not one day become silver bugler, and be the one to perform the "Last Post."

We left after church on Sunday morning for two nights at the castle. Upon our arrival, there was Nanny waiting by the front door. Bless her! I had tears in my eyes as I leapt from the car.

"You've grown," she told me as I gave her a kiss on the cheek. I felt like giving her a bit of a bear hug, but something told me it might not be the appropriate thing to do. "Only you, Nanny, could possibly notice an additional quarter inch, or whatever it is I've grown."

"Oh, but I do!"

I was riddled with self-doubt in my first two years at St Aubyns. "I wish he would be a little more forthcoming," Mr. Gervis wrote in his headmaster's report at the end of my third term. "I hardly know the sound of his voice, and am only greeted with a series of grunts when I ask him any question." Fortunately there was no time to dwell on it. The days were organized in such a way that every boy knew exactly what he should be doing from the moment he woke up in the morning to the moment he went to bed at night.

Of course, if you were not doing what you were meant to be doing, there was a strong chance you would be doing something you should not. My lack of self-confidence failed to stop me, when I was more senior, from joining in such intellectual activities as baiting the local "oiks" (boys from the non-private, distinctly less posh local school) who appeared from time to time at the entrance to our playing fields to see how much taunting they, or we, could get away with. Throwing bangers (not sausages but tiny exploding fireworks) at each other the evening of Guy Fawkes Day and not getting caught proved to be remarkably therapeutic. And should one dare attempt—as I did on two occasions—a strictly forbidden foray past the shooting range, out through the school's side gate, followed by a quick sprint down the main road to the sweet shop, returning with illicit cargo without being discovered, the thrill was even more pronounced. To have been caught in either of these wicked misdemeanours would undoubtedly have led to a painful encounter with the stick.

Compared with home life the atmosphere was a little harsh at first, but familiarity with the system and rising seniority brushed aside those initial anxieties after two years. St Aubyns had a happy atmosphere, a distinctive and charismatic group of schoolmasters (especially my geography and Latin teacher and cricket supremo, Walter Thursby-Pelham) and, over five years, helped me to discover the academic, leadership, and sporting strengths I wasn't aware I had.

By the time my third summer term rolled around, I'd managed to become the opening bowler and middle-order batsman for the Colts cricket XI, silver bugler in the school band, and was keeping up in the classroom. Ambition had joined forces with the castle way and exerted a levelling effect on the latter. This was possible only in the competitive and hierarchical environment of boarding school, where the senior boys became responsible for the juniors and the top sports players garnered all the accolades.

Normally no one chooses to pick on the opening bowler. Nonetheless a big fat oaf called Ker challenged me to a boxing match and I couldn't say no, even though he was huge, because I would have looked like a coward. What lay behind his challenge was the fact that I had knocked around a boy smaller than me, Bailey, in a brief fight instigated by the boxing coach himself. It had not been my intention to hurt Bailey—and I didn't—but I was not of a mind to lose the encounter either. Ker and I arranged to fight in the small space behind the history teacher's classroom, which meant I wouldn't be able to make use of my speed and we'd be obliged to stand there and biff each other like prizefighters. We decided to have "seconds" as they used to do in duels in the old days, to check our gloves and call for help if necessary!

It turned out to be a strange contest, with both of us keeping up a constant stream of threatening repartee modelled on Muhammad Ali's but not as funny. It kept us busy, though, and actually slowed down the fighting dramatically, which was perhaps its intention. We finally laid down our gloves after about fifteen minutes of periodic hard-hitting fisticuffs, and though I'd been hurt, it seemed my opponent was not left entirely unscathed. With honour apparently satisfied, we continued about our business, and it was only a comment from Mr. Strawson, my English teacher and tennis coach, which later informed me that my not declining the contest had gained approval in the masters' common room.

Being in the choir was useful because just before chapel on Sunday, when the rest of the school were in their pews, I was able to listen to the last few tunes of Alan Freeman's *Pick of the Pops* top-twenty show on the tiny pocket radio which had been in one of my previous Christmas stockings. It was essential to listen quietly, of course, because such behaviour was strictly *verboten*. But the radio's size allowed it to be quickly stuffed away under my robes when the vicar arrived with Mr. Gervis for the warm-up prayers.

I often wrote to Nanny about my near misses, and she would respond by telling me to take good care of myself and stay out of trouble, which generally wasn't that hard to do. On the rare occasion that Mr. Gervis did require my presence in his study to rebuke me for a committed transgression, there was no brutality in his administration of the stick.

When at home, during school holidays, the castle way's operating system returned to its hard-wired dominance, there being no framework to counteract the slings and arrows of outrageous grown-ups who controlled the keyboard. In other words, no one paid any attention to the fact that at St Aubyns I'd become "somebody." Why would they?

Triumphs on the sports field, such as they were, were witnessed and applauded by a limited audience—the school and the visiting opposition. David, ever the sports fan, graciously took an interest in my cricket adventures, particularly one that occurred on a euphoric sunny day in June 1964. I was opening bowler for the first XI cricket team, and that day was able to achieve what few bowlers do—take the wickets of the entire opposing team with the exception of a run-out. In cricket-speak, nine wickets for twenty-seven runs. We won the match with five minutes left on the clock.

Leaving the field amidst cheers, handclapping, and backslapping galore, the first person to make a beeline for me was the deputy headmaster, Mr. E. A. K. Webber, a wavy-white-haired, walrus-moustached, gravel-voiced old man with a twinkle in his eye and aptitude for tearing his tweed jackets and forgetting to do up his fly. Holding out his hand, a broad smile extending to the many corners of his craggy face, he said, "Congratulations! You'll never do that again in your entire life!" It was intended as a compliment, of course. But after all the furore had died down, it dawned on me that it could just as easily have been a warning. Such heights are rarely scaled, and seldom matched.

———

Mr. Gervis wrote in the school magazine of October 1965: "A. J. M. Russell goes to Stowe. His two elder brothers, David and James, were here and we feel sad that there are no more brothers to come. But his mother is godmother to several future boys and we shall, therefore, hope to keep in touch with the family. He was captain of cricket, in the soccer XI and shooting VIII, and played for the rugger XV. He was in the choir until his voice broke and he then carried the Cross. In the band he was silver bugler longer than any boy; nine times in all, eight times in succession. He won the lawn tennis cup, was captain of hockey and a Section Commander."

After five years of making my way from small fry to the top, it was now time to go back down to the bottom and start the process all over again at Stowe School for boys, crucially without the companionship of my close friends Soames and Steel. Like a large number of St Aubyns pupils at that time, they were going on to Eton.

In a peculiar twist of fate that shed a light not just on the way things were then done in the upper echelons of private education but also on the incomprehensible workings of my family, I was offered a place at Eton two weeks before I sat my Common Entrance exams (the all-important examinations for gaining entrance to a top public school). Because I was captain of cricket I'd been invited by a friend of the headmaster to accompany him up to London to watch the England v. New Zealand Test Match from the comfort of a private box at Lord's. It was quite a thrill watching the game from such an exalted position. The grown-ups present, mostly men, a couple of ladies, were thoroughly agreeable from the outset.

"How do you do?"

"How do you do?"

"How do you do?"

"How do you do?"

"Hello, how are you?"

"Isn't it simply glorious?"

"I'd say!"

Everyone drank copious amounts of champagne or red wine from the moment we arrived until teatime. At lunch I was placed between Mr. Gervis and a rotund, jovial man dressed in a three-piece tweed suit, and we discussed cricket and school at some length. On the train back to Brighton, Mr. Gervis informed me that this particular gentleman was a housemaster at Eton and he had offered me a place in his house. What did I think?

I didn't know what to think. I was unable to fathom that something as important and difficult to come by as a place at the world's most famous school could be attained by sitting demurely with an unfamiliar bunch of grown-ups watching cricket for five hours, with a one-hour break for lunch. My father had been sent to Stowe by his mother—Eton had indicated it wished to distance itself from the "Russell baby" association—and, as a result, David and I went there too.

In 1965 the difference between going to Eton and going to Stowe was the difference between flying First Class Pan

American, and Aeroflot. The one had a well-established (founded in 1440 by King Henry VI) aura of distinction and a high success rate in achieving the goals of its customers. The other was suffering from low self-esteem, diminished public regard, and providing an indeterminate outcome for its clients.

When my father arrived at Stowe in September 1935, the headmaster, J. F. Roxburgh, had already won the twelve-year-old public school an extraordinary reputation. Michael Bevington (head of the Classics Department) writes for the Stowe School Web site: His aim was to produce a modern public school concentrating on the individual, without the unpleasantness of fagging [a system by which younger boys act as servant-cum-dogsbody to older ones] or arcane names then common in other schools. Instead he sought to instil a new ethos enthused with the beauty of Stowe's unique environment where the best of traditional education would be tempered by liberal learning and every pupil would "know beauty when he sees it all his life" (Roxburgh's words). Pupils and staff would relate in a civilized and open way, showing confidence and respect based on Christian values. Such was Roxburgh's success in developing this vision that he was recognized as a formative figure in 20th Century English education, "greater than Arnold" (the nineteenth-century headmaster of Rugby) in Gavin Maxwell's (the author of *Ring of Bright Water*, among other books, was a Stowe alumnus) words.

Essentially, in a few short years Roxburgh turned Stowe into a contender for inclusion in England's elite hierarchy of private boarding schools such as Eton, Harrow, Winchester, Westminster, Rugby, and Shrewsbury. But after World War II, which claimed the lives of many old Stoics, the school went into decline. It wasn't until forty years later that the restoration came, both in education and for the glorious eighteenth-century buildings themselves. The school got its mojo back under Jeremy Nichols (a former Eton housemaster) in the 1990s, and then, expanding and improving as never before, under the current headmaster, Dr. Anthony Wallersteiner.

Stowe has now regained, perhaps surpassed, the old Roxburgh heights, becoming not just a contender but a leading member of the elite group. In the mid-1960s, however, there was clearly no contest between the distinction and expected outcome of going to Eton or going to Stowe.

"Look, Anthony," Mr. Gervis said kindly. "This is an important and very difficult decision. It needs to be studied carefully, but unfortunately there isn't much time. Leave it with me, and I'll find out what your parents think." I had a feeling this was going to be awkward, and I was soon proved right. Days went by, and I never heard another word. I tried to summon up the nerve to ask Mr. Gervis, or to write to my parents to ask what was going on, but my inhibitions froze all action. I said nothing to anybody about my dilemma.

It's hard to fathom how—having displayed over five years some healthy determination both on the sports field and in the classroom—I could have left unanswered the question of the Eton offer. I think what lay behind the confluence of silence might have been associated with my father having gone to Stowe after being turned down by Eton, and what was good for him must be good for me. No further discussion needed. But did he ask Mr. Gervis, a kind man and superb headmaster, not to discuss the affair with me as the case was most assuredly closed? Carrying my reserve to optimum negative levels, I felt unable to confront Mr. Gervis and did not write a letter home about it. What I did do was stay a long time inside my shell, feeling outraged that the principals had failed to involve me in their deliberations.

I will never know what benefits, if any, going to Eton might have given me. If, however, there was one school that might have been able to combat the effects of the castle way once and for all, Eton could well have been the place. Its ancient rules and harsh discipline, not to mention high academic requirements and reams of boys from backgrounds equally, if not vastly more, privileged, than mine, might have been the medicine I least wanted but most needed. Perhaps foolishly, perhaps selfishly, my father must have thought otherwise.

11

RECORD ROUNDABOUT

During the period when St Aubyns was beginning, valiantly and moderately successfully, to conduct my education, my burgeoning love of music and its hold on my psyche led to significant new events on the home front. Chief amongst them was a second barnstorming of the grown-ups' tea citadel, as well as the development of a profound new connection, close to Egerton Terrace, called Record Roundabout, where I made, and almost lost, a new best friend.

I was not meant to be like this. I was not, by nature, inclined to cause a rumpus: I did not stir the pot, tie Nanny's shoelaces together, go out of my way to frighten my mother's poodle or defy castle way mores. I was eight and a half years old and had just completed my second, the winter term, at St Aubyns, during which we had all played a lot of football and kept up the now familiar tight schedule of lessons, meals, prep, and bed. A film was shown in the gym most Saturday and Sunday evenings, which was very good news. I could have done without the less than stellar comedies by the popular actor Norman Wisdom, but the World War II tales of heroics *Reach for the Sky* and *The Dam Busters* appealed to my advanced patriotic sensibilities. There had been the odd encounter with intimidation in far-flung windy corridors, but generally the speeding-cricket-ball-fallback excuse worked well, and the eleven weeks had sailed smoothly by.

Now, almost eleven months after my introduction to the full-blown tea ceremony, in which Lady Huntley, Guysy-Wee, and I had made toast as if our lives depended on it and I had been invited to Nassau, I was, once more, preparing to enter the lion's den. This time I was armed not with my trusty "Glute" but with a copy of "Only the Lonely," a pop song of breathtaking sweep and grandeur sung by an American called Roy Orbison, who had to have the most beautiful pop-singing voice ever. I had not received a formal invitation, so I considered my plan to be a bold one, akin to storming the beaches armed with a 45 rpm disc.

"Look sharp," Nanny said. "If you're going to go, it's five minutes past five."

Was my uninvited appearance at tea a gesture of defiance or my first real attempt at self-expression? All I knew was that I was fixated on a high-level meeting with both the grandees in the drawing room and the highly polished mahogany radiogram perched in the far corner, next to the Louis XV desk and opposite the Chinese screen. Entering through the double doors, I received the customary welcome of polite indifference and not the looks of surprise I had anticipated. I let this minor affront go, not wishing to stall my momentum.

"Hello, darling, how nice of you to pay us a visit," my mother said.

"Darling, come and give me a kiss," Granny said, "and have a piece of cake."

I crossed the room for kisses, pleased that I had remembered to wear my St Aubyns long grey flannel trousers, which at least made me feel less of a chump around the grown-ups. The drawing room was as warm and toasty as before, log fire crackling and burning, and guests, court, and family dotted around the room with subtly orchestrated informality.

"What is that you have with you, darling?" Granny asked as I munched on chocolate cake with as much decorum as I could muster.

"It is the best new record, Granny, and I want to play it for you, if I may."

I spotted the Duchess of Roxburghe looking at me from the sofa as if I had just let one go, and even Morg, sitting as usual on Granny's right, wore a quizzical expression. My mother appeared intrigued by the situation, as did Johnny G and Guysy-Wee. Lady Huntley, Woody, Bottle, and my father remained neutral but cast furtive glances about the room, while the Wiltons stayed stolidly aloof, he seemingly asleep. Granny, though, was thankfully alert to the needs of the moment and said without hesitation, "Let's hear it, darling. I don't know anything about this Mr. Orbison, but if you say he's good I'm sure he's simply marvellous."

The assembled company cleared their throats and focused their attention upon me as I made my way over to the radio-gram, all the while suppressing an urge to turn tail and run. Fortunately my mother had previously shown me, when no one was around, how to operate the machine (playing Perry Como tunes endlessly), so at least I knew what to do. I turned the player on with one of the big buttons on the front and opened the lid. I placed Roy on the upright middle prong and brought the lever over to rest on top. I moved the play switch to the right and waited for the clicks. By now the drawing room had been silent for a minute. One click, two, down went the disc, over came the arm, down went the needle; first, a soft scratchy sound and then—"Dum-dum-dum-dummy-doo-waa"—we were off; intimate back-up singers, gentle beat, tinkling piano, and lastly, Roy's startlingly pure voice: "Only the lonely . . ." I stood back from the record player to better appreciate the music and watch the reaction. My mother and Johnny G were clearly enjoying the tune, in fact Johnny G gave me the impression he was quite familiar with it already. He tapped his feet and twirled one of the sleeves of the navy cashmere sweater which was draped over his shoulders and loosely tied in well-established *beau monde* style. The rest of the audience looked as though they were sitting in a dentist's waiting room, which I found discouraging as the tune was only halfway through. I caught Morg's eye, and he was kind enough to wink, which helped.

The record's crescendo was spectacular, but it, too, elicited no response, so I waited anxiously for the tune to end and for the gramaphone to reverse its starting procedure. As I put the disc back in its sleeve, I was caught off guard to hear a very subdued round of applause, emanating first from Granny and then picked up by the room. It lasted mere seconds but confused me greatly. Surely it wasn't for me; it must be for Roy, but he wasn't present. Besides, "enthusiasm" was not the word that sprang to mind when assessing the overall reaction to his record.

Almost immediately conversation resumed as if the whole nasty business had never taken place. Trying not to blush but failing miserably, I beat a hasty retreat back upstairs to the nursery, but awarded myself the mildest pat on the back for having given the pot a gentle, but carefully considered, deeply felt stir.

I rarely settled down to think hard about whether I had, in material terms, everything I needed, because I thought I did—except for records. If I ought to have been giving greater consideration to the needs of people in less fortunate circumstances than mine, life inside the bubble promoted no such thoughts. As the weeks drifted by, there were constantly new 45s I craved to add to my collection, but my minuscule pocket money always fell drastically short of covering even my most urgent requirements. Christmas, Easter, and my birthday provided three occasions to stock up, but the maddening gap from May until December was barren and hard to bear. My brothers suffered similar iniquities, although their pocket money beat mine by a mile, so they had a little leeway in purchasing power. My sole recourse was to gather a half crown here, a half crown there (after the Roy Orbison "Only the Lonely" incident Morg apparently now considered me past the "singing for reward" stage) and wait until I had the magic six shillings and eight pence. As soon as I did, and I was out of the clutches of boarding school, I beat a path to see my new friend, Richard, at Record Roundabout to listen and make a purchase.

Record Roundabout was just about the friendliest little shop you could imagine. The window decoration consisted of LP sleeves, and as the shop was right next door to Simpson's, the greengrocer, Nanny and I had had many opportunities to admire the display before (reluctantly in my case) continuing with our mission to pick up vital supplies (porridge, tapioca, little things Miss Preston must have overlooked) for the nursery kitchen. One day, when Nanny was deep in conversation with Mrs. Simpson, I had gone in, causing the bell to *ding-dong*, and been straightaway enchanted by the cosy atmosphere and the sensation of being in a place for people who really loved music. Richard had been tucked away behind a half-curtain listening to classical music while attending to paperwork and had ignored me for quite a while, causing familiar feelings of discomfort to resurface. But then, after I'd flipped self-consciously through the racks along the walls and on the countertop, he had leapt up and been all smiles and enthusiasm. He was a handsome man with a deep voice and, as it turned out, a fondness for wearing heavy and hairy sweaters instead of a shirt. Over time, I became aware that he was also a "confirmed bachelor" with a passion for Mahler.

Richard and I quickly became firm friends. Often, when I did not have the requisite amount of money or token, he would simply tell me to take the record (or records) home with me and pay him when I could. This trusting relationship brought an element of joy to my world which had not always been so much in evidence. And then one day I almost threw it all away.

It was December and cold outside so I put on my duffel coat, letting Nanny know where I was going and that I would be back in under an hour. A brisk walk up Egerton Terrace, a Georgian cul-de-sac where all the houses were four or five storeys, painted toothpaste-white, had black railings and porticoed steps in front, and walled gardens at the back. We lived in number 24, the last house on the right, the only house in the street with a garage. On through Egerton Gardens, the cherry and plane trees winter bare, and in no time I arrived at Record Round-about, where it was as warm as toast and classical music played.

"It's Mahler's Ninth Symphony," Richard told me from behind the curtain, neither taking it off nor lowering the volume. After two or three minutes I admitted defeat:

"Do you have 'It's Now or Never' by Elvis?"

"I certainly do," Richard said, jumping up and skimming through the round rack on his countertop and withdrawing the single in question. As he did so I spotted the other 45 I wanted just as badly but did not have the money for, "Let's Think About Living" by Bob Luman, an American country singer. On the spur of the moment, without thought for the consequences, I decided to steal this record if I could. But I needed time. I had to think how I was going to do it. I needed Richard to go back to his desk, behind his curtain, to leave me space to carry out this dastardly plan. I knew it was wrong. Ever since the "trash-mag" folly in Bembridge with Nanny, which had left me a quivering wreck for ages, I had told myself I would never do such an idiotic thing again. But there I was, lost in my compulsive "I want/must have" way of thinking, and I really, really wanted Bob Luman's record, so good-old-fashioned common sense momentarily flew out of the window. Again.

"I'm going to look around some more," I said, and Richard went back to his desk and the Mahler, which I was beginning to find a little trying. I started flipping through the same rack on the counter with great deliberation as I felt a nasty creeping sensation of nerves taking over my whole body. Keeping one eye on Richard, who seemed to be busy with his office work, I pulled the 45 out of the rack and looked at it for a moment, still not sure if I was going to proceed. Then I slipped it into the right-hand pocket of my duffel coat, my hand shaking like a leaf. I thought my face had gone beetroot and my feet felt rooted to the spot. The sensation of guilt was appalling, and to make matters worse, Richard stood up. I panicked hopelessly and completely. I took the record back out of my pocket, convinced Richard knew what I had been up to, placed it on the counter together with the Elvis 45, and rushed out of the shop without saying another word. Once outside I ran half the way home, engulfed by waves of embarrassment and shame, tempered only by a blessed relief at having left empty-handed.

Richard was a kind man. When I plucked up the courage to go back to Record Roundabout several months later, convinced I would need to apologize profusely before any further transactions between us could conceivably take place, he greeted me in such a way that it seemed virtually impossible to begin by saying I was sorry. "My goodness! Where've you been? I've been worried that you might have gone back to shopping at Harrods, or somewhere, for your records!"

We resumed our friendship as if the Bob Luman incident had never happened, although I couldn't help but wonder, the first few times I handed over money or record tokens, what Richard must have been thinking.

12.

A CASTLE WAY LETTER

In January 1961 I wrote a letter to Granny B, hoping that it would act as a harbinger of significant future "audiences" at which I envisaged us sitting together in her boudoir and discussing "high-level things." I would admire her Louis XVI bureau *plat et cartonnier* (after, of course, she had explained the reasons why I should be admiring it), and we would chat and get along famously as if all those years of saying little to each other had been a mere preliminary to establishing a fine, friendly relationship.

But my nerve failed me. Nothing in the past suggested that my grandmother had ever wanted to spend time with me. Also, and this was assuredly the rub, it seemed obvious that the letter would be discussed with my parents, because of what I had written about them, and possibly with other members of the court who would doubtless be keen to voice an opinion.

The whole point of writing the letter would then be destroyed by one controversial paragraph. Of course that paragraph could have been left out, but the truth was I wanted my grandmother's help. It never entered my mind simply to go up to her one day and say, "Granny, I would like to speak with you about something important." The system did not work that way, and neither did I.

Dear Granny B,

I hope you won't mind me writing to you like this but I find it easier to put some things down on paper rather than say them. Also, we don't really see each other a great deal, and when we do you always appear to be so terribly busy.

As you know, I think, I'm almost nine years old now and sort-of looking forward to moving into the Maiden's Tower during the summer months but I'm also really going to miss the nursery and staying in the castle. I've always loved the way it feels to press down on the front door's big handle and step inside on to the smooth stone floor and soak up the atmosphere of the entrance hall. The swords which hang each side of the door remind me how old the castle is. Sometimes I take one down to pretend I'm a knight for a minute, but Nanny takes it away from me before I can do some damage. It's amazing how heavy they are. I usually check the box which holds the croquet balls and mallets to make sure nothing is missing. Perhaps one day you'll let me play a game with you and Mummy and Morg? My favourite tapestry is the one in the entrance hall above the long oak table. All those fierce-looking men on horseback with the archers on foot and the woods behind. Sorry if this letter goes on a bit but there are a lot of things to say and as we've never actually had a proper talk I thought this would be a good way to mention them.

Thank you for letting me have lunch in the dining room sitting at the table with the grown-ups for the first time the other day. Woody was very nice to me and told me many interesting things especially about how Monsieur Boudin had suggested building panels around the lovely Aubusson rugs which hang on the wall to make them look like paintings. I saw you and Monsieur Boudin and Mummy and Daddy walking round the Maiden's Tower recently but I didn't want to interrupt because you all looked as if you were concentrating on important things and making notes and discussing. Are we moving into the Maiden's Tower because now I have a little sister there isn't enough room in the castle nursery for us all? It makes sense. It's a shame Vanessa will never know what fun the castle nursery is and I'm really going to miss the views although they're not at all bad from the Maiden's Tower, as you know.

I want to tell you I think you seem very nice and very generous. You organize so well and everything always looks wonderful and runs like clockwork. You get everyone to do what you want them to do and still remain popular. It's funny how all your guests, Mummy and Daddy too, joke about not being able to make plans in case you need them. I don't know if you're aware of this but all the people on the estate think the world of you, and Mummy tells me how kind you are to all of them.

I hope you don't mind my saying so but another thing I find really funny is how you make sure you have the four you want for cards following tea and after dinner. I once heard Borrett whispering to a guest, "Are you available for bridge, m'Lord, after dinner?" and I thought to myself, "Why doesn't Granny ask? I'm sure he'd say yes." Anyway, I like playing gin rummy and pontoon, especially when we have chips and pretend to gamble. I know you and your guests play for real money which must make it more exciting—but no fun when you lose!

I've been meaning to tell you about my bike accident last September and what really happened. I hope Mr. Elves didn't get into trouble because it wasn't his fault in the slightest. I was going down through the stable yard at top speed leaning low over the handlebars pretending they were the racing type and Mr. Elves was driving up the hill coming towards me in his green Austin van but because he hadn't yet gone past the aviaries we couldn't see each other until he came round the corner and it was too late. It was a head on prang right outside the estate office. I flew off my bike on to his bonnet, banged into his windscreen and tumbled on to the road ending up a few feet away from his left front wheel. If anything, I think Mr. Elves was going quite slowly. He helped me in to Miss Brown's sitting-room where I lay on the sofa for a while to recover. I felt a bit biffed around. I don't remember who picked me up and *brought me back to the castle but I do remember you and Morg and goodness knows who else coming into the nursery bathroom to see if I was in one piece or needed a doctor. I must have passed the test because the rest of the evening went by in a nice calm way. Mummy read to me and I heard Cliff Richard's new hit "Nine Times Out of Ten" on the wireless. Did you spot the Scalextric laid out on the floor?*

I probably shouldn't be saying this but now that I have had lunch and dinner a few times with Mummy and Daddy in London, sometimes with David and James, sometimes not, I have noticed that Daddy often says unkind things to Mummy. He thinks he's being funny but I don't think he's being funny at all. He thinks we're laughing with him but I'm not laughing with him; in fact, I'm angry with him. He puts Mummy down, tells her she's foolish, makes fun of her. It makes me feel horrible. I want to stand up for her but don't know what to do. I can't say anything because I feel tongue-tied around him, incapable of standing up for myself. I don't know why. Does he do things like this to Mummy in front of you? I hope not because she does not deserve it. I think she's clever and kind, just like Nanny. Please tell Daddy to behave properly if you see him being nasty to Mummy because someone has to. You wouldn't believe how awful the atmosphere can be in the dining room on these occasions.

Back to Leeds. I know we're only moving across the croquet lawn but I want you to know I've loved living in the castle even though it's mainly been Nanny and I with every-one else popping in and out of our bubble. Did you know that when no one's around during the week I explore all the guest bedrooms and bathrooms, and sometimes I go up in the lift to visit Mrs. Walsh and she shows me the rooms where all the maids sleep? Also, I sometimes visit Mr. Bor-rett in his pantry and have a peek into the kitchen if no one's there. Everywhere I go feels different and yet it all fits perfectly. It really is a wonderful place and even though it's somewhat huge it still has a friendly feeling. I like the old four-poster beds and the big oak furniture and I'm glad you hung the picture of you with Mummy and Auntie Pops in the library because I look at it when I'm playing backgam-mon with Guysy-Wee. I love the library bar with the mir-rors. "Can I get you a Coca-Cola, Master Anthony?" Borrett asked me the other day and he brought me a heavy glass of Coke with ice and a slice of lemon on a silver tray. I enjoyed that. I hope we'll be able to come over for lunch or dinner every now and then in the future.

Boarding school was initially a shock. I thought Hill House was bad enough, but being away for weeks on end, sleeping in dormitories with so many other boys, was ghastly at first but it didn't take too long to get sort of used to it and now I've made some friends it isn't quite as bad. I'm hoping I'll be able to invite one or two to stay once we've settled down in the Maiden's Tower and everything's ready. Mummy tells me the place was used for bachelor guests in the past who would have to be very clever to get into the castle late at night to pay their respects to the ladies. I hope you'll tell me more about this one day.

The duck launching was the best fun and I'm sure everyone there thought so too.

Much love,
Glute

I should have sent the letter. It might have opened the door to a sparkling new form of dialogue with my grandmother—assuming, that is, it would have resulted in her wishing to talk to me at all. It surely would have sent up distress signals on my mother's behalf, alerting the powers that be to a sympathetic fifth column lurking in the nursery whose patience was running out but whose warrior skills had not yet matured. The slights my mother was obliged to suffer, from my father and other members of the court, had to be curtailed. Granny B must have known about this disrespectful behaviour, but she would not have known the opinion of the boy with the Davy Crockett pistol. It might not have altered much, but it could have helped in some small way.

13.

THE MAIDEN'S TOWER

If the castle was positioned at twelve o'clock, then the Maiden's Tower sat squarely at three, and without suffering undue strain or stress, or even having to break into a trot, one walked from door to door in approximately a minute. Initially I found this comforting, almost a form of compensation for having been booted from the mother ship in the first place.

In keeping with tradition, I asked no one about the precise reason for our move across the croquet lawn to new digs. In return, and, in keeping with the general rule of thumb, no reliable source from the castle hierarchy vouchsafed an explanation. My theory behind the uprooting was that my new baby sister, older brothers (now thirteen and fourteen), Nanny, and I had outgrown the nursery. I would hazard a guess that disturbing the peace played a role. Granny B and the court were getting older and her health was not as robust as she would have liked. Clearly we were now upsetting the orderly manner of things, and castle way calm needed to be restored.

No one had mentioned the Maiden's Tower for years. We passed her on our walks, appreciated her Tudor good looks from a host of different vantage points, but never ventured inside until one day word was passed down that she was to become ours, and that there was work to be done. Exactly how much work was revealed when my brothers and I were permitted a cursory inspection and stumbled into a heavily cobwebbed, crumbling interior with no discernible layout beyond a central staircase and a vast billiard room, table intact, with the country's largest stuffed pike glaring down from the wall through its glass encasement, somehow still managing to look ferocious despite its predicament.

The Maiden's Tower looked just the same from the outside when we moved in in 1961 as it had in 1509 when Catherine of Aragon had come to the castle before her marriage to Henry VIII. The building had housed her Maids of Honour, which may, at a later date, have given it its name. Granny B, Monsieur Boudin, and my parents redid the interior from top to toe, carefully and exquisitely transforming it into a fabulous country house, a place where ancient and new sat side by side in perfect harmony, and the triumphant glow of a job well done was immediately apparent.

The entrance hall was long and tall, stone floored, and suggested baronial splendour, though the Maiden's Tower, or MT, as my mother almost immediately christened her, had an intimacy which belied her spaciousness. A wide, handsome oak staircase led to seven bedrooms and seven bathrooms on the upper floor, each with its own colour scheme, high-quality antique furniture, and magnificent views. My sister, Vanessa (who was one year old when we moved in), and Nanny shared the pink; down the corridor James and I shared the blue, and David was next door in the yellow. The green guest bedroom with its large double bed, my father's manly quarters, and my mother's pink-and-green suite of rooms completed the circle save the cupboard by the top of the stairs, which housed the cleaning lady's array of equipment, and had steps to the roof and battlements.

There was nothing not to love about the MT, from the Ping-Pong, Scalextric, television, card corner, bar-billiards, and music-infested playroom to my upstairs twin-white-cupboarded, fancy-dressing-tabled, blue-and-white-curtained and headboarded bedroom, with racing lithographs on the walls and windows looking out over the castle, croquet lawn, moat, golf course, and woodlands stretching far off into the distance.

The court situation became more elastic as weekends came and went. Now that we were all on top of each other, in a manner of speaking, no longer separated by corridors, arches, and hallways or controlled by the strictest of castle way rules, there developed an almost festive atmosphere to family life at the MT, greatly enhanced by the presence of my little sister. Vanessa not only gave Nanny a whole new lease on life (the pink bedroom and bathroom becoming a jungle of baby bottles, nappies, and knitting) but also appeared to have tempered, at least for a while, the grotesque remarks ("Oh Susy, do pipe down, you don't know what you're going on about" and far worse) my father liked to address with airy abandon to my mother, in front of us all.

Weekend drinks before lunch in the combined drawing room/dining room, which stretched the whole length of the house, were an instant hit with court regulars and visiting guests alike, who clearly loved being able to let their hair down in the informal atmosphere my parents created. The bar, artfully located just outside in the hall, hidden discreetly behind a solid wood door, opened for business without fail at noon. Whereas Borrett and his troops held the fort in the castle, my father performed the task of shaking and mixing, stirring and squeezing, thoroughly adept at satisfying all requests that came his way. Once the glasses were filled he brought them in, two by two, taking great care not to trip on the small step at the entrance to the room.

Everyone wandered in on the weekends unannounced, and the peals of laughter and general din emanating from these gatherings usually provided more than sufficient cover for my brothers and me in our playroom (formerly the billiard room, pike and billiard table removed) to make some noise ourselves.

For a while I only had ears for Johnny Kidd & the Pirates, whose blistering "Shakin' All Over" would probably have caused Perry Como's short-back-and-sides to stand on end. Though still blissfully ignorant on virtually all matters of a sexual nature, I was starting to recognize a pattern in the music to which I had become addicted, and shaking certainly seemed to play a large part in it. Pop stars (Elvis, "All Shook Up") were constantly finding themselves quivering wrecks, and without exception the cause of their inability to remain still was a girl.

Playing doctors and nurses with a young lady quite some time before, underneath the bed in James's room in London (he being away at school), had taught me a little about feeling particularly nice all over as a result of delicate ministrations to a region previously kept as private as possible. Still, I had never felt "the shakes all over me," as Johnny Kidd did when a girl moved "right up close," so I obviously had a great deal to look forward to—unless, of course, it was only pop stars who got to shake.

"Oh my goodness!" Johnny Galliher exclaimed one day, touching his cheeks with both hands and rolling his eyes. "We are going to get a tremendous dose of salts, are we not?" Borrett, looking gravely concerned, had just been over from the castle to announce that Granny B was waiting for everyone in the library, he having already telephoned the MT ten minutes before to say she was on her way down to lunch. This was not good.

I'd been standing in front of the massive stone fireplace (with "1529" carved into the cross-section, almost at head height) observing the before-lunch drinks extravaganza in full swing, wondering how long it would all go on before the castle way interrupted the singsong, or perhaps even changed the tune.

The Wiltons, the Warrenders, Lady H, and Johnny G downed their Bloody Marys and headed for the front door, with Lord and Lady Dudley (the former actress Maureen Swanson), my parents' houseguests, chasing them on their way, howling with laughter. It was obvious that these before-lunch cocktails at the MT were drawing the ire of the authorities who recognized, perhaps, a form of popularity contest developing between mother ship and impertinent vassal. It was amusing to witness the grown-ups acting as if they'd been caught being naughty in class, but it remained the one minor castle way infringement permitted to endure.

The far end of the MT drawing room was the music area, with a long sofa, armchairs, and mullioned glass doors that led out to the swimming pool. Expensive-looking stereo equipment hugged the wall, and Quad speakers stood just in front. My father liked to put on Mahler after lunch and spend a couple of hours looking gloomy. My mother preferred (though not at the same time) to smile and hum along to Ray Conniff and his orchestra, Andy Williams, and the obligatory Perry Como.

My parents were so far apart in their likes and dislikes, habits and personalities, that sometimes their charm, good looks, and fondness for a stiff drink seemed to be all that they had in common. Smoking and drinking were pleasures their World War II generation indulged in, and they, along with practically everyone I saw around them, enjoyed both vices to the fullest. I never saw my parents, their friends, or any member of the court particularly drunk, but my mother always had dry sherry in the morning, wine at lunch, a cocktail before dinner, and wine with the meal. Her delicate nature and vulnerability, so susceptible to teasing and torment, frequently needed setting to rights. She never insinuated to me that she was by no means the happy camper our privileged situation in life would have led me to expect. As I grew to understand, it was not in her nature to speak in a derogatory way about others, especially family or the court. But I had borne witness to the gross unkindness shown to her in Nassau, and on other occasions since, and the barbs directed her way never entirely ceased for the rest of her life.

Living as a family a hair outside the castle's heroically ample bosom—yet still in thrall to its way—inaugurated a period of adjusting to the new setup. We had our own front door, our own staff (who lived in the basement apartment), and for the first time in our lives the seven of us (Vanessa in a high chair when she was able to remain upright and bang her spoon) sat down to lunch at a beautiful long refectory table the opposite end of the room to the music area, two days in a row at weekends, and made what passed for civilized conversation. Perhaps this should not have appeared such a strange phenomenon, but it was new to us. My father always seemed on much better form when guests were present, especially when David, James, and I had our friends to stay. He worked harder on being witty and worldly-wise, elements of his social armoury he particularly prized but that were on display less frequently when only the family was present.

Both my parents came to the table puffing on cigarettes, lit up fresh ones between courses, and launched a final brace before returning to the drawing-room area for coffee. Four cigarettes apiece, a three-course lunch washed down with a bottle of red wine (we boys drank Coke), two full, tiny pewter ashtrays, and a very smoky dining-room became the order of the day. David never smoked; he didn't care for it. Not so James and I. We puffed happily away in the playroom whenever possible, blowing smoke up the chimney and stubbing out our finished cigarettes on a ledge inside the massive brick fireplace which also stored the logs for the drawing-room fire. We thought nobody knew what we were up to until one day my mother angelically said over lunch, "Darlings, you must stop putting your cigarettes out inside the fireplace; you're going to set the house on fire. And while we're on the subject, I wish you wouldn't smoke at all. It's bad for you, and it's such an unattractive habit."

I never thought to argue the point. For many years my mother was a heavy smoker, and it probably was the cause of the cancer that later developed in her mouth. Her mother also was a smoker and, during her later years, was laid low by severe respiratory problems. People then knew smoking could cause health problems, but the social stigma attached to the habit was still thirty years or more in the future.

One thing I'd been fearful of—that I might feel disconnected from the castle and castle life in general following our move to the Maiden's Tower—did not happen. What became increasingly apparent, though, was that the chief insidiousness of castle way mores lay in their ability to shut out the norms of everyday life. With three more years ahead of me at St Aubyns, there was still a lot to learn. The question was how, and from whom? When everything was taken for granted, at all times, by everyone, who was going to be my guide?

Morg was the first guest to stay the night at the MT, which was symbolic of how much we loved him, and of his unique place within the Leeds Castle community, where his special gift of friendship was given to everyone without thought for rank, position, or circumstance. If ever the expression "light up a room" applied to anyone, it applied to him because his presence and personality were not just impressive but also generous, warm-hearted, devoid of self-reverence, and suffused with a sense of humour which crackled and popped and always hit the right notes with a *ping*. He dined, he stayed the night, he signed the guest book, and then returned to his room across the croquet lawn, leaving behind a contented household to revel in the unique aura he had bestowed, like a papal kiss, upon their domain.

Granny B relied on Morg for counsel in virtually all matters. He performed a role for her similar to that which the Duke of Edinburgh performs for the Queen. He was consort, adviser, closest friend, and, in many ways, a husband in all but name. He was the one member of the court I always hoped would come over to the MT drinks extravaganzas because his uplifting presence allowed me to forget my unease around some of the less than charming, overly unctuous courtiers. But he seldom did because he knew it would be disloyal to Granny B.

Morg's career in politics had seen him rise to the top of, and remain for many years a potent force in, the Conservative Party. But after the war he avoided the limelight, choosing to devote himself more to the needs of Granny B and the castle. When he came to see us at the MT it was always a personal visit, just him, dressed in his customary tweed jacket, sober tie, corduroys, and shiny brown brogues. He was very close to both my parents, and they adored him like a second father. Frequently he played croquet with David, James, and me, giving us the benefit of his stellar wit and wisdom for an hour or more on sunny afternoons. We laughed when he dropped his mallet and wandered over to a large bush at one corner of the MT to have a much-needed and highly indiscreet pee, humming and often reciting loudly a dirty limerick for our benefit: "There was a young fella from Kent / Whose prick was so long it was bent / So to save himself trouble / He popped it in double / And instead of coming he went."

To have been able to spend considerably more time in the company of David Margesson would have been ideal, but castle way procedures resolutely, frustratingly, barred the way.

———

Between 1960 and 1965 things started going wobbly in Great Britain for the old-school-tie aristocratic caste who had become serenely comfortable in their top-dog role hundreds of years before the actual invention of the necktie in 1660. (The story goes that a bunch of Croatian soldiers turned up in Paris that year for a parade wearing brightly coloured handkerchiefs around their necks. Their acute fashion-forward awareness was swiftly adopted and, naturally, fine-tuned, first by the French, then by the English.)

English "society" probably changed more between 1963 and 1970 than during the titanic struggles of the century's first fifty years. But neither at the MT nor at boarding school were political, cultural, or anything that might laughingly be termed philosophical discussions raised as a matter of course. They did not enter the classroom beyond passing reference, and they failed to put in an appearance at our dining-room table—which was strange considering the number of political and business heavyweights who regularly assembled for weekends at the castle and whose presence was keenly felt, often at MT cocktail time.

When President Kennedy was assassinated in Dallas on November 22, 1963 (midway through the winter term at St Aubyns), I saw the grim, grainy pictures and read the story on the front page of the *Daily Express* before heading off to morning chapel. Although it came as a huge shock ("What *is* the world coming to?" I could hear Nanny expostulating), I still felt alienated from the event and its implications for the United States and the rest of the world. I was focused at the time on work, sports, my friends, and the imminent replacement of "She Loves You" by the Beatles at the top of the charts by their next single, "I Wanna Hold Your Hand," a feat unsurpassed in the annals of pop music.

Sir Alec Douglas-Home, 14th Earl of Home, became British prime minister in October 1963 and was the last aristocrat to do so. He was obliged to renounce his title in order to put his name forward for the job, but he did not come out on top as a result of people voting for him. He was appointed by an inner circle who thought his background made him ideally suited to the task. In the general election the following year the voting public disagreed—by the smallest of margins—and sent the pipe-smoking, mackintosh-wearing, lower-middle-class Yorkshireman Harold Wilson to 10 Downing Street for the next six years. He had been director of economics and statistics at the Ministry of Fuel and Power during World War II, when Woody had been secretary of mines and secretary for petroleum.

The "Swinging Sixties" then began in earnest. Mr. Wilson wasted no time ingratiating himself with the swingers by including the Beatles on his New Year Honours List in 1965. Amidst great fanfare the band trooped off to Buckingham Palace to receive their MBEs (Member of the Most Excellent Order of the British Empire) from the Queen, much to the fury of several distinguished former recipients who returned theirs in disgust at what they saw as the cheapening of the medal. I would have preferred to see all the Beatles created peers of the realm (lords) with hereditary rights and have done with it. It would have provided essential viewing to witness Lord Lennon debating foreign affairs with either Lord Carrington or Earl Jellicoe (Conservative leaders of the House of Lords in the mid- and late 1970s), and, of course, we'll never know what breadth of knowledge and keen insight the 1st Baron McCartney might have brought to the House if given the opportunity.

During these years we had a few changes of staff at the Maiden's Tower. The kitchen and staff sitting room were off the entrance hall, and downstairs were the bedroom, bathroom, cellar, and back door leading out to the service drive, where all deliveries to the MT and the castle took place. My father kept the key to the cellar always on his person for fear that couples who came to work for us might have designs on his wine and spirits.

Watts was a half-decent butler with an unpredictable personality and lively manners. He was very short with a face resembling a chewed-up cigar, but somehow he had managed to find himself an attractive wife who also knew how to cook. Upon our return from church one Christmas Day we discovered him dressed in full regalia—tailcoat, striped trousers (at the MT the butler was asked to wear normal jacket and trousers), and wearing his medals from World War II. He reeked of whisky and staggered from kitchen to dining room, carrying spoons, plates, and dishes with great uncertainty, all the while muttering and mumbling under his malodorous breath.

Having somehow succeeded in serving the turkey and vegetables, which had been neatly carved and laid out on a serving dish by his long-suffering wife, he stepped back from the table, cleared his throat noisily, and proceeded to make a speech, first on the welcoming nature of our family, followed by a disquisition on the greatness of the British Empire. Much to everyone's amusement my father allowed this spectacle to reach its natural conclusion, which meant waiting until Watts had run out of things to say, which he did after some five minutes. He then bowed modestly and stumbled back to his quarters, not to be seen again until the following morning.

Watts and his wife were not dismissed for this irregular behaviour because it was becoming increasingly difficult for my parents to find good couples. Working in a household as staff had lost most of its appeal by the middle of the 1960s, on top of which the number of country-house owners who could afford to maintain their properties, let alone fill them with domestics, had dwindled after the war to a fraction of what it had once been. Being someone's servant connoted a form of deference the age had pugnaciously set out to destroy, and history emphatically notes its success.

We were fortunate. Thanks to the skill of her advisers (and, perhaps other indeterminate factors) Granny B's cocoon of wealth remained relatively intact. And so, from inside my gilded bubble, I observed and absorbed the revolution of Socialist Members of Parliament, rock stars and hairdressers, playwrights, theatre producers, movie stars, television personalities, photographers, fashion designers, models, and footballers taking over Great Britain's airwaves and headlines with my ears tuned in and an idealistic foot planted firmly in two camps.

14.

TERROR AT THE GALLOP

In January 1963 I was given the chance to test my mettle by going fox hunting in Ireland with Granny A and the infamous wild and woolly Galway Blazers. Terrifying as it appeared, the opportunity could not be turned down—or indeed avoided. I'd never been to Ireland, so the prospect of staying in Dunguaire Castle with David and James for a few days right after Christmas seemed like fun. But I was far from convinced about the hunting. My brothers had gone the year before and said it was great, although James's comments about the jumps—"Holy Moses! You should see the size of those walls"—had not exactly been encouraging.

I also had reservations about Granny A's boot-camp approach to life. David claimed to have worked out a satisfactory antidote, which basically entailed saying yes to whatever he was instructed to do but modifying what he actually did to suit his original plan. James permitted little to upset his apple cart and charmed his way out of most difficulties. Although

I believed I possessed elements of both brothers' worthier characteristics, being much younger I had not yet figured out how to put them into practice. One thing I felt quite sure of, though, was that castle way thinking was in for a drubbing.

Colonel Hislop, a powerfully built, jovial man with a huge moustache and a firm manner, with whom I'd been taking riding lessons since the age of seven, had done his best to bring me up to a standard where I'd be capable of handling two days out with the Galway Blazers. I'd attended the Colonel's riding school near Bearsted, five miles from Leeds, once a week throughout the previous summer and winter holidays, and by the end of this strict regime he had me clearing jumps in the show-jumping ring practically as high as the top of my pony's head and cruising round the cross-country course with confidence and a modicum of style. He told me I'd be just fine, especially if I kept myself at a sensible distance from the gentlemen who drank more than one glass of port before the off. It turned out, though, everyone drank more than one glass of port before the off (apart from Granny A who did not drink), which made it difficult to follow that particular piece of advice.

Entering the reception area at Shannon Airport, Ireland, all three of us heard our grandmother before we saw her.

"Over here, boys, over here!" her melodious yet firm voice rang out across the hall.

She need not have spoken. Granny A stood out wherever she was. There in Shannon she could have been the Blarney Stone incarnate, such was the manner in which her presence appeared to shrink all those around her into specks of insignificance. She was dressed in her customary long gabardine skirt, dress shirt, waistcoat, tweed jacket, hat, veil, and shiny black boots, and the crowd waiting to meet their friends and family parted like the Red Sea for Moses as she strode towards us with a huge smile.

"How *are* you?" she inquired, ignoring the formality of kissing but hugging us all powerfully from a great height and pounding our backs with wild enthusiasm. Greetings dispensed with, she summoned porters with a wave of her riding crop as she sailed off towards the luggage conveyor belt, assuming, quite rightly, that we'd follow. It was just a few moments before our suitcases appeared, one after the other. Granny A instructed our bemused porter how to load his trolley and then, as we headed for the car, exhorted the poor fellow to walk quicker, walk slower, in fact to walk in every possible way except the one of his own choosing. Our conversation was minimal because Granny seemed intent on conducting our exit from the airport as if it were a military exercise: "Left here, right here, mind that dog, follow me, catch up!"

Fortunately the car ride took only one hour and a bit, so when we arrived outside the walls of Dunguaire Castle and

Granny parked her Volkswagen Beetle on the grass verge, James and I were still just about able to manoeuvre our limbs and step enthusiastically out of the back seats into the bracing wind.

Looking around, it struck me that this was a supreme spot. Whichever bloodthirsty warrior had built the place four hundred odd years ago had known his onions (or potatoes, as the Irish might say). On one side the picturesque Galway Bay, her waters breaking gently against the rocky shoreline; on the other, as far as the eye could see, the famous rolling hills and fields criss-crossed by grey and ragged stone walls. Here, I felt, time really stood still—or used to until Granny A came along! She opened the gate, and we lugged our suitcases across the grassy courtyard. Looking up at the battlements, I was reminded of some of the best crossbow shoot-outs from my favourite *William Tell* television programmes.

The main tower, indeed the only tower, looked strong enough to withstand a direct hit from a meteor. Inside, I had the same impression. Apart from the kitchen, a ground-level extension of the tower, all rooms led off the narrow, solid stone spiral staircase. The castle felt as if it would fit comfortably into the nursery wing at Leeds, and had an ambience more suited to Sparta than to the Rome of Augustus. The thick stone walls were dark grey and gloomy, and the few mullioned windows that there were gave little light. The furniture was in keeping with Granny A's rugged but tasteful approach: antique, well suited, and, in the case of the chairs, difficult to sit on in comfort for longer than ten minutes.

The first floor was the drawing room; the second, Granny's area; the third, and top, our room. Only three floors hauling my case up the narrow, winding stone stairs and I felt as though I'd conquered a straightened-up version of the Leaning Tower of Pisa.

"There you are," said Granny. "What took you so long? Your bed is over there. I was telling the boys that beds must be made before you come down to breakfast. Your drawer is this one."

She indicated with her riding crop the bottom of a nice-looking chest of drawers. Then she strode out of the room, instructing us to unpack and report to the kitchen in half an hour for high tea.

James regarded the ensuing free time as the perfect opportunity for a cigarette. David cautioned against such a move, citing the unopenable windows as reason enough. James decided otherwise. I went over to have a look, and sure enough, there was a terrific view of the bay and not a latch or a handle in sight. Although by no means a keen proponent of icy draughts blowing through my bedroom at night (quite enough of that at school), I was intrigued that Granny, a massive devotee of the great outdoors if ever I knew one, should wish to have her castle sealed up like an Egyptian tomb.

I was having a quick puff of James's cigarette when Granny's voice echoed from below: "I can smell that." Seconds later she marched into the room: "How dare you smoke in my house?!" I'd never seen anyone look so angry and talk so quietly at the same time. She took the cigarette from James, holding it between her thumb and forefinger as if it were a diseased goat's testicle, walked into the bathroom, and flushed it down the loo.

"Don't ever let me catch you smoking again," she said and left, leaving the three of us speechless and staring at our feet.

Oozing guilt, we soon afterwards stepped into the spacious, brightly lit, rectangular kitchen and stood rather sheepishly for a while by a long wooden table awaiting instructions. Granny was peeling potatoes with speed and precision and appeared not to notice us. Standing next to her, deftly slicing a large slab of beef into neat little cubes, was a short and rather wide Irish lady with red hair and a wicked accent. Both talked without pausing for breath and without waiting for the other to finish a sentence.

"Make yourselves useful," Granny said over her shoulder, "and lay the table, if you please."

Rinsing the potatoes and moving on to the carrots, she informed us with a series of points, nods, inferences, and verbal directions as to where everything was. Her anger was gone. She was smiling and vigorously applying herself to the next important function of the day. Whatever she had meant by high tea at six obviously had little to do with the preparations under way.

Watching Granny and her cook, whose name was Mary and who happened also to be the woman who came in to clean, chatting away like old friends, was a revelation. How come, I thought, everybody back home was intimidated by Granny A and made allowances for her, and yet this little woman from the local village of Kinvara, who looked half her age, seemed to get on with her as well as I did with Nanny?

We ate at eight o'clock. The food was excellent, and there was much laughter and gaiety. Granny could be as funny as anybody I knew, and this night she was in full flow. By nine thirty I could stay awake no longer and was allowed to skip clear-up duties and go to bed. Tomorrow we were getting to know our horses, and the day after was the hunt. Something told me I was going to need as much sleep as I could get.

I was improperly dressed. Also, both I and the pony assigned to me were half the size of everybody else. David told me the clothes didn't matter and I looked very distinguished anyway. Granny told me I sat well in the saddle and my pony would handle the rest. I wanted it all in writing.

It was ten fifteen on a grey morning, and I was surrounded by fifty or sixty ladies and gentlemen on horseback and perhaps fifty more on foot, most of whom were knocking back glasses of port with abandon. As I had never before attended an equine cocktail party outside a large country house right after breakfast, the humorous side of the event did not elude me entirely. But I was a little concerned that in the heat of the chase, the somewhat excited and inebriated throng might fail to spot me altogether. If anybody needed some port it was I, but with Granny on patrol that was out of the question.

In keeping with my freshly minted, slightly more outgoing persona, I did my best to look relaxed and in control of the situation as I walked my pony around. I raised my riding hat to a brace of good-looking ladies who may or may not have noticed. Having seen other gentlemen do this and get an enthusiastic response, I surprised myself by brushing aside my shyness and putting in a little practice for the future. Surrounded by a sea of black jackets, black hats, white stocks, and high black boots, I compared my outfit against everybody else's. My jodhpurs were pretty much all right. It was the tweed jacket, shirt, tie, and short dark brown boots that caused grief. The outfit didn't look bad, but it didn't look right either. It was the same old problem; getting stuck with the hand-me-downs. At least nobody appeared to be looking at me strangely.

I trotted over to Granny, who was talking to a man in a bright red jacket, which for some reason was called pink. I had a feeling he was the local big cheese whose large and very attractive manor house provided the backdrop—and, I daresay, the port—for the enormous gathering. Just then, I heard the *yap-yap-yapping* of the hounds for the first time, immediately followed by the blare of a hunting horn, expertly blown. Around the corner they came—goodness knows how many hounds—and in the middle of them all their boss, also in a pink jacket and riding a powerful-looking grey.

"Never overtake the Master; it simply isn't done," Granny reminded me with the look of a hanging judge. "Stay close to me," she went on, "and don't forget, give your pony his head."

This sounded remarkably like "If in doubt take your hands off the wheel," but I nodded and promised to heed her advice as best I could. If I had been a soldier in the trenches during World War I, I imagined this is how I would have felt just before going over the top. And I was meant to be enjoying myself!

David and James came up. James looked very smooth. Black horse, black jacket. A touch of devil may care about him. David seemed in his element, immaculate and raring to go. "We're off," they both said. And we were.

A sense of urgency and expectation hung in the air. Heavy clouds and a slight chill provided an ominous additional touch to the proceedings. As we *clop-clopped* our way down a narrow country lane lined by hedgerow, I noticed my pony's behaviour had taken on a rather authoritarian air, quite absent up till now. I wasn't sure if this was a good thing or not. His whole demeanour seemed more alert, even aggressive, and when I let the reins hang loosely round his neck, he marched on without missing a beat. Clearly he was not out with the Galway Blazers for the first time.

For half an hour or more we cantered gently across fields, jumping the occasional wall or gate, or walked and trotted down the lanes as the hounds attempted to pick up the scent of a fox. Up front the Master of Foxhounds led the way, issuing commands and goading his pack to greater efforts in a voice that sounded like the mating call of a hyena. I was riding close behind Granny, admiring her dash and elegance, when suddenly a mighty howl went up from the hounds and I knew the moment of truth had arrived.

The Master's horn began to wail with a vengeance. I looked

around and noticed many riders adjusting their riding crops and making sure their hats were firmly in place. I did the same. My pony broke into a gentle canter without my asking. The whole field was now moving forward inexorably, momentum and speed slowly building like an ocean wave. I heard the crack of whip against rump. The thud of pounding hooves grew louder as each second went by, and the field of riders formed a kind of egg-shaped mass. If it was not exactly like a cavalry charge, I thought it must be close.

As we were approaching a gallop, I was caught up in the most exciting, hair-raising thing I'd ever done in my life. I was loving it. And I was terrified. The first wall was coming up. It was a big one. Everybody was shouting at their mounts. I wanted to but couldn't. I tried to focus. Just a few strides now. My God, it looked huge! "C'mon boy!" I called out. *Whoosh!* We went up. We went over. We made it. No pause, maintain speed. "Yes!" I bellowed at my pony. "Bloody great!" I couldn't believe the rush. I was near the middle of the field, a bit to the left. I could see D and J and Granny. I felt as though I were surrounded by people possessed. The roar of hooves was now constant. The next wall loomed. I gripped tighter with my knees. "C'mon boy!" I shouted again through clenched teeth. There were huge horses on either side of me. No time for panic. *Whoosh!* Over. Made it. How can my pony keep up? I wondered. He's half the size of the rest of the field.

We were going downhill now, slowing. There was a stream and a wall just beyond. It looked tricky. I watched Granny delicately cross. Four, five strides, up and over the wall. I gave my pony his head and held on tight to the saddle. We slipped a bit in the water. A couple of good kicks, more for my benefit than his, and we cleared the wall. We quickly picked up speed, and again I was struck by how strong my little pony was. Somehow I had made it towards the front of the field. I was close to Granny A once more. She looked stunning galloping side-saddle with grace and breathtaking skill, her face beneath her veil and black top hat a vision of unbridled joy and determination. The fear and the thrill were both so intense I couldn't tell which one had the upper hand. I saw the next wall. It didn't look big. We took off a little late. There was a drop, a large drop, on the other side. Too late. I felt myself going. I couldn't hold on. I went over my pony's head and landed hard on the grass.

Everything became slow motion. Horses thundered by. I couldn't tell how long I remained on the ground. I felt battered but not in pain. I got up and dusted myself down, happy not to have broken my neck or been kicked or trampled underfoot. There were some hunt followers who'd been standing close by and had witnessed my fall. One of them retrieved my pony, who'd been kind enough not to disappear into the wild blue yonder. I picked up my hat, which had performed its task to perfection, and after warmly thanking my helpers, climbed back atop my trusty steed.

I caught up with the hunt an hour and a half later. I knew the direction in which to head, but when a very attractive public house appeared before my eyes as I rounded a bend in the road, the opportunity to recharge my batteries with an iced

Coca-Cola proved irresistible. The landlord allowed me to tether my pony to a fence at the back, which I found hilarious—just like in a cowboy film. Entering the pub, I removed my hat and was introduced to the landlady and their two daughters, who were about my age and quite pretty.

They were all very friendly to me. One of the girls brought me a Coca-Cola, and I told them about the hunt and my fall. They thought it was amusing that I should decide to drop in for refreshment before rejoining the other riders. I told them that I had found the whole affair quite scary but also incredibly exhilarating. They taught me how to play poker-dice and for almost an hour we had an enjoyable time chatting away. Saying good-bye, I told them how much I hoped I would see them again, but I never did.

Had I grown up between London and Dunguaire Castle and not between London and Leeds, it is easy to imagine that most of my spoiled habits would have been ground to dust, all the weak spots in my personality whitewashed with marine-like thoroughness, and all my many other imperfections swatted into eternity. Granny A was that kind of person. My contacts with her were limited, however. I went to stay at Dunguaire only twice. Contrary to what I believed as a child, my father and his mother quickly got on each other's nerves when under the same roof, so Granny A's visits to see us were infrequent and brief. Granny A also avoided coming to Leeds as much as possible because she and Granny B had as much chance of seeing eye to eye on just about anything as Wellington and Napoleon.

If my father blamed his mother for inflicting the "Russell baby" stigma on him, he surely had a point. Nevertheless, when he was a child she had proved herself to be an extraordinary mother, considering all she had been obliged to contend with.

15.

FRENCH CONNECTION

F ollowing a now well-established pattern, the court was
spending August, and parts of July and September, at
Granny B's villa in Cap-Ferrat. Both my parents rou-
tinely were in the South of France for two to three weeks
during that time, dutifully soaking up the sun and adhering
to the strict timetable of breakfast in bed, morning swims, sun-
bathing, cocktails, luncheon (sometimes taken with friends on
the Cap, Beaulieu, or Èze), afternoon rests, shopping, cards,
evening drinks, changing for dinner, and dining on the terrace
or with friends on theirs. After that Granny went gambling in
Monte Carlo, or to the casino in Beaulieu, accompanied by a
small, devoted coterie who shared her enthusiasm for the tables
or were merely needed to act as escorts.

I was shipped off to the Côte d'Azur for another solo spell
of Granny, the court, and me because Nanny was on holiday
in Bournemouth, David and James had gone off elsewhere
together, and I was left dangling like a seven-hour roast for

a two-week period in mid-August, my long weekends with Soames and with Steel having come and gone, and nothing else appearing on the horizon until the family returned to the castle to recuperate from it all towards the end of the month.

My mother and I flew down to Nice on a British European Airways (BEA) Comet, which took off like a Ferrari at Le Mans and had seats as comfortable as our new Jaguar. When the doors opened and we walked down the steps, I reeled from the heat of the afternoon sun and the powerful smell of jet fuel which filled the air. I had felt exactly the same sensations the summer before, when my brothers and I had been invited to stay with Granny and the court at Château Saint-Jean, which she had again rented before finding Castèu Cansoun de la Mar in nearby Villefranche. On that occasion I'd finally learnt to swim in the oval pool and been presented with a pair of goggles as my reward from a glowing Auntie Pops. Peter Lucy had taken us sailing on his and Aunt Audrey's gorgeous yacht, and David had been bitten by a giant jellyfish just off the rocks by the jetty, necessitating a house call from the doctor and a day in bed.

Mr. Brewer, a small man of gentle disposition and neat appearance, was waiting for us after we had passed quickly through passport control and customs. He had brought Granny's Mercedes 600 (driven down from Leeds laden with trunks and suitcases) round to the front of the terminal, and I helped him put Mummy's two large cases and my smaller one in the trunk. The remarkable scenic drive along the coast I re-

membered from last time, starting with the panoramic cres-
cent and azure water of Nice's Baie des Anges and the
Promenade des Anglais. My mother told me that it was the
English who had first had the good sense to "discover" the
South of France as a sophisticated getaway a century ago,
which, though less astounding than the much-ballyhooed ex-
ploits of Captain Cook and Dr. Livingstone, still struck me as
a good thing. As we left Nice behind, the view of the Medi-
terranean and the town itself was captured for a brief moment
from high atop the bluff, a shimmering landscape, gone too
fast, but firmly embedded in the mind. Winding our way
along the coast, my mother and Mr. Brewer had lots to discuss—"How is Mrs. Brewer? I know she hasn't been well
lately." "Oh, she's much better, thank you, Madam. In point
of fact she's . . ."—so I continued in silence to soak up the
vistas and the villas and the bougainvillea-studded hillsides
that soared up into a cloudless, incandescently blue sky. With
very little traffic in our way (almost unrecognizable as the same
stretch of coast today), we soon arrived at Villefranche-sur-
Mer, where, way off in the distance, at the mouth of the bay,
silent, grey, and still, was a mighty warship. "She's American.
They visit quite often," my mother explained.

I was reminded of a similar sighting in Venice a few years
previously and volunteered a similar reaction. "Amazing!"
Driving around the bay I noticed rowboats with outboard mo-
tors and half a dozen small yachts anchored or tied up along
the quay, which was lined by colourful houses and full of little
shops and a brace of adjoining restaurants, their tables laid

for *alfresco* dining. On the far side, where Granny's villa stood, adjacent to other houses of similar style and proportion, a number of larger motorboats were moored. Up in the hills to our left, there were villas dotted about, and the old town of Villefranche, passing below us, looked very pretty. There was no time for further inspection. Ignoring the sign to Saint-Jean-Cap-Ferrat, Mr. Brewer turned right; we went down a slight incline, past a couple of gates, and then turned left into Cansoun de la Mar.

Ah ha! I said to myself, here we go again, taking in the rigid formality of the tree-lined driveway and the looming pink mansion with steps, arches, columns, and balustrades much in evidence, gardeners discreetly gardening in far-flung corners but otherwise not a soul in sight. As soon as our tyres came to a genteel halt on the soft gravel, Borrett and Johnny, accompanied by a young footman whose face was new to me, appeared from nowhere. My mother and I stepped out of the car's hot interior into the equally warm late-afternoon sun.

"Good afternoon, Madam; good afternoon, Master Anthony. I trust you had a pleasant journey."

"It was fine, thank you, Borrett," my mother said, as did I, adding a "Mr." as I had been instructed to do. Amidst a gaggle of pleasantries and general chatter, the three men, all in shirt-sleeves, a phenomenon I had never encountered before, whisked our luggage away, and we followed them into the hall.

Accustomed as I had become to Granny B's lavish ways, I found myself surveying the opulence of my surroundings with more of a critical than an appreciative eye. The grand, curving staircase, all marble, came straight out of my pictorial history book of tsarist Russia, as did the gleaming cut-glass chandelier which hung like a trussed whale high above my head, and the combination was less than welcoming.

Just then Granny wandered through an archway at the top of the stairs, smoking a cigarette through a long holder, with her hair in curlers and dressed in a towelling bathrobe. First Borrett in shirtsleeves, now Granny practically in a nightie. As Nanny was prone to comment, "Whatever next!"

"Hello, Mama," my mother said to Granny, and we went up to greet her.

"Darling, forgive my appearance. We're just *en famille* to-night, and Irene is doing my hair. Hello, Glute, are you well, darling?"

"Yes thanks, Granny" was all I had time for before she went on. "Darling, when is Geoffrey coming? We have Noël and David coming to dinner next week, and I need him here."

"He's still with Francis [my godfather Sir Francis Peek] in Nassau, Mama. They're making progress with the hotel, but he's not sure when he'll be able to leave."

"Oh, how maddening! Glute, darling, I'm afraid I shall need you to help out. Are you familiar with Noël Coward and David Niven?"

"Sort of."

"Well, never mind. Your mother will tell you what you need to know, and you'll be fine."

"I will?"

"How old are you now?"

"I'm just twelve."

"Well, there you are."

"Really?"

"Darling, you did say it would be all right for you and Glute to share the twin bedroom? There's plenty of space."

"Of course, Mama."

That was an interesting development. Up until then, merely entering one of my parents' bedrooms had been an irregular occurrence, tolerated if a particular situation called for it (and the hour was not too early) but generally not encouraged. It turned out our room had ample space to accommodate a family of four. We had a view of the terrace and the garden and a bathroom twice the size of any bathroom I had ever seen, with two basins and a loo with its own door. A maid who spoke only French helped us unpack. In my case this was a three-minute affair. For my mother it was a complex undertaking lasting at least one and a half hours, and involving much tissue unfolding and refolding once garments had been removed, great deliberation about their ultimate destination, and careful filling of cupboards, shelves, shoe racks, bathroom drawers, and countertops with soaps, scents, and a dazzling array of makeup and miscellaneous essentials. It was riveting. My mother spoke to the maid all the while in what sounded like an excellent French accent, and I wondered how she had managed to do that.

"How come your French is so good?" I asked her.

"Darling, I'm sure I've spoken to you about Madame Southier, haven't I? She was your grandmother's governess in Paris and became Auntie Pops's and mine at Leeds, where she lived for many years. She died when you were quite little, but you would have known her."

"Perhaps. Were all your lessons in French, then?"

"Mostly, yes. Auntie Pops didn't enjoy that, but I thought it was marvellous, and Madame Southier was an absolute dear, although she could be quite severe."

"That has to be a better way to learn French than sitting in a classroom with twelve other boys and a bad teacher with a worse accent."

"Well, you must make an effort, darling. It's difficult at first but it will get easier if you really try hard."

Apparently everyone dined late in the South of France so it was a quarter to nine when we went down to join the party. My mother looked glamorous in a Pucci dress and pearls, and I looked decent enough in cotton long trousers and a white shirt. Surprisingly I'd been allowed to keep my blond hair longer than usual, which I thought made me halfway good-looking, and after a successful cricket season at St Aubyns I had a little more confidence in my step. As we approached the drawing room there was no escaping the familiar voices of Woody and Morg, or the sulphurous tones of Mickey Renshaw.

They all stood to welcome my mother and acknowledged me with pats on the shoulder or even a handshake. Lady Huntley was there, down from her house in Èze, talking quietly to Grace Dudley. Bert Whitley was on his way from

Beaulieu, as was Mary Lasker from the Villa Leopolda, the grandest villa on Cap-Ferrat, which she had taken for the summer. If this was what my grandmother called *en famille*, then I dreaded to think what lay ahead.

The first thing I learned as cocktails were refreshed and a Coca-Cola miraculously appeared at my right hand on a silver tray carried by Borrett, was that we were all going to lunch with Mrs. Lasker the next day. Morg showed an interest in hearing about my summer term at boarding school. So did Mickey Renshaw, who archly commented on what young boys got up to when gathered under one roof far from home for extensive periods of time, which earned him a disapproving scowl from Morg. I pondered briefly what Mr. Renshaw was referring to, but Granny interrupted my thoughts by making her entrance, accompanied by Mrs. Lasker and Mr. Whitley, the three of whom must have been ensconced in one of the adjacent sitting rooms having a private pow-wow.

As did my mother's secretary in London, Mrs. Lasker looked like a big bird but with even bigger hair and very expensive jewellery. Mr. Whitley was short, balding, and wore the expression of a pug with dash and hauteur. He had on his customary dark red trousers, perfectly pressed, and a navy cashmere smoking jacket. Granny wore a cream silk long dress with sleeves, and a little off-white cardigan on her shoulders to guard against any chill that might have had the temerity to show up.

Everyone sat on the terrace at one long table, covered in a

white linen tablecloth with white linen napkins and off-white candles in glass-encased silver candlesticks. Garden lights cast shadows across honeysuckle and oleander and up into the *pins parasols*. The sound of water lapping against the quay and breaking gently on the rocks could be clearly heard, and I imagined Woody's flotilla bobbing like ducks in the bath.

"Yes, I have a Boston Whaler for morning swims and short excursions, and a Bertram for longer rides with small groups of people," he told me at dinner as I sat between him and my mother at the opposite end of the table from Granny. "Perhaps you would like to come with Mickey Renshaw and me for a swim tomorrow morning before we go on to lunch with Mrs. Lasker?"

"Yes I would. Thank you. Mummy, will you come?" My mother explained that she would go in the car with Granny in order to be "ready" for lunch. Woody translated for me, a look of amusement on his face: "The ladies, you see, need to avoid spoiling their carefully prepared hair and makeup and wardrobe, whereas us men can quickly, with no fuss, have a shower and change, comb our hair, and be ready in just a few minutes."

"So I should bring swimming trunks, a comb, and my things for lunch?"

Having never had a shower in my life, not even at St Aubyns, where we had baths, I did not relish the prospect of standing around naked in front of Woody and Mickey Renshaw, or of seeing them and all their bits. "Where does one have a shower at Mrs. Lasker's house?"

"There are changing rooms by the pool on the lower level. It's rather a lovely villa; you'll see."

I went to bed uncertain about the following day's programme.

At breakfast I sat alone on the terrace, at a round table set for one. Before me lay a fresh linen tablecloth and napkin, an array of marmalades and jams in small glass jars, bread, butter curls in a tiny crystal dish, croissants, milk, and, at Borrett's insistence, two fried eggs. It was eight o'clock, the sun already warm, and I wondered where the big table had gone. I had approximately three hours to fill by myself, the same as the Nassau routine, so I took my time. My mother hadn't stirred when I tiptoed out of the bedroom after a quiet visit to the bathroom. That had been odd, too. Having a wee with one's mother asleep just a few feet away, albeit on the other side of a closed door, was yet another first.

Before settling down to read, I went down to the jetty to inspect Woody's boats and test the water. For a villa this size it seemed improbable that a swimming pool would not exist, but no pool was there. Apparently Granny liked to swim off the rocks—an event I was looking forward to witnessing. In the meantime I sat for a while at the end of the quay and soaked up the warship's silhouette and the paradisiacal surroundings. If truth be told, I imagined I could very rapidly grow tired of all this, because I would have preferred to be sharing my brothers' escapades. Or would I? During the Nassau trip I had discovered there was something to be said for enjoying all this luxury, albeit on my own. But the more I experienced the breadth of my grandmother's empire, the more difficult it was to know what my twelve-year-old self really wanted.

I was reading on a comfy chair in the main drawing room when Woody strolled in wearing a silk dressing gown and slippers and asked me if I was ready. Apparently, despite his appearance, he was and thought I might not be. Leaping to my feet, I responded, "Absolutely," and picked up my rolled-up beach towel—which housed my luncheon outfit together with a change of swimming trunks—grabbed my goggles, and followed Woody down to the quay. Mickey Renshaw, looking like an emaciated stork in skimpy bathing trunks and nothing else, lay spread-eagled across the Boston Whaler's back bench.

"Good morning, Glute, and how might you be today?" he enquired, standing and offering me a hand onto the boat. Swiftly and skillfully Woody stepped on board, started the engine, stepped back on the quay and untied the two ropes from their moorings, and was back on board steering us away from the rocks.

"Glute, would you be very kind and bring in the fenders, those white buggers dangling over the side?" Woody asked. I managed to accomplish this task without falling overboard and then seated myself on the white plastic bench behind

Woody and Mr. Renshaw, who stood at the driver's console as we picked up speed and headed out into the bay. For a minute or two I just sat there enjoying the roar of the outboard motor and watching Villa Cansoun recede into our wake, her pinkness highlighted against the surrounding greenery and the grey stone walls of nearby properties.

Woody had removed his dressing gown to reveal a pair of bathing trunks remarkably similar to Mr. Renshaw's, to the extent they existed at all. No sooner had this thought crossed my mind than, to my horror, both men proceeded to remove what was left of their modest coverings altogether. I had no idea where to look. No more than three feet in front of me stood two very tall men—both of whom I had previously only seen dressed formally in jackets, trousers, and ties—stark naked, their ageing posteriors shaking and wobbling all over the place like two of Miss Preston's classic blancmanges, chatting to each other as if I weren't there or at least giving the impression that it shouldn't matter that I was.

Curiously, they both held their trunks in front of their willies as if such coverage would pass muster with the censors (and keep their private parts private). Despite my valiant efforts not to look and keep my gaze fixed on the pretty tree-lined hills of Cap-Ferrat, I could not avoid catching a glimpse now and then of both men's protrusions, neither of which struck me as an obvious candidate for the Guinness Book of Records. This peculiar impasse reached new levels when we dropped anchor in what felt like a secluded spot and Woody asked me, "Now then, Glute, are you ready for a little swim?"

It was the first time either of them had said a word to me since we left the quay. Now that we weren't moving they both dispensed with any attempt to hold their trunks in place. "You should try swimming with us au naturel," Mickey Renshaw said to me, smiling broadly. "It's delightful. I'm sure you'd love it." Thoroughly stymied by the situation I said nothing, and so, leaving me to my own devices, both men dived into the sea and swam elegantly away from the boat, in the same direction, in a synchronized, aerodynamically correct crawl.

Such were the limitations of my swimming abilities I was obliged to take a more deliberate path into the water by way of the steps. As I swam I gave some thought to the possibility of someone with binoculars watching us from high atop the hills. I wondered what conclusion they might draw if they spotted a brace of naked older men in the water near a young chap steadfastly attached to his swimwear. I was simply too shy to swim naked with Woody and Mr. Renshaw, though both seemed to think I might enjoy doing so.

Much vigorous rubbing down and drying of bits ensued when Woody and Mr. Renshaw climbed back onto the boat. The two of them were still clearly amused by my embarrassment and kept up a steady repartee about the glorious sensation of being naked in the water. "One's balls feel so liberated," Mickey Renshaw said with feeling.

"*Chacun son goût*," I managed, which made me feel better and surprised them both.

———

The dock for the Villa Leopolda was round the other side of the Cap, and there were a couple of men in white shirts and white trousers waiting for us as we approached the quay. Fortunately Woody and Mr. Renshaw had put their swimming trunks back on.

Amidst a flurry of *"Bonjour, messieurs"* we were, indeed, led to the swimming-pool area, where I waited for the men to shower off the salt water and put on their lunch clothes—I'd had enough nudity for one morning.

Self-consciously I stood under the water with my trunks still on, rapidly undressed to towel myself dry, and slipped on my shirt and shorts as if performing against the clock. Stepping outside into the bright sun, I discovered that Woody and Mickey Renshaw were nowhere to be seen. One of the men in white was waiting to lead me on to my next port of call. I couldn't believe it. Just when I needed a full military escort, I'd been dumped. What was with these people? I asked myself. Did the castle way make no provisions at all for the feelings of others? (Precious few.) Was it so wrapped up in its convoluted mechanisms that the trials and tribulations of its younger members were of no consequence? (Seemingly so.)

I found myself being led up many steps, through beautifully landscaped gardens with tall hedges and flowers everywhere. When we eventually reached the top, I was immediately confronted with probably sixty grown-ups, most of whom I had never seen before, milling around the columned terrace. *"Voilà, monsieur,"* the man in white said, and left.

I waited for someone to spot me, gaining greater sympathy for ducks who found themselves out of water as each moment went by. I noticed one or two people casting an eye in my direction, but after swiftly concluding they could be of no assistance, they carried on with their conversation. Finally, to my relief, my mother emerged from the crowd, glass in hand, saying, "Darling, *there* you are!"

Yes, I'm here . . . have been for a while.

"Hello, Mummy. Who are all these people?"

"They're friends and houseguests of Mrs. Lasker's, darling. How was the boat trip?"

"A bit odd, actually. After a decent start I had the good fortune to be treated to Woody and Mr. Renshaw putting on a bum-and-willie show."

"What *do* you mean, darling?" My mother had noticed people watching us and seemed to want to rejoin the crowd.

"They thought I'd like to swim naked with them. Of course I didn't. It was all a bit embarrassing."

"Come along now, darling, let's mingle; we'll have a chance to chat later."

Our way through the throng was interrupted countless times by friends who wished to have a few words with my mother, most of whom peered at me briefly but said nothing.

Luncheon was a very grand affair. Six round tables were laid under the awnings, which covered two sides of the house with spectacular views of the sea below and the coastlines both East and West. A platoon of men in white served food the likes of which I had never encountered before, and as a result I ate very little. My mother sat on my left and talked to me throughout, which was saintly because the woman on my right contributed purely snide criticism all the time we spent in each other's company. "Have you never eaten lobster before, young man?" came at an early stage, and "Try not to mess up a Grand Marnier soufflé in such a vulgar fashion," came later as I mashed my pudding in a vain effort to make it look as if I'd eaten something.

At our table alone I heard French, Italian, and English being spoken, and two of the guests had American accents. I glanced often at Mrs. Lasker across the terrace, but the nature of things saw to it that an encounter was avoided. My mother told me that, like Granny B, she was very much involved in raising money for medical research, and that she was an art collector of some repute. I noticed that people treated her with the deference that was always accorded Granny B, and it was interesting to see them at the same table, important-looking men hanging on their every word like courtiers, which, of course, they were.

All the men were dressed in colourful shirts and linen trousers. The ladies wore light dresses and minimal jewellery. But by the end of it all I'd had more than enough sophistication for one day, on top of which all anyone had wanted to talk about were the North Vietnamese attacks on U.S. destroyers in the Tonkin Gulf. My interests lay in securing a ride back to the villa, in a motor car, with my mother, as soon as possible. "Of course, darling, but I'm sure Woody and Mr. Renshaw would be happy to take you back."

"I'd rather not, if that's all right?"

I rode home with my mother, Granny, and Morg, who discussed the upcoming dinner with David Niven and Noël Coward in endless detail. I sat up front with Mr. Brewer and discussed Mrs. Brewer's scones, which, to my mind, had taken on legendary status down at Leeds.

My father turned up the afternoon of the Coward/Niven dinner party, thus depriving me of my first stargazing experience. Truth to tell, his arrival also rescued me from another agonizing social conundrum: To be there or not to be there? Difficult to say, particularly when given the choice.

Shunted to the smallest bedroom in the house, I had a few words with my father: "My dear sir, are you having a lovely time? Does the South of France agree with you?" ("I think it's great!"), before having an omelette on a tray in my room and spending the early part of the evening leaning out of the window straining to catch a glimpse of the famous faces and listen a bit to the conversation. I saw Noël Coward: His pink blazer and midnight-blue trousers were easy to spot, as was his mellifluous, theatrical voice and ever-present cigarette in a holder. As my eyes roamed over the many other coiffed and bejewelled guests, everybody's words soon melded into a sea of cocktail-party chatter and I went to bed, falling asleep to the sounds of raucous laughter drifting up from far below, wondering what I was missing.

16.

BEATLEMANIAC

It is a strange and wonderful thing how some music can penetrate the inner sanctum of the mind and envelop one's entire being in a warm, spiritualistic glow. Beethoven's Fifth Symphony did it for some; Wagner's *The Ring* held sway with others; Frank Sinatra and Elvis Presley had legions of admirers. Beatles music did it for me. Although I shared this sentiment with a large number of other people, the experience was distinctly personal for each of us. More often than not it was impossible to put the intense appeal into words. One listened. One felt. And it was good. One put the LP onto the turntable, soaked up both sides, and, in a transported state, repeated the process if time and circumstances permitted.

In April 1963 David had returned from Stowe for the holidays, wandered into the playroom at the MT clutching a copy of *Please Please Me*, the first LP by the Beatles, and told me that the group had recently played at the school and had been a sensation. It was immediately clear why. From the opening "One, two, three, four" to the final shattering chord of "Twist and Shout," the record was a masterpiece of unbridled energy and musicality the likes of which I had never heard before. Then *With the Beatles,* their second LP, arrived a few months later, and a new set of superlatives had to be found.

It soon became obvious that I would need to redefine the term "Beatlemaniac" when the second half of the word started to take on substantive meaning. At the age of eleven, with all policeman, fireman, explorer, and Canadian Mountie aspirations left unceremoniously on the trash heap, I decided that when I grew up I was going to play in a very famous band. Nobody attempted to disabuse me of this notion until three years later, when I was at Stowe, and by then it was far too late. The seeds had long since been planted, and only the most drastic of interventions could have halted their growth. My housemaster, Mr. Gilbert, suggested on several occasions that I was starting to display all the signs of being stupid, irresponsible, and in urgent need of a more mature outlook on life, but he might just as well have been talking to his dog. My parents, too, misread the nature of my ambition or simply thought I was "bound to get over it."

My mother used to wonder out loud, as we sat in front of the television watching *Thank Your Lucky Stars* or *Ready Steady Go!,* if the Beatles or the Rolling Stones ever had baths. I found this curious and could only answer, "Why not?"

"Oh, but darling, do look at them," she would say, her tone

awash with concern. "Their strange clothes and all that long hair. So unkempt!"

If I had been allowed to I would have grown my hair and dressed the same way. I would have enjoyed seeing the court's reaction if I had turned up for tea one day wearing a high-collared floral shirt, crushed velvet suit, scarves, and Chelsea boots, and with hair down to my shoulders. I expect Morg would have mumbled after I'd left, "Dear fella's completely lost his marbles!" But there were no outward signs at Leeds during the 1960s that anyone was suffering even the mildest onset of culture shock. No one was paying particular attention to the new cultural forces that were rapidly emerging and that would sweep away their kind of world forever.

Thankfully, my obsession was not completely dismissed by the family. When the Christmas holidays arrived, my mother announced with great fanfare that Aunt Cicili had procured tickets for the Beatles' Christmas Show at the London Odeon, Hammersmith. Together with Granny A, she would be taking her boys, John and Michael, and David, James, and me to the concert. Though eccentric at first glance, the fact that Aunt Cicili and Granny A were to be the grown-ups in charge seemed oddly appropriate. Their forceful and enquiring personalities led them to want to find out for themselves what the fuss was all about.

Thursday, December 31, 1964, found us sitting at 6:15 p.m. in the dress circle of the Odeon, surrounded by screaming teenage girls. And the concert hadn't even begun. Every time the curtain, a heavy, reddish, velvety-looking affair, moved, the girls went crazy with anticipation. The atmosphere was as electric as electric could conceivably be. Then add more.

I was sitting between James and Granny A. He was as caught up as I was in the ever-increasing frenzy; she appeared content to sit straight backed, her hands resting on top of her umbrella handle, observing what must to her have seemed utter madness, as if she were studying reptiles through thick glass in the zoo.

Jimmy Savile, the compère, walked out onstage in front of the curtain, and after trying to tell a joke, announced the Mike Cotton Sound. The curtain rose, the music started. They were good, but they weren't whom we'd come to see; and you couldn't hear much because the girls screamed for them too. The Yardbirds were on next, and the audience loved them. Even the men started making a noise, cheering and clapping to the pulsating blues sounds. The blond lead singer, Keith Relf, blew his harmonica and dived about the stage like a man possessed, and their guitarist, Eric Clapton, played guitar solos which boggled the mind. They were genuinely exciting, and the scream level rose. Freddie and the Dreamers, whose songs I found quite dreadful, closed the first half, and I watched in bemusement their tiny singer, who danced about like a circus clown amidst the continuous bedlam.

The Mike Cotton Sound came back to open the second half, but by then I wasn't really listening to what the other groups or singers were doing. I was simply waiting for the Beatles to appear and pondering which of my favourites I hoped they would play. When the moment actually arrived, and they walked out on stage waving and smiling, the roof was lifted high into the sky by a surge in decibels akin to three thousand steam engines blowing their whistles in unison at the same time. I sat mesmerized, enraptured, in a state of total bliss.

Ringo climbed up and sat behind his drums. John, Paul, and George plugged in their guitars and struck a few chords. The din was stupendous, the screaming out of control. Directly in front of me a girl was howling like a demented banshee, her hair a tangled mess after she had spent the previous ninety minutes rearranging it in a way that only a Force 10 gale could outdo—and then only at sea. I glanced down our row and noticed that Aunt Cicili, like Granny A, was registering no more than a mild interest in the proceedings. I hoped I was mistaken and that their fixed expressions were simply misleading. John and Michael, David and James, like me, sat and stared, mesmerized.

I recognized the guitar intro to "I Feel Fine," and suddenly everything that had gone before passed for polite enthusiasm. Every teenage girl, or younger, gave the distinct impression of having gone stark staring mad. They clutched their hair, they shook their heads, they jumped up and down in their seats. They cried as if their pet hamsters had just been eaten by the cat, and they continued to scream as if their lives depended on it.

Although we were high up and quite far from the stage, we were in the middle and the view was perfect. *The Beatles.* Holy cow! Now they were playing "She's a Woman." Was it the third song, the fourth? Damn! It was so hard actually to hear the music at all. I watched the stage intent on missing nothing, but though I knew the words and melodies by heart, it was only intermittently that I clearly picked them out. Paul did all the talking between songs. John played the fool a bit. George did his little skip occasionally. As they played and sang, I was as happy as I could ever have wished to be. It was magic. Just for this brief moment in time I, and a few thousand like-minded individuals, were breathing it in.

"Thank you . . . thank you very much . . . we're going to do one more," said Paul. "And this one's called 'Long Tall Sally.'" Good grief! Surely not the last, I said to myself as triple pandemonium erupted from the first few rows to the last. They seemed to have been on stage for only such a short time. The song was flat-out rock and roll, and the hall, myself sedately included, was beside itself. "We're gonna have some fun tonight . . . have some fun tonight," went the refrain. Blimey! Why did this have to end?

After a final bow, final wave, they left the stage. Gone. The lights went up, handkerchiefs came out, dabbing eyes, wiping away sniffles.

Still somewhere far away and not wanting to come back down to earth, I stood up just as Granny A gave the girl in front of us a gentle prod with her umbrella and spoke to her in an angelic tone of voice: "You know, my dear, it's only the plain girls who scream."

17.

STOWE VERSUS HOME FRONT

The following year I went to Stowe. I'd visited David
there and he'd shown me around, but I had found
the place austere and cheerless. Even the school's
spectacular setting and architecture had left me curiously un-
moved and despondent over what the future might have in
store. Now was the time when a health and safety warning on
the side of the Leeds Castle luxury brew (it was a home-grown
blend and not available to the general public) was needed. I
had imbibed all my life (no one said it was not safe for children) on an epic scale, but unlike cigarettes (Smoking Causes
Cancer) the brew manufacturers never had the gumption to
provide the necessary cautions on the side of their powerful
product's tin, such as: "The luxury brew has been known to in-
duce powerful delusions of grandeur which can, if not treated,
last for a great many years and prove harmful to achieving
success in meeting life's myriad challenges. The brew is

known to have further unintentional side effects including, but not limited to, obscuring reality. Be aware that the luxury brew will one day cease production without any possibility of being replaced. Consume in moderation and learn to be self-sufficient."

The magisterial grandeur of Stowe, Palladian, palatial, and exquisite in form and *façade*, once the country seat of the Dukes of Buckingham and Chandos, in 1965 a boarding school for six hundred boys, swiftly passed me by. I'd been a successful big cheese at St Aubyns, so becoming a small fry all over again wreaked havoc with my new but still tenuous self-confidence. The drab Corinthian columns which graced the school's North Front, so greatly admired but, through my eyes, so badly in need of a clean, typified for me every aspect of my new seat of learning. What's more, despite being only ninety minutes' drive northwest of London, Stowe attracted the coldest, wettest, and dullest weather imaginable.

It was my winter of discontent. Twelve weeks of frigid acclimatizing to new rules, new faces, new systems, new accommodations, new teachers, new world. New friends helped. Richard and I had arrived on the first day at the same time in the new boys' dormitory at the top of the house, both of us carting our trunks up the never-ending stairs, he aided by his stepfather, Enzo, a sculptor, and me by David, now an old boy, who had kindly driven me up in my mother's Jaguar to offer as much moral support as he could.

After the sad farewells, Richard and I had walked round the main building, impressive, indeed stately in its institutionalized form, particularly the domed assembly hall where they say the Beatles had signed autographs and former pupil David Niven had somehow deposited a master's car, minus its wheels. I straightaway admired Richard's insouciance and willingness to look on the bright side, while I still seethed at my parents' lack of consideration offloading me in such a gloomy and inhospitable place.

Clearly my attitude was unfortunate, even crass, but an unrealistic view of my place in the world had dogged me for years, and things had perhaps been a little too easy. The vast comforts of the castle way softened up the beneficiary almost to the point of no return. Although I didn't like myself for doing it, I soon found myself comparing the amenities and splendours of Leeds Castle with the bleak, authoritarian shabbiness of Stowe. Such thoughts I was obliged to keep strictly to myself, not wishing to become public enemy number one before I'd even got started.

Richard's jokes were quite good, and he was kind enough to find funny my laboured attempts at humour, even when I suggested how much better the place must have been two hundred years before. Lanky and possessed of a fine Roman nose, he liked the same music as I did, and our friendship took off on a high note.

Peter, a year older than me, black haired, wild eyed, and preternaturally self-possessed, became my friend later in the term. We discovered that we not only shared the same tastes in music and fondness for an occasional Player's No. 6 cigarette, but also his father was the star stylist and owner of

Olofson's, the salon on Brompton Road where my mother went to have her hair done every week. Furthermore Peter lived with his mother, the actress Pauline Olsen, in Rutland Gate, which Nanny and I had always passed through on our way to and from Hyde Park for our walks all those years ago.

It was soon apparent that spending time with older boys had the undesirable effect of upsetting the "all in the same boat" connection with my year's crop of new boys. Peter and Richard did not become friends with each other, so from the word go I found myself in the familiar position of operating with my feet in separate camps.

At St Aubyns there had been no such thing as free time. Each day had a set timetable which was rigorously adhered to. At Stowe, however, when you weren't in the classroom or playing scheduled sports, your time was your own, and it was up to you how you managed it. This meant that when I wasn't dozing through science or math class, or playing rugger, squash, hockey, or hurling down cricket balls in my capacity as opening bowler for the Colts "A" team during the summer term, I could more often than not be found strumming my acoustic guitar in the music room at the far end of the west colonnade. One reached this room by passing through the junior changing rooms, which were always liberally perfumed by the aroma of unwashed socks, sweaty jockstraps, and other sports accoutrements. It was also, distressingly, the venue of choice for prefect beatings. Fortunately I was summoned only once for a thrashing by the head of house, after receiving a chit for disobedience during house-room prep. During the administration of the six resounding thwacks, I maintained a running dialogue apparently containing sufficient humour to slightly derail the concentration of both my tormentor and his slouched witness, thereby lessening the unpleasantness of the wretched scene.

It was Christmas Day 1965, and my first term at Stowe had come and gone. I was standing in my Maiden's Tower bedroom, luncheon over, staring through the windows at the rain as it fell in its usual dreary fashion on the still-immaculate croquet lawn. Off in the distance the red flag on the ninth green twisted listlessly in the wind, sodden, bowed, like a condemned man tied to the stake. Beyond, the cluster of towering cedars maintained their ancient, dignified presence, but they, too, were shrouded in a blanket of grey drizzle and melancholy.

Within the MT walls the gloom outside was matched by an all-encompassing sadness, felt in every corner, in every room. Word had come from Nassau that Morg had died. The shock was excruciating and real. The household had dispersed, each to his or her spot, to cope with the news. I felt I wanted to cry, needed to cry, and wondered how it was that someone in whose company I had, over thirteen years, spent only a limited amount of time could have formed within me such a deep, emotional connection. Natural leaders with great charisma often inspire intense devotion in those around them, even from a distance. I didn't have proper conversations with

Morg any more than I did with Granny B; castle way bylaws saw to that. But I knew him well enough to understand what my family had lost.

If this was how Morg's death affected me, what must it have been like for my mother, who had adored him since she was a child? And for my father, who had perhaps looked upon him as a form of surrogate father for the one he never had?

I went to my mother's bedroom, knocked on the door, and found her preparing to set off on her rounds distributing Christmas presents to all the old friends and retainers who worked on the estate, as she had done every Christmas Day since I could remember. She told me to come in as she reapplied makeup and fussed about, doing her best to pretend things were normal. Neither of us mentioned Morg.

"Can I come with you this year, Ma?" I asked. Normally David or James went with her to keep her company and help with the chatting and carrying the presents.

"Yes, darling, of course. That would be very nice of you." My mother had such a sad look on her face and seemed so utterly bereft that I wanted to say or do something to help, but nothing came to mind. So I told her I was going off to find my brothers and load up the car with the gifts so we'd be ready to leave when she was.

This was the first time since the war, to my knowledge, that the court had not spent Christmas at Leeds. Granny B's bronchitis and Morg's cancer had brought about the decision to leave for the Bahamas early to escape the harsh English weather.

I knew deep down that it was more than just Lord Margesson who had died—such was his aura, his charm, his sense of humour, and his genuine concern for all of us and everyone who worked at Leeds. Without ever overshadowing Granny B's position as the castle's dominant personality and patron of all things great and small, Morg had embodied the spirit and the splendour that was Leeds. He had been there before the war, when the castle was one of England's most sought-after weekend invitations among leaders of society, government, and the arts. He had been a constant and reassuring presence throughout the postwar period, when Granny B had entertained and conducted her affairs, in general, on much more modest levels than in the early years.

It was the tallest, strongest, brightest-burning candle in the whole castle firmament that had finally flickered out. The place would never be the same.

"What on earth are you going to do with that?" asked Mr. Gilbert, my Temple housemaster (also known, bizarrely, as Prune), who accosted me one day during my second (Lent) term, outside the house prefect's study.

"Play music, sir."

"Play music? With *that?*"

The object of Prune's scorn was my new acoustic guitar, a gift from my parents for passing my Common Entrance exams the year before. Prune and I never got on well. He insisted on letting me know, once, how much he preferred

David. "He was very nice," he'd said in his strangely squeaky voice, "but you're"—there he had paused as he sought the *mot juste*—"nasty!" This I found less than encouraging—indeed, infuriating, and somewhat confusing as well—and it further exacerbated my general ill feeling towards Stowe. "Nasty" was not a word I would have applied to myself at the time, or at any time, but Prune chose not to explain himself. In my usual fashion I told nobody about it: Never let on. People do not want to know. Get a grip. Your parents may be losing it, Morg gone, Stowe a total drag, but who doesn't have a problem?

"Absolutely, sir. The Beatles, and many other groups like them, are being very successful and making lots of money playing music on instruments like this."

"I don't know what you're talking about." Prune genuinely did not know what I was talking about. He was old school in the classic sense and probably considered any music post-Bartók to be rubbish. It turned out, though, that dismissing what I cared about most was not to have the effect he was hoping for.

I was on my way to the music room. There, my trusty and essential chord book and the sheet music for Donovan's "Catch the Wind" shared the rickety upright piano's music stand, and I succeeded in learning to play the tune in one afternoon, attracting quite an audience in the process. Some of them appeared to like what they were hearing, especially Peter, and before the term was over he and I had formed a group with Max and Oliver, two like-minded new friends in

Temple. Once we had laid our hands on some half-decent equipment—a struggle for all four of us and accomplished, in my case, by bidding farewell to six months' allowance in a single afternoon—we spent the next three and a half years endeavouring to replicate the finest pop music ever made with the drive and determination of an Olympic rowing team.

Max was tall, red-haired, and athletic. He was from Yugoslavia, which gave him a slightly exotic air, and his obsession with the ladies was second only to my brother James's advanced preoccupation in that field. When he wasn't talking to me about beautiful blondes and brunettes over a Dunhill International cigarette down by the Temple of Concord—an activity greatly frowned upon by the authorities and likely to result in a nasty beating or even expulsion if apprehended—he was writing love letters to them in Serbo-Croat, head bowed in concentration over his desk.

Oliver was of normal height, a ready wit, a keen sportsman, and an Englishman to the core. Of the four of us he was perhaps the most scholarly and even tempered. That might have explained his decision to be the bass guitarist and his fondness for "Wasn't Born to Follow" by the Byrds.

My first year at Stowe ended in July 1966 with the Kinks' crafty record "Sunny Afternoon" at number one in the top twenty and Britain's prime minister, Harold Wilson, raising taxes and nationalizing the steel industry.

Although Ray Davies's masterful tune and lyric captured to perfection English working-class distaste for English upper-class dismay over Wilson government strategy, it seemed quite clear to me that all those new rich-and-famous Swinging Sixties superstars were, in fact, well on their way to establishing a new aristocracy. And the old aristocracy was so enamoured of this new one that it soon was hard to tell them apart as they all swanned around in velvet suits and Cuban-heeled boots at country house weekend parties and fashionable London gatherings!

In the still fully operational English class system, the long-established mutual respect between the upper and working classes was, sensibly, finding new and exhilarating outlets for its expression: "What a piece of work is a[n English]man! How noble in reason, how infinite in faculty!"

It was, of course, important if one was going to be a member of a pop group at school to choose a name for the band that denoted cool and spoke volumes about the ludicrously avant-garde life style and philosophy of its members. In my case this was garnered from fourteen years' indoctrination in the castle way, and an indulgent, extraordinarily kind Nanny! After much going round in circles the four of us had settled on Source of Controversy. It might not have been as cool and avant-garde a name as we hoped, but the band was certainly controversial with Prune and with all our parents. If proof were needed that Prune might have had a point, even Oliver, the scholar, failed to achieve the two-year-mark examination results everyone had expected he would, and by quite some margin.

Max, Oliver, and Peter shared a study, but because I was a year behind them I had to linger in the house room, keep my books in a locker, and do all my work at one of the long tables with roughly twenty-five other boys my age or younger. I often found myself knocking on their door, asking if I could have a coffee and work on a tune with them. Sometimes I wasn't sure if I was welcome. Sometimes I wasn't sure who my friends were back in the house room. Sometimes I just felt like saying, to no one in particular, "I have to get out of this fucking place," because anger and frustration at being somewhere I resented being had replaced the achievement highs and happiness of St Aubyns. I felt I had no control over or say as to what happened in my life. Even if I had felt able to speak my feelings to anyone, the nature of those feelings—*I should have gone to Eton with my friends from St Aubyns. . . . I'm above the rest, the castle way makes it clear*—would have left me more isolated than ever.

Granny B was having the very devil of a time in Nassau maintaining the level of privacy she had sought throughout her life. Since the early 1960s "unsavoury characters" (many of them friends and associates of Sam Clapp) had been doing their level best to "take things over" (both phrases attributable to my mother's fine sense of humour and astute assessment of the situation). Every multimillionaire "developer" known to mankind had been showing up with a burning desire to destroy the natural beauty of Paradise Island and transform every square inch they could lay their hands on into a resort hotel and casino. In brief, gangsters and their cohorts were moving in, and something had to be done.

Granny was briefly, but not for long, able to beat gangland to the punch by purchasing first the Porcupine Club, which had had the dark cloud of a foreign conglomerate with high-rise projections hovering ominously over it, and then Gray-leath, the stupendous eleven-acre property adjacent to her beloved Harbourside and one of the many former homes of her South of France friend the wealthy Canadian Dorothy Killam, a house that could have become the target of the very worst of the worst.

Granny gave Grayleath, which had a sensational garden and an Olympic-size swimming pool, to my mother and Auntie Pops, which was very kind of her although it was never at all clear to me what opportunities might present themselves for the family to gather under this far-off, exotic roof. To the Porcupine Club and its members, a mildly run-down home away from home "estate" for semicolonial types who liked to play a little tennis and drink a lot of gin on the wide, rickety veranda, she gave carte blanche to carry on just as before.

She personally breathed a long and heavy sigh of relief at not having to contend with the grim possibility of being spied upon in her private domain from a nearby eleventh-floor suite. For the umpteenth time I marvelled at how simple it all seemed for the castle way's operating system to keep the world, and all its associated complications, at bay.

Holidays accentuated the Stowe-versus-home-front comparisons, and none more so than the Easter 1967 visit to Paradise Island. Grayleath was a sumptuous addition to the "empire." Over the period of a year it had been redecorated, air-conditioning installed, and the garden pruned and trimmed with the precision of a Curzon Street barber. So when we all turned up in April, everything looked miraculous, and I, aged fifteen, proceeded to drink copiously from the luxury brew.

Unlike Granny's Harbourside, our house was on the north side of the island, close to the beach, so we had an Austin minivan at the dock to drive guests and luggage the quarter mile up through the garden. This was quite nice because, no matter how much water it received, the grass was always bordering bed-of-nails-like to walk on, especially after a few hours of hot sun had dried it out.

Eleven acres on Paradise Island was a considerable amount of territory, and the garden was awash in palm trees, cork trees, shrubs, climbers, and flower beds dotted in all the right places with oleander, hibiscus, porterweed, dogwood, and yellow elder. The whole thing was a picturesque riot of Bahamian tropical splendour, and it reminded me, in a peculiar way, of Granny B's wood garden at Leeds with its winding grassy paths and lush weeping willows. Both gardens were uniquely beautiful and tranquil and were in perfect harmony with the dwellings which abutted them and breathed their air.

Grayleath was almost U-shaped, built of wood, and painted soft white. The gently slanting grey slate roof, brushed by tall palms, gave the spacious single-storey house a charming and unpretentious appearance. All the rooms were airy, the furniture colourful, the bedrooms had pretty wood panelling, and the card room/music room/second drawing room was a festival of green and white from the sofas, armchairs, and plushest of carpets to the cascade of greenery seen through wide windows, whose shutters were kept open by day. The walls of the long corridor off which all the bedrooms led were trompe l'oeil paintings of Bahamian landscapes, and the veranda overlooking the pool was tiled in black and white, windowed, and casually furnished with wicker chairs and an abundance of plant life. One could be swimming in the transparent turquoise sea, trot up the soft white sand private beach (hosing down one's feet at the tap by the steps on the way), and be by the freshwater pool in less than three minutes.

For part of our stay David's friend William (son of my godmother Lady Buckhurst) and my friend Camilla (daughter of my godfather G) beefed up the family complement of our parents, David, James, Vanessa, Nanny, and me. James was disinclined to reveal his reason for not bringing a friend, male or female, but I suspected it had something to do with his not wishing to mix what he saw as the incompatibility of his "hip" new circle of friends with the eccentricities of our family.

All went well for ten days. We were handsomely looked after by Clive, our charming black butler, and a bevy of housemaids who wore pretty blue-and-white-striped dresses and pressed white aprons. We swam, we sunbathed, we ate, we drank; friends of our parents came over from the mainland for lunches, bringing their teenage daughters, all of whom spent their entire time chatting up and making eyes at James, who successfully raised their temperatures by addressing them with winning indifference.

We visited Huntington Hartford at his Ocean Club, which he was enthusiastically transforming into a hotel enterprise of elaborate luxury, topped off by his purchase of the Cloisters, a fourteenth-century French Augustinian monastery, from William Randolph Hearst, which was reassembled on the thirty-acre property to startling effect. Mr. Hartford was kind enough, on one occasion, to show us at some length his skill in interpreting our individual personalities with a set of tarot cards. The laboriousness of this display and its ludicrous conclusions rendered that afternoon's digression a wearisome affair and made me wonder if Hunt was quite all there.

After two weeks James was getting bored and asked David and me if we'd fancy renting a speedboat for a day. I was full of enthusiasm for the plan, David less so. He urged caution, primarily out of concern for our lack of boating experience, not to mention the expense. James informed us that he'd had plenty of experience in handling small boats (something I was unaware of but only too happy to go along with) and that he believed he had sufficient funds for the rental.

Quite how James knew where to go and what to do was left unsaid, but without David and without informing our parents, he and I set off one morning walking through the Porcupine Club and over to the Paradise Island hotel property, where boat rentals were available at the small marina nearby. My brother signed papers—insurance, no doubt, and other noteworthy legal matters—handed over a large amount of cash, left his British driver's licence with the man in charge, and in we climbed to a heavy-looking, seen-better-days black wooden speedboat with an enormous outboard motor. Much to my relief, James reversed away from the dock with consummate skill, easing the boat gently into the harbour. He then put it into forward, and we set off on our journey around the island, passing under the new bridge which had caused Granny, and other island property owners, so much concern over the inevitable crowds to come.

Although the boat felt like an old tub, and each bump on the water resonated like an elephant stomping its foot, the ensuing half hour was exhilarating and almost as charged as a day out with the Galway Blazers. We left the eastern end of Paradise Island behind and headed out to sea before turning in a wide arc and making a run for the north shore.

"How on earth do you know how to do all this?" I shouted at my brother as he let me take the wheel once we were clear of any other boats or obstacles. "I have friends with boats," he told me. "I've learned a lot with them and done tons of driving."

The sight of our beach from far out at sea, and the ragged line of palm trees swaying in the breeze as we approached, was magnificent. "So what's the plan?" I asked.

"We'll gently make our way past the reef up ahead, a couple of hundred yards off the beach, then, when we're close enough, let's drop anchor and have a swim. How about that?"

"Okay. I have a feeling Ma and Pa are going to be pretty angry because we didn't tell them what we were doing."

"I'm old enough to make decisions for myself. Don't worry. It'll all be fine." We approached the beach as slowly as possible, but the current was clearly taking us there faster than we would wish. On top of that, James suddenly shouted, "Shit! I can't tell how deep it is. We must be too far out to drop anchor now, but if we wait too long we're going to end up on the beach."

"Oh dear," I said helpfully.

"Dear-oh-fucking-dear is right!"

We were fifty yards away from the shore, and I could clearly see the steps and parts of the house through the palm trees when James told me to drop the anchor. Though it was incredibly heavy, I managed to pick up the iron monster from the bow and toss it over the side. It seemed to hit sand before running out of rope, but did nothing to stop our forward momentum. The waves were small but insistent. James put our vessel in reverse, but that had the effect of turning it around and little else, so now we were heading for the beach, backwards. Realizing that he must save the outboard motor if he could, my brother put the boat in neutral, and we both did our best to manipulate the anchor in such a way that it would get a grip on the bottom. To no avail.

Gently the bow touched sand, we rocked a little, then the stern swung round, becoming parallel with the beach.

We were only a few feet from the shore, the propeller firmly wedged. Our boat was going nowhere, and James and I were *dans la merde*.

At lunch our father played the role of the hanging judge as only he knew how, silently deliberating as to whether the gallows fitted the crime, while Ma, David, Nanny, and Vanessa made valiant efforts not to give off the unseemly air of onlookers at a public execution.

James and I sat side by side and stared sullenly at our plates. Only Ma made halfhearted attempts at polite conversation, but there was not a great deal, apparently, to talk about. Not until the end of the meal did my father commence his summation, and it was a real corker, laced with vitriol and withering condemnation. The tone of delivery was measured and calm, but, like his mother, Pa had always been able to be devastatingly forceful without raising his voice. My insides turned to jelly, and I imagined my face turning puce. Stealing a glance at James, whose Ray-Ban sunglasses provided him with a smattering of cover, I noticed that he, too, uncharacteristically, found himself floundering in the eye of the storm. The nursery incident, when I was still in my high chair, returned from out of the blue to dislocate my thoughts, and I wondered if my brother was having unpleasant recollections of that same morning.

Before lunch and before our dressing-down, James and I had been instructed to contact the marina and do what had to be done. Sixty minutes after the accident our boat had been towed off the sand by a brace of highly amused Bahamians whom I later wished had joined us for lunch and explained to our father the more jocular side of the story. Our parents wrote a cheque for the damage; the amount was never revealed, and the incident was never spoken of again. If James was punished in some way I never found out how. I had my next month's pocket money withdrawn. This came as a severe blow because the group needed more equipment, and I was obliged to pay my share.

Castle way programming never let up and sometimes produced a surprise. Three months later I was issued a free pass ("Of course you can go") and tourist-class ticket to fly to still–Communist Yugoslavia for a summer holiday with Max. It never once crossed my mind that my trip to Eastern Europe and my parents' to the South of France to join Granny B for the same two weeks was anything more than coincidence.

Images of dark, empty streets, floodlit by night, spooky Communist spies playing deadly cat-and-mouse with dour Western counterparts—lifted, naturally, from the best espionage films of the day like *The Spy Who Came in from the Cold* and *Funeral in Berlin*—filled my head during the flight.

Zagreb turned out to look as grimy, run-down, and depressing as any of the Russian towns I had seen in films, newsreels, or photographs. Whatever grandeur my hotel once possessed had disappeared. The giant foyer gave the impression of having been ravaged by an occupying force, its columns peeling, its scattered furniture decrepit and sad. My room was large; an exposed lightbulb dangled from the high ceiling, and the bed's ancient springs made their presence felt. From my window I looked down on streetlights, tramlines, stationary trams, and lumbering streetcleaning trucks whose hoses and giant brushes were the only soundtrack to the night's desolation. I actually found myself wondering if my telephone was bugged or a secret camera was watching my every move. Maiden's Tower comforts seemed far away but the spirit of adventure was intoxicating.

In the morning I paid my bill in cash and, lugging my small suitcase, set off for the station, which Max had told me was five minutes' walk from the hotel. I had not gone more than a hundred yards when suddenly I heard a loud yell from behind that made me jump. I turned to see a soldier, carrying a rifle, running directly towards me, his greatcoat flapping around him like a doomsayer's robe, waving, pointing, manifestly indicating that I should halt. Immediately I pictured sinister men in black leather jackets, interrogation cells, and demands for an admission of guilt. Then, before panicking completely, I racked my brain for clues as to what I could possibly have done wrong.

Puffing a bit from his exertions, the soldier arrived in front of me, and the fact that he failed to unsling his weapon, point it at me, and order me to kneel on the ground with my hands behind my head brought immense initial relief. He did, though, speak loud and fast in his native tongue about something that was surely of great importance. I replied with the obligatory, "I don't understand you, I'm afraid."

This provoked another lengthy outburst, accompanied by frenetic waves in the direction of the hotel.

"I paid my bill. Paid . . . my . . . bill," I said, eschewing previous generations' methodology of "If they don't understand English, speak louder" in favour of slower and clearer enunciation. Now that I was sure the soldier was not going to shoot me, I relaxed a little and paid attention to his fresh young face, which wore an expression just as confused as my own. He started tapping his pockets and pointing at me, indicating I should do the same. Then he began to mime opening a door with a key. My room key was still tucked snugly away in my jacket pocket, my foolishness laid bare for the soldier's appreciation. I gave him the key, but before he turned to go back to the hotel he smiled at me again, and to my astonishment and immense pleasure, doffed his military cap. Extraordinary! I thought. It's as if I'd never left home soil. Without even so much as a nod or a wink, the castle way had accompanied me to dour Communist Zagreb! How daft was that? And how daft was I for thinking it?

After two and a half years at Stowe, all I really was sure about was that when my best friends and I were playing music—Oliver on bass, Max on drums, Peter on lead guitar, me on rhythm guitar and lead vocal—I felt like a different person, joyful and uninhibited. For me it was patently worth the enormous effort which went into it and, I thought, any potential fallout which might come from it.

Prune thought otherwise. He banned us from rehearsing for the entire 1968 Lent term, which sent me into a paroxysm of rage. He wrote to my parents towards the end of my third year: "It is a very difficult decision to make. . . . Anthony certainly has the intelligence, but I doubt whether he has the drive or even the inclination to make the University. . . . It would seem to me that the best plan is at least to start a fresh two-year course. . . . I have never been popular with his study companions (all of whom are too old for him) because of my continuous opposition to this pop group nonsense. . . . I remain still convinced that it has detracted from their work results. . . . Anthony, having deserted his own contemporaries, will not find it easy to return to the fold. . . . He should be in the 1st XI next year, but that would not be any great pull for him."

I saw this letter for the first time almost forty years after it was written. So Prune had thought, correctly, I did not want to go to university. It had been an assumption on his part because we never discussed it. But I did feel that the sooner I was playing in a band professionally, far removed from the halls of education, the better my life would be. I knew Prune thought my friendship with older boys was wrong, but the decision to hold me back a year—again, not discussed with me—in the hope of stirring me to greater efforts and better results in the classroom, had a demoralizing effect of such proportion that I saw only hopelessness stretching far over the horizon.

I had been headed for the first XI cricket team the following summer. Contrary to Prune's belief that it "would not be any great pull," or matter very much, to me, I remained fanatical in my love for cricket and was still reasonably good at playing the game. If any of the authorities at school or at home had asked me for my views, I would have told them they were right about my infatuation with music having a detrimental effect on my work; but they were wrong to think that making me start the year again would solve anything. The one thing I was quite sure of was that if there was an important task before me, I would pull out all the stops to get it done. That included changing gears, reversing priorities, or whatever ad hoc phrases the principals tossed out like spiteful confetti as they sought to address the nature of my shortcomings. Just as at St Aubyns, I was confident I could get the job done, both academically and on the sports field. But the principals either overlooked or were unaware of such capabilities, so the opportunity to prove them once more was denied.

I was instructed to begin my A-level course (two years of advanced-level studies in three specialized subjects) again in the winter of 1968. Now I was surrounded by boys a year younger than me, in the classroom and in my house, and, as Prune had stated in his letter, it was not easy to "return to the fold." In fact, with castle way thinking scornfully dismissive of my new "seniors and betters," the situation at Stowe continued to deteriorate.

And then it got worse. Thanks to a bout of flu, I turned up two weeks late for the start of the 1969 summer term only to find a pair of opening bowlers firmly ensconced in the first XI. What I had dreamed of for a year, believing it, clearly in error, to be mine for the offering, had gone up in smoke. *Merde!* Something was rotten in the state of . . . Buckinghamshire, and I didn't know what it was.

18.

Do What?

"The time has come," the Walrus said,
"To talk of many things:
Of shoes and ships—and sealing-wax—
Of cabbages—and kings—
And why the sea is boiling hot—
And whether pigs have wings."
(Lewis Carroll)

During the holidays, school tension was replaced by parental tension. I don't know what my mother and father said to each other when they were alone, but in my presence there appeared to be no limit to my father's capacity to wound with words. They had separate bedrooms in London and at Leeds; they seldom went on walks together in the country, and I always felt at the lunch or dinner table that my mother was one comment away from receiving an unpleasant, barbed response. My brothers and I were constrained in verbal straitjackets, never daring to confront our father's quiet authority. Fortunately, when friends came to stay at the Maiden's Tower, or I met up with them in London, tensions evaporated and industrious pleasure seeking ensued.

At sixteen, Soames and I were still best friends and not bad looking in a freckle-faced, hair-in-a-fringe, pouty-mouthed, grey-flannel, upper-class sort of way. We were above-average height, slim, and moderately athletic. We shared a profound and character-building appreciation of cricket and popular music. We were both inclined towards exuberance, but whereas I was shy and often hesitant to carry out our mutually conceived plans of derring-do, Soames was bold and brazen and instigated exciting escapades at the drop of a hat, or, indeed, his trousers!

When we'd gone off to different public schools, I'd feared the separation would change things between us but it didn't. We exchanged letters during term-time and saw each other a great deal during the holidays. On this particular occasion we were sitting in my parents' Egerton Terrace drawing room at two o'clock in the afternoon, having just devoured with wolfish enthusiasm a classic example of Miss Preston's toad-in-the-hole, followed by rhubarb fool and washed down by enough Coca-Cola to evaporate a tiger's front row of teeth, contemplating what to do next.

"How about a boff?" Soames suggested, chuckling and guffawing like a dirty old man.

A boff? I said to myself, trying not to appear startled by

this suggestion from out of the blue. I was familiar with the word, but not with the actual deed. My brother James talked a lot about boffing. Sometimes I thought he talked about nothing else. I had it on good authority, however, that he was an expert on the subject; I, on the other hand, was not yet out of the starting gate. "Do you have anybody in mind?" I asked, knowing full well the answer but needing time to think. Surely Soames hadn't gone off and done something drastic without telling me first?

"Actually, I have," he said, his face taking on a familiar, conspiratorial sheen. "My brother's given me the address and telephone number of a prostitute in the West End. He said she was terrific."

"But you haven't been before?"

"No, don't worry. I wouldn't sneak off without you. You're still a virgin, aren't you?"

I nodded.

"So, me too. Isn't it time we did something about it?"

"Since you put it so eloquently, I suppose it is! How much will it be?"

"My brother said five pounds. Why don't I call and find out?" Extracting a piece of paper from his pocket, Soames dialled the number. We looked at each other and started to laugh. He had to control himself when someone came on the line.

"Hello . . . yes, I'm calling to make an appointment with Yvonne, please. . . . My brother Mr. Soames gave me your telephone number. . . . Two . . . this afternoon. Three thirty is fine. . . . Yes I do. . . . Thank you, good-bye. Oh! hang on—I forgot to ask—what's the . . . er . . . yes, that's it! Okay, thanks, goodbye!"

For a second or two neither of us said a word. A momentous decision had just been made: One minute we were guzzling rhubarb fool and discussing goodness knows what; the next, we were embarked on a life-altering mission. This was what best friends were for. You did things together you wouldn't normally think of doing with anyone else.

"It's a fiver," Soames said, putting the telephone down. We both leapt to our feet and dived into our jacket and trouser pockets looking for the all-important cash.

"No problem," I announced, fishing out two five-pound notes and an array of singles. "I've got fourteen, no, fifteen pounds. Wow! Three goes!"

"But we've got to get there and back, and I've only got six pounds."

"Okay. One go, and I'll take care of the cab."

"Cabs."

"Cabs. I say, serious money."

"Serious business."

Soames went off to pee, and I rushed upstairs for a brief chat with Nanny. Taking the stairs two at a time, I reached the fourth floor in seconds. Nanny was in the nursery knitting and listening to the radio, as was her custom. "Nanny, we're going out. I'll be back around teatime, in case somebody wants to know."

"All right, dear. Now, don't you get up to any mischief,"

she said, peering over her half-moon spectacles and smiling.

I rejoined Soames downstairs in the hallway, checked for keys, and we left. It was a fine day. We walked up Egerton Terrace with a spring in our steps. I was experiencing a mixture of intense excitement and mild apprehension. I knew Soames felt the former because our conversation was loud and animated. I wondered about the latter.

We hailed a taxi, and Soames instructed the driver in his deepest, most dulcet tone, "Thirty-one Maddox Street, if you please."

"Righto!" the driver said, returning his sliding window to the closed position.

"Are you worried about coming too quickly?" Soames asked me with a constipated grin.

"Of course," I replied, "but what can one do? I shall close my eyes and think of England."

"I'm going to have a wank right before." Again the dirty-old-man chuckle. "That should do the trick."

"Good grief. Where?"

"I don't know. We'll have to see."

This idea struck me as a little extreme, but I let it go. I had my own mental preparations to make, and as we drove round Hyde Park Corner a few pertinent questions came to mind: "Who's going to go first?" I couldn't decide which was preferable.

"You go first."

"So you have time to . . ."

"Exactly."

"I may not take very long." The closer we got, the more anxious I became.

"Doesn't matter. Let's just see what happens." Soames's right knee was shaking uncontrollably. Clearly he was as nervous as I was.

"Are you nervous?"

"Not at all."

The cab stopped. We climbed out, and I paid. It was a narrow street, less salubrious than most in this neighborhood. Mainly four-storey buildings that had been converted into offices or flats, or both. There was a coffee-and-sandwich shop two doors down. A few steps led up to the black door of number thirty-one. We walked up, and Soames pressed the appropriate bell. We waited. About one minute later a grizzled and grey-haired old lady, wearing a battered blue gingham summer frock and cook's apron, with a cigarette dangling out of one corner of her sagging and heavily lined mouth, opened the door. She stood there, the door wide open, smoking her cigarette but saying nothing. We took this to mean we should enter. We lingered in the cramped hallway while she shut and bolted the door. Everything was dark red—the striped wallpaper and the carpet—and there was a smell of joss sticks. Directly ahead was a staircase and two wall sconces which cast a dim and shadowy light. Still saying nothing, the lady hobbled past us, indicating with a wave that we should follow.

At the top of the stairs was a twenty-foot-long corridor with three closed doors, two immediately facing each other, and one at the end. Hunting prints adorned the red-striped walls. The lady opened the door on the right and showed us into a living room. There was a mantelpiece and fireplace with an electric fire turned off. A hunting print hung above. Matching sofas, in dark red material, were positioned on each side of the fireplace. Bookshelves, full of paperbacks, lined the walls, occasional tables were dotted about, and the floor-length curtains, in darkest red, were drawn and had the appearance of heavy silk. It was not your standard doctor's waiting room.

"Wait here, please." The old lady's voice was cracked and smoky. She left, closing the door.

Soames immediately went behind the far sofa and crouched down. I sat on the near sofa and attempted to relax and keep my mind off premature ejaculation. I tried to picture what Yvonne would look like, and what she would say.

"Are you doing what I think you're doing?" I asked Soames, not quite believing what I was seeing, or rather not seeing since only his head and shoulders were visible.

"I am," he grunted back, darting furtive glances at the door, praying, no doubt, that it would not open until he completed his task. "Do you have a Kleenex?" he gasped.

"No, but there's a box on the table straight ahead of you."

For some reason Soames's extravagant behaviour had a calming effect on me. I picked up a magazine and leafed through it, adopting the pose of a "regular." Just as Soames finished, there were sounds in the corridor. Doors opening and closing. Voices, male and female. He grabbed the Kleenex, hoisted his fly, and sat down.

"All done?"

Soames, a peculiar expression on his face, had no time to respond before the door opened and, preceded by a waft of expensive perfume, Yvonne came into the room. I stood up to look at her and was rendered speechless by her startling resemblance to one of my mother's best friends.

"Allo," she said, in a charming French accent. "I am Yvonne, and you are . . . ?" she asked me first, holding out her hand. We introduced ourselves. Her handshake was soft and feminine. She was small, well rounded, and attractive. Her thick brown hair was elegantly coiffed, and her floor-length silk *négligé* was the palest blue.

"Would you like to come first, chéri?" She took my hand without waiting for a reply. I exchanged Cheshire-cat grins with Soames and followed her out of the room. She led me gracefully down the corridor and opened the door to her bedroom. The dark red theme continued, greatly enhanced by antique mirrors, a handsome commode, delicate French armchairs, and voluptuous pillows and cushions. The light was soft and subdued.

"Why don't you undress while I wash?" Yvonne suggested in a matter-of-fact way as she headed for a small basin in the corner, dropping her *négligé* on the bed *en passant*. I complied. My mind was rushing in every direction, and I was deeply grateful to Yvonne for telling me what to do. I didn't wish to appear shy, so I removed my clothes as rapidly as I could, a task made difficult by my inability to take my eyes off the naked woman wandering around the room, acting as if everything was as normal as could be. Which, for her, it was.

Not since my last highly agreeable session of doctors and nurses, conducted at the age of six after tea in the privacy of my brother James's empty bedchamber, underneath the bed, with my equally youthful female friend of the time, had I been naked in a bedroom with a female. Through my sole remaining article of clothing, Willy was registering his approval.

"Come here, please, and I wash you too."

I was not sure that I had heard Yvonne correctly. "Do what?"

"Come to the basin, please. I need to wash you too."

I walked to the basin, slowly. Everything started to take on a dreamlike quality. I thought I needed to pinch myself but before I had time, Yvonne pulled down my shorts, took my startled willy in her hand, and proceeded to wash him in soap and water. This came as such a surprise that the poor fellow, instead of standing to attention like a guardsman on parade, did the exact opposite and shrank ignominiously to a blob. Yvonne pretended not to notice, smiled reassuringly, and completed her task with a few dabs of a conveniently located pink hand towel.

"There, chéri. We're ready. Now, come with me." She took

my hand once more and guided me to the bed. "Make yourself comfortable," she said, shifting through a pile of photograph albums on the bottom shelf of the bedside table.

Lying on the pink sheets—there was no blanket—up against a mound of pillows, I attempted nonchalance at being naked and looked around the room. I asked myself how I was doing so far. Quite well, the answer came back.

Yvonne handed me an album and removed her bra. I didn't know whether to open the album or watch her, so I did both. Her breasts were magnificent; large, but firm and exquisitely round. Willy was, again, displaying a keen interest. The photographs were all of naked men and women doing what we were about to do. Yvonne slipped off her panties. Her nakedness was enthralling and fabulous to behold. She climbed onto the bed, and for the first time I felt her skin against mine. It was like velvet.

Quite unexpectedly, in one fluid motion, she descended to my nether region and took Willy in her mouth. Oh my! This was something else—this was most assuredly something else! I kept a tight grip on the album, but I was not looking. Through her delicate ministrations, Yvonne had my complete and undivided attention. I wondered what degree of heroic self-control was required to prolong the pleasure.

Yvonne stopped. Unlike myself, she had the situation totally under control. She moved up the bed, put the album away, and lay next to me, on her back. "Put yourself inside me, darling," she said, in the same tone of voice Nanny would use telling me to work hard at school.

"Do what?"

"Move on top," she murmured "Gently."

I obeyed, as gently as I could. I knew what I was meant to do, but it wasn't clear in my mind precisely how to do it. I had no need for concern. Yvonne placed Willy where he needed to be, and as he slipped inside the secret territory, Willy and I were both immediately struck by the warmth and softness of the surroundings. I was gripped by new and brilliant sensations. Yvonne guided my head to a position by hers on the pillow. There was no kissing. I savoured her smell and the intense eroticism of the moment and began to move against her with ever-increasing strength of purpose.

The finale, which arrived soon after, was an anticlimax. It was the one great feeling I already knew. What I wanted was a lot more of the others. I was, however, pleased with myself for holding out much longer than I had anticipated.

"Well done, darling," Yvonne said sweetly. Assuming she said that to everybody, I slipped a five-pound note into her hand, got dressed, and left the room.

On the ride back home Soames and I compared notes.

"Fantastic," he said.

"Incredible," I agreed.

"Did she . . . ?"

We went through the details. Nothing was left out. Certain things were embellished, according to taste. It transpired that we had both received identical returns on our investment with the notable exception that Soames, due to his pre-session indulgence, had taken rather longer to conclude matters than

I. He told me Yvonne had congratulated him on his performance.

I said, "Me too."

"Do what?" Richard asked me.

"Come for the weekend and watch a day's shooting. I think you might find it fun."

"What do you shoot?"

"Pheasants mainly, sometimes the odd duck, rabbits."

I was calling my Stowe friend from the telephone in the Maiden's Tower playroom following a ping-pong marathon with James. I'd forgotten Richard hated the idea of killing anything but I thought he would enjoy witnessing the spectacle and spending some time at the MT. "Hey, why not?" he said. "Thanks. Sounds great."

At the age of eleven or twelve I had discovered that the act of firing a shotgun and hitting a rapidly moving target was a satisfying sporting endeavour. There were less appealing features, however, such as standing around in the freezing cold for hours, waiting for the pheasants to make an appearance, which they were often reluctant to do. In addition, being obliged to spend the day in the company of some suspect individuals who had paid a tidy sum for the privilege of "a gun" at the castle shoot, frequently reduced my enthusiasm for the sport faster than Uncle Bobby could say, "Large gin and tonic, please" to the Park Gate Inn barman at, all being well, one o'clock on the dot.

I mulled over this vaguely inconsequential matter on a crisp December morning while standing at my number-one peg on a pathway facing Church Wood. Behind me was a wooden fence and, off in the distance, Leeds village church, its eight-hundred-year-old Norman spire clearly visible across the ploughed fields and meadows. Before the gamekeeper's whistle-blow announced the beginning of the morning's last drive, I spotted Richard, my weekend guest, making his way up the path towards my position, warmly dressed in rainproof garb, scarf, gumboots, and a peculiar striped woolly hat. He was smiling but also looked confused. "Good morning. Congratulations on finding me!" I said.

"Hello, Anthony, how are you? Your mother very kindly dropped me off where all these people were milling around, and one of them told me how to find you. Nice chap, fairly tall, wearing thick tweeds and glasses."

"That sounds like the gamekeeper's son, Peter. He's a very nice man."

"Who are all those other blokes?"

"They're the beaters. If you like I can give you a rapid little scenario of what's about to happen."

"That would be an excellent idea. I have absolutely no concept whatsoever of what's going on here."

"Okay, any minute now you'll hear a whistle blow, telling everyone the drive, which is the last one of the morning, has started. What that means, basically, is all the beaters who've been forming a long line, from one end of the wood to the other—the opposite side to where we are here—begin slowly walking through the wood beating the trees and the undergrowth with their long sticks in order to cause maximum havoc amongst the pheasant population and send them bursting up into the sky and, with any luck, drive them forward over the eight 'guns'—the seven others all being spread out to the right of me—you can see someone just over there, if you look, I think it's my uncle Gawaine—and then whoever they fly over gets a chance to shoot at them, hopefully with some degree of accuracy."

"How do you avoid shooting your uncle? He's not that far away."

"You never shoot sideways and low, always forward and up or behind you and up, and you stick to an arc of about forty-five degrees on each side—that way, no one on the ground is endangered."

As I spoke I demonstrated the movements to Richard, who, quick as a wink, backed off, thinking I was about to fire. "Don't worry, this little peashooter makes a pathetic bang," I told him, indicating my 20-bore shotgun, formerly David's property but now mine since he became the proud owner of a secondhand Churchill 12-bore. "And anyway it's not loaded yet."

Just as I finished speaking, we heard the distant whistle and I loaded up, popping two cartridges into my shotgun from a belt around my waist. Similar to the huntsman's horn, this was the moment when expectation mounted, and in shoots across the land all armed personnel went on maximum alert, ears straining for the flap of feathers and the tremendous shouts of "Forward!" from keepers and beaters. At

Leeds laws of probability kept the adrenaline levels at more subdued levels than at some of England's famously well-stocked shoots.

"Nothing much will happen for a while," I went on. "They beat around and stir things up. Sometimes the odd bird is discovered loitering conspicuously and is dispatched up into the sky with terrific hullabaloo. Normally one has to wait until they've advanced at least halfway through the wood, pushing the birds further in front of them before they—the birds, that is—come to the conclusion that flight is their only remaining option. My number here at the beginning of the line—you'll notice this distinguished looking stick with a 'one' inserted into the notch, means I'm unlikely to see much action because the middle 'guns' are usually the lucky ones—but you never know. I'm always optimistic."

Assorted blandishments, cajoling, and threats could now be clearly heard as the beaters reached what probably was the halfway mark in the wood. Quite a number of birds started to fly over the line and for several minutes the crackle of gunfire filled the air. Very briefly a pheasant headed directly at me, but before it was in range it veered off towards Uncle Gawaine, who gave it short shrift, rising casually off his shooting stick, firing one barrel, and sitting back down before the bird hit the ground with a thud a few yards behind him.

Then, as if by way of compensation, a rabbit suddenly scurried out onto the pathway down to my left about twenty-five yards away. It paused and twitched its nose, as rabbits are prone to do, and—thinking I had no more than a second before it disappeared forever—I turned and fired my 20-bore in one motion, one-handed, one shot, and killed the rabbit stone dead.

"Good Lord! That was amazing," Richard said from the safe position in which I had asked him to stand, three feet or so behind me. "A Wild West show at Leeds Castle!"

Chuffed to the nth degree by the shot, I found myself pondering whether I should have fired in the first place, and, more to the point, would I be able to perform the exact same shot again? "I'm sorry," I told Richard, "I'm afraid I somewhat broke the rules I just explained to you. I could see it was a clear shot, there was no one on the path or nearby, but still—I hope I didn't freak you out."

"Oh boy, I'm so glad I saw that, Anthony. Despite my being totally anti–killing anything, it was still pretty cool. You know I'm just a hippie at heart, but, wow, this is all too much—the castle, this lifestyle, it's not something I could even have imagined."

"My mother drove you up the front drive past the castle after collecting you from the station and bringing you to join the shoot?"

"Absolutely, assuming the road we came up was the front drive because there was no shortage of roads leading in a bunch of directions. My God, the castle is stunning—it blows my mind!"

"It never fails for me either."

"What's it like living in a place like this?"

The question came as a surprise. I couldn't recall anybody

asking me something similar, certainly none of my other friends from school. I knew their parents had to be sufficiently well off to send them to an expensive public school such as Stowe, but I was equally aware that Granny B's "empire," crowned by Leeds Castle, was in all likelihood unmatched by any other Stowe family. However, because Richard was so open himself, I answered him straightforwardly, if a little self-consciously. "We don't strictly speaking live here. We come for weekends, but during the holidays I am here a lot. It's got everything but, if truth be told, I feel a little isolated from time to time. It's like being in a cocoon where every conceivable luxury is provided but no one knows you're there. And when you step out into the big wide world you find yourself a little . . . I don't know . . . unprepared. Don't get me wrong, I know what a lucky bugger I am to have grown up with all this . . . sometimes, though, I wonder. . . ."

I stopped speaking as peculiar thoughts entered my mind telling me to pipe down, I was not talking to Sigmund Freud. Richard had time to observe, "I think I know what you mean"—and I thought he did—before a final whistle told us the drive was over and it was time for lunch. We walked down to pick up the rabbit, but before I did Richard took a moment to crouch down and inspect the damage I had inflicted.

"I don't see the bullet wound," he said, utterly mystified.

"It was a clean shot. I think you'll have to look very closely to find the pellets which killed him."

"Perhaps not today."

19.

HEAVEN AND HELL

It was all so simple. Everything was taken care of. Bills got paid; standards were maintained. All we had to do was stay out of trouble and soak up the fun. Slaving to achieve academic bull's-eyes or a scratch handicap at golf (having a private course on one's doorstep should have helped) were never the priorities they should have been for my brothers and me.

By the time James's twenty-first birthday party rolled around on July 22, 1969, and the Maiden's Tower and swimming pool area had been decked out to resemble one of the King's Road's more fashionable discothèques for the celebration party, the three of us had the castle way imprint up to our necks, so there was a need to keep our wits about us and manage the beast. David was working for Hodder & Stoughton, the London publishers; James, characteristically, had become a salesman on commission for the flamboyant Bernie Cornfeld's Investors Overseas Services, then the hottest (and later to be discovered highly questionable) purveyor of mutual funds on the planet. I, a little mournfully, was ticking off the clock at Stowe, but looking expectantly to the future. Opportunities abounded. To have thought otherwise would have been absurd.

James had told me that he and Charlotte, his spectacularly beautiful blond girlfriend, would pick me up at one o'clock and we'd all go out to lunch. It was now two fifteen, and I was beginning to wonder if something had gone wrong, not to mention the rapidly disappearing image of steak-and-kidney pie that had lodged itself firmly in my mind halfway through chemistry class that morning.

I'd been parading up and down the west colonnade on a cold and windy first Saturday in October since five to one, witnessing the comings and goings of people and automobiles across the North Front, hoping that at any moment James's sleek new red E-type Jaguar, his twenty-first-birthday present from our parents and Uncle Gawaine, would rumble into view, coming majestically to a halt directly beneath where I patrolled, virtually outside my study window.

Stowe School, Buckingham, my seat of learning for four years now, still mightily impressive to look at, its North and South fronts a breathtaking amalgam of massive steps, crowns, Corinthian columns and porticoes, crescent-shaped colonnades, and a brace of neoclassical façades equal to any in the country, with hundreds of acres of exquisitely landscaped gardens, lakes, bridges, and temples adding further luster to what few would dispute is an architectural gem. But through my eyes, sadly, it remained a soulless leviathan with few redeeming features beyond the friends I had made there.

As opposed to St Aubyns, where the castle way, work, and sports had developed seamlessly into coordinated ambition, at Stowe the three became quickly separated and found themselves competing unfavourably with electric guitars, bass, and drums, and the most exciting, mind-altering music ever. I had drifted into being a sometime indifferent student without caring all that much about it.

At two-thirty, cold and a little frustrated, I decided to return to my study for coffee and toast. Knowing James and Charlotte, it seemed reasonable to assume that the previous night, with the "deb" season in full swing, they had enjoyed a busy evening on the town attending a bevy of cocktail parties and dances. My brother's mantelpiece at his house in London was permanently under siege from large engraved invitations. It stood to reason that they had surely left the city that morning much later than anticipated.

As I waited for the kettle to boil, some of the more memorable events of the last few months popped into my head, chief amongst them James's incredible birthday party, the Americans landing on the moon, to be followed only a few days later by Senator Edward Kennedy driving off a bridge on Chappaquiddick Island in Massachusetts with a secretary called Mary Jo Kopechne in the passenger seat. He survived, she drowned, and the rest was shrouded in mystery. In August almost four hundred thousand people had attended the Woodstock Festival in upstate New York, braving what must have been stupendously uncomfortable conditions since it poured half the time, and sanitation was reported as being medieval. But good vibes and music from the stratosphere had transformed the festival into an instant legend, and I wished I had been there. In Vietnam fifteen hundred Viet Cong had been killed in a twenty-four-hour period, and the unbelievable Rod Laver had won the United States Open tennis on September 8, becoming the first man to win the Grand Slam twice.

Through my study window, the only part of the room above ground level, I could see the school starting to congregate along the touchlines to watch the first XV rugger match scheduled to begin at three. My study mate, Trevorrow, an amusing anti-authority type, had gone out with his parents for lunch, so I had the place to myself. About ten foot square, the room accommodated in cosy fashion two desks, a couple of bookshelves, a small sofa, coffee table, record player, and a corner by the door for the kettle and portable gas burner. Nine or ten such rooms lined the corridor underneath the west colonnade and provided the social hub of all mid-level-to-senior boys in the house.

At five to three I put my navy blue overcoat back on, wrapped a long scarf round my neck, and went back up to watch the rugger. Joining some friends from another house, we offered some frenzied vocal support as Stowe kicked off and thirty supposedly civilized young gentlemen set about battering and bruising each other with furious abandon, attempting to trample the opposition into the mud—stomping on hands, booting testicles, jarring knees with bone-crushing shoulder tackles, all the while trying desperately to score by crossing the opponents' line and touching the ground with the egg-shaped ball.

Aside from demonstrating one's enormous masculinity, I could never fathom why anybody volunteered to play this peculiar sport. Oliver assured me there was no better game on earth, but as I watched them all charging around in the freezing cold like demented bull terriers, I simply thought, rather them than me.

Midway through the first half, I looked over for the umpteenth time towards the main drive, and there, miraculously, it was: the best-looking sports car in the world with the best-looking couple I knew seated within, rolling gently past the pavilion, heading, as I had suggested, for the slip road adjacent to my study block. I felt a surge of excitement combined with immense relief. People around me had turned to stare, some asking if I knew who it was. "Indeed I do!" I said, deriving fantastic pleasure from telling them.

James and Charlotte, both wearing leather jackets and jeans, got out of the car and took in their surroundings, the epitome of good looks and rakish cool, and as we walked towards each other I knew that image would lodge itself in my memory forever.

"I'm really sorry," James said. "We were a little late setting off." I kissed Charlotte and she apologized too. "Look, we've cancelled our dinner so we can take you out for supper instead. Is that all right?" she asked.

"That's terrific, thank you, but are you sure? I don't want to upset your plans."

"Absolutely," she went on. "We're staying with friends not far away, so we'll join them later in the evening."

"Excellent," I said. "So how would you like to watch the rugger for a while?"

"Too damn cold, I'd say," James stated. "What do you think, darling?"

"I'd love a cup of coffee, if that's possible," Charlotte suggested.

Coffee in the study it was. Despite his former prowess on the rugby field, James had long since transferred his allegiance to sports of a more drawing-room-like nature, with the occasional foray, when time and company permitted, onto the golf course or tennis court. Furthermore, this was the first time he'd come to visit me at Stowe, and I wanted to show him around. In fact, I wanted to show him—them—off.

We mounted the west colonnade steps, walked past the tuck-box room (where Peter and I had, long ago, got our friendship off to a resounding, nicotine-infused start surrounded by locked-up sweets and biscuits by the ton), past the junior changing rooms, and entered the main building through a sturdy door painted dark green. The relief from the cold was immediate. Going by the head-of-house's two-floor private domain, we went down the stairs to the study block.

Gratefully ensconced in the warm room, I made coffee, James lit up a Dunhill International cigarette, an exotically packaged affair, and Charlotte made her ravishing self comfortable on the sofa. "This is not bad. Not bad at all," James said, looking around the room and puffing away Humphrey Bogart–style. "May I presume that is yours?" he judged accurately, pointing to the larger, neater, and more antique of the two desks that faced each other underneath the window.

"How could you possibly tell?" I grinned at him, not needing a reply. "Perhaps I'll have a puff myself since you're here. Normally one has to troop off into the wilds when the urge for a cigarette strikes."

"Go ahead." James passed me his luxury brand and gold Dunhill lighter.

The car was an E-type 4.2 (2+2), which meant, in theory, that two people could sit in the back. As I squeezed into a semi-contorted sideways position, I ruminated upon exactly how small those two people would have to be. Images of stuffing myself into Granny A's Beetle in Ireland also came to mind. But the E-type was a monstrously exciting car: visually sensational, fast as lightning, and rock solid on the road. It was six thirty and completely dark as James accelerated hard down the three-quarter-mile-long dead-straight section of the main drive. In a flash the speedometer nudged eighty miles per hour, although it felt more like fifty. My brother was a very good driver who inspired confidence in his passengers.

The ten-mile-drive along narrow country lanes, past Silverstone race track, to the Green Man for supper was a rapid and exhilarating experience. The Green Man was a classic English country pub, low beams and dark wood abounding, the walls plastered with hunting prints and portraits of inebriated gentlemen wearing Edwardian frock coats, talking to their dogs. Much to our surprise, we were able to commandeer a small table in the corner. Despite the room being jammed to the rafters, this crowd of revellers clearly preferred to drink standing up. Food, if food was on the agenda, would come later.

James and Charlotte drank beer, while Coca-Cola remained my beverage of choice. Steak-and-kidney pie was available and ordered for three, along with mashed potato and peas. Good things do come to those who wait!

I sat back and enjoyed the company, observing, as always, the wonderful rapport between James and Charlotte, their obvious closeness, and thought, it doesn't get much better than this. We talked at length about what I'd shown them of the school, eliciting no more than neutral observations from either, which told me they already had an understanding of my feelings on the subject. We laughed a lot about the birthday party, a sensational affair which had succeeded in shocking our parents, and others, by both the appearance and behaviour of many of the guests, some of whom had had the misfortune to be interrupted by members of the older generation while having enthusiastic sex in their motor cars.

It was past nine o'clock when they dropped me back at

Stowe. I'd told James about a Spinners concert taking place at the school the weekend after next. We both really enjoyed the folk group's music, and he told me he was going to try and come. I loved being around James. His style, his joie de vivre, was always such a kick. We said good-bye, and they roared off into the night.

Two weeks later I was in my study working on a history essay—Trevorrow was also busy at his desk—when someone knocked on the door. I couldn't imagine who'd be paying us a visit at eight thirty in the evening. The door opened, and a junior boy informed me that Mr. Vinan, my new housemaster, wished to see me in his study. Not, to my knowledge, having transgressed significantly in the recent past, I had no idea as to why my presence might be required. I put on my jacket, went up the stairs, turned left into the main thoroughfare between our house and the North-Front entrance hall, and after a few paces wheeled left to face Mr. Vinan's study door. It was ajar. I knocked and immediately heard him say, "Come in."

He was seated at his desk, an expression of rigid blankness on his face, holding the telephone to his ear but not speaking. Without looking directly at me, he stood up, came round the desk, holding the telephone out towards me. "It's your father," he said.

As I took the phone from his hand, he immediately strode out of the room, closing the door behind him. Mystified, but with a creeping wariness, I spoke tentatively into the mouthpiece. "Hello."

Something was wrong. My father sounded strange. Then he said he had bad news. "It's pretty rough. You'd better brace yourself." My mind raced. What could have happened? There was a desperate quality in my father's voice that I had never heard before.

"It's James," he said. "He's had a motor accident . . . it happened this morning . . . he was killed."

A physical force hit me in the chest. It felt like a boxer had just punched me with all his might. I gripped the telephone harder and gulped a few times, as if something had become wedged in my throat. Suddenly the room felt claustrophobic. My father was still talking, but his words had become a blur. My mother came on the line. When I heard her voice, I could control myself no longer. I burst into tears. She tried so hard to be strong and to comfort me. But I could not be comforted. Nor could I speak. After a few minutes we agreed to hang up and call again in the morning.

I had understood that my parents had gone to my godfather Sir Francis Peek's house in the country for the weekend. It was Friday. The accident had occurred that morning in north London, and the police had taken most of the day to track them down.

As I walked out of the study, the weight and brutality of the news started to invade every fibre of my body. I needed air. I went out, through the dark green door which only two weeks before I had passed through so happily with my brother and his girlfriend. It was cold and raining, but I felt neither. I walked and cried through the night. Only the lights of the school reminded me where I was.

For the first time in my life I had come face-to-face with the shattering nature and force of crushing sadness. James was dead. For the time being I was inconsolable, and there was nothing I, or anybody, could do. I cried until there were no tears left inside me. I called out his name until my throat was raw. When I returned to my house I was soaked and dishevelled from top to toe. I had no energy or inclination to clean up. It was the middle of the night. I dumped my clothes, put on my pyjamas, ran a towel over my head, and went to bed. I must have exhausted all my reserves. I slept.

Sunlight, cruel, demanding, insensitive, insistent, streamed through the tall bow windows of the castle dining room, casting corners filled with Chinese porcelain into dark shadow but saturating the eight of us seated at the polished mahogany table with bright, unwelcome intensity. My parents and Granny B were wearing sunglasses. I'd never seen that at the luncheon table before. Conversation was sparse. Words did not come, or at least not the kind of words that meant anything, or helped at all. Woody, so eloquent by nature, was almost silent, as were David, Vanessa, Nanny, and I. The depth of misery which hung palpably in the air was draining, debilitating. It had been eight days since the accident. No one mentioned James. The shock was still too present, the pain too raw.

My mother spent the afternoon in her bedroom in the Maiden's Tower while my father went, on his own, for the longest walk anyone recalled him ever taking. No one actually announced what they were going to do except Nanny, who understood that Vanessa should not stay cooped up unnecessarily on such a gorgeous day. David chose to read in the drawing room, and I went upstairs to be alone in the blue bedroom I had shared with my brother so happily, for so long.

I opened the cupboard by his bed and felt the tears well up seeing the familiar jackets and jumpers he'd worn only in the country. Going to the window, I saw my father striding out across the golf course, his pace a good deal quicker than usual.

"Good night sweet prince: / And flights of angels sing thee to thy rest!" I was reading *Hamlet* at school and couldn't dislodge Horatio's beautiful farewell from my mind.

But the past was now a shattered mirror. The protective shield of innocence was gone. Why, now, did I start thinking about how so many of Granny B's friends were no longer around? How so many loyal retainers, some going back three generations, were also no longer around? How Granny's health was deteriorating, her weekend house parties greatly reduced? How Uncle Gawaine, for reasons always unclear, had displayed no interest in living at Leeds? How Her Majesty's Government—I was reliably informed—was waiting in the wings, anticipating an 80 percent windfall on the estate when Granny B died, thereby removing any possibility of the castle's remaining a private home?

I had stared out of these same windows in a state of

extreme unhappiness that Christmas Day we learned that Morg had died. I was thirteen then. I was seventeen and a half when James died, and such was the shock to my system that I felt I would never be the same. His death left me wanting even more to be like him, in some way to try and fill his shoes. It was unrealistic to think I would ever come close, but I had to try. His death took away the guide I needed most when it came to understanding how to effectively, winningly, rock the boat. His charm, spirit, candour, and smarts had, over time, softened the castle way's grip on our household, and on our lives.

20.

THE UNWARY BENEFICIARY

I left Stowe in 1970 with a brace of decent A-levels in English and History. My father insisted I follow the rules and organized a job for me at Cooper Brothers and Co., Chartered Accountants, overlooking the fact that mathematics was something I'd never quite got the hang of. I knew that reminding him would be an error because he simply would have instructed me to pull my finger out and not be an ass, just as he had done on the two or three other occasions he had offered his counsel in the past. So I spent a year and a half wrestling with ledgers, charts, and figures in the heart of the City of London before admitting total defeat and quitting, probably as much to the relief of my employers as myself.

At twenty-one I came into the first portion of my trust fund (thanks to Granny B's generosity), and I moved out of David's Bayswater house into my own in South Kensington. Dreaming all the while of playing in a band, I found myself a job with J. Walter Thompson advertising. I had my sights on a post in the creative department as a copywriter, which a vocational guidance test my parents suggested (I wish they'd done that before the accounting idea) had proclaimed was my ideal job. But there was a two-year wait before I was permitted to take the copywriting test, and that was just too long.

The emerging pattern, clear to any interested party but entirely absent from my own thinking, was that the castle way's operating system, automatically downloading updates and adding additional layers of code, like Hal in *2001: A Space Odyssey*, was in charge of the ship and had been so, emphatically, since I was five.

In less than three and a half years I walked away from two potentially good careers simply because I wanted to and because I could. How many people are similarly blessed, or cursed? I had a house, I had a trust, and I wanted truly, madly, deeply to be a professional singer-songwriter. No laws were laid down by my parents as to how long this (to them) incomprehensible choice of occupation should be allowed to continue before the cash spigots were turned off. Perhaps that was because they had other more crucial matters on their minds. Their divorce in 1971, after twenty-five years of marriage, had come as a bitter blow to my mother, who appeared to be the last one to find out about my father's less than clandestine affair with a much younger French woman, a relationship that had been going on long before James's accident. Fortunately, after suffering a near–mental breakdown, my mother found happiness with Col. Edward Remington-

Hobbs, a small-business owner, whom she married in 1972. They, too, spent twenty-five years together until his death in 1997.

The bubble in which I had existed did breed a mind-set all of its own. It had enveloped me everywhere I went. It had told me I was richer (without needing any actual money) and better than the rest. It had told me that I could have everything I wanted and that my position at the top of the heap would remain sacrosanct and unchallenged forever without my having to achieve a thing. Those had been unsuitable thoughts for a child on the cusp of being sent off to boarding school for the next ten years, but for a young adult seeking a way to make his mark such thoughts had moved into the realm of the dangerous.

Four years after my brother's death, I was playing in a band in London, performing in pubs and clubs and the occasional far-off university, happy at last and brimful of confidence in achieving success down the road. Regrettably, I was again ill prepared for the realities of life when, in 1974, I met with Ahmet Ertegun, the legendary, charismatic cofounder and chairman of Atlantic Records, a friend of my father's, to see if he would consider signing me to his label.

"How do you plan to make it?" he asked me in the drawing room of his London house after listening to four of my self-composed demo recordings. As always, he was dressed in a perfectly cut suit with formal shirt and tie—so unlike most other music executives—and exuding a powerful cocktail of bonhomie and hard-nosed professionalism. He was leaning forward in his chair, staring at me through oval glasses which emphasized the size of his eyes and the force of his gaze.

My plan "to make it," if it could be called such, was to get a record contract, have hits, and go out and play them in front of enthusiastic audiences. Instead of dismissing me out of hand, Ahmet said, "I'm going to put you in the studio with Dave Dee (who'd been a pop star himself with Dave Dee, Dozy, Beaky, Mick, and Tich) as producer, and I want you to record five singles for me. Your best tunes." His hoarse growl seemed to convey a modicum of optimism about the outcome, and he made no mention of "paying dues"—the act of playing the clubs, building an audience, and becoming a seasoned performer—as one or two well-known musicians, including Eric Clapton, later did to me. But with great kindness and generosity he gave me the opportunity to see if I could come up with something to disprove what his instincts were telling him: The kid may be good; he certainly has ambition; but he's been brought up in a different world; he's naive about the music business; he's naive about life. His heart's in the right place, but his head tells him all the wrong things—no "blood, toil, tears and sweat" required. Atlantic Records eventually turned me down—and the castle way's operating system marched on.

It is one of life's more regrettable features that the most

important life decisions are often made when one is young, irrational, lacking in experience, and (oh dear) frequently plain dumb. One's upbringing either fills or leaves empty the common-sense larder, either promotes or ignores the importance of being serious, either nurtures or casts aside the essence of self-awareness. In all three cases the castle way maintained a lofty indifference, thereby ensuring less than desirable outcomes most of the time. I was consumed with ambition and, according to some, not a bad singer and player. A top London producer wanted to turn me into "the next David Cassidy," but I insisted on playing my own brand of self-written melodic pop. I should have listened: It might have opened the door.

Three years later Mick Jagger informed my glamorous French girlfriend, Florence (whom our mutual friend Taki Theodoracopoulos, the famous playboy, journalist, and gossip columnist, christened "the High Priestess of the Jet Set"), that I would never make it in music because I was too posh, too damn spoiled, too *right side of the tracks*. He even said to me once—with a slight sneer—"Of course, *I* didn't grow up at Leeds Castle!"

Music helped me distance myself from the castle way, but it was too ingrained to disappear over the horizon never to be heard from again. Its power as a curse upon motivation and normalcy had resulted in my first twenty years on Planet Earth becoming a minefield of mixed-up emotions and complicated mind games. The creature comforts were never less than dazzling, but detecting and disarming the mines had been left almost entirely to Nanny, and her expertise in this field was, on the surface, rather limited.

But if Bertrand Russell was correct that "the point of philosophy is to start with something so simple as not to seem worth stating, and to end with something so paradoxical that no one will believe it," then Nanny was clearly onto something. "There, there," she would reassuringly tell me whenever things were looking grim. "I expect you'll muddle through." She wasn't, of course, trying to be rude or put me down by mapping out my entire future in one curt phrase, but it turned out she was right on the money. No bright lights. No glittering career. The castle way and I kept close and consistent watch over one another, and like ragged misfits we muddled our way through a sometimes enterprising but generally mismanaged life. Family welfare (a trust fund periodically topped up) and an inheritance when my mother died in 2001 virtually guaranteed that the huge holes in my understanding of how the world works would remain untouched by toil and trouble. I have travelled umpteen times to the fleshpots of the world but failed to make intelligent use of the proverbial silver spoon. It's obvious now that the castle way and rock music (just like the castle way and family holidays) were never going to see eye to eye despite my best effort to make them.

21.

THE MAN AT THE GATE

Shakespeare, in his most famous sonnet, chose to compare the beauty of his undisclosed subject to a summer's day, and that element of perfection was everywhere to be seen, and felt, when I visited Leeds Castle on a sublime Monday afternoon in August 2009, not having been back since my mother died in April 2001.

My wife, Catherine, and I had been staying with my brother, David, a local councillor and businessman, and his wife, Tia, an antique collector and gardening maestro, in their fine Georgian house on the outskirts of Rye, a picturesque medieval town on the Sussex coast. David's life had also been crucially touched by the castle way and its hard-line programming, but, never one to make a fuss, the furthest he ever cared to go in expressing his feelings on the subject to me was, "I suppose we were brought up a little soft." Academically and intellectually very bright, I'm sure the careers my brother started but didn't quite finish, including publishing and property development, would have turned out very differently but for the troubled waters of our castle way upbringing.

My wife and I decided we would visit my mother's grave at St Nicholas's Church in Leeds village before continuing on our way back to London. After spending half an hour in the pretty churchyard, where natural meadow grasses flourish year-round and the gravestones are dotted haphazardly about as if indulging the untidiness of death, we entered the magnificent eight-hundred-year-old Saxon/Norman church, with its massive twelfth-century tower, high steeple, and intricately carved rood screen separating nave from chancel, and a flood of childhood and adult memories came rushing back, prompting me to suggest to Catherine that we should drive over to the castle to see if they would let us in without, perhaps, having to pay the £16.50 entrance fee.

Granny B had devoted her life, and vast amounts of money, to exquisitely restoring and maintaining Leeds Castle's splendour. Before she died, in September 1974, she bequeathed it to the nation with an endowment of one and a half million pounds. I was not at all ready to start becoming a paying customer.

With few exceptions (golfers for the most part) all visitors now arrived at the new front drive main gate, two hundred yards off the A20 London-to-Dover road. The park drive, which bisects the other two, runs uphill past the cricket pitch directly towards Leeds village, was unattended but had a barrier for which one needed a pass card. I sensed that the back drive golfers' entrance, just off the narrow country lane to Broomfield village, would provide a calmer negotiating forum, and so it turned out to be.

We pulled up alongside a grassy verge which bordered what had been the seventh hole of golf (castle guests and family, for aesthetic and convenience purposes, always began their morning nine holes at the third hole because it was an easier, shorter, more pleasing walk, across grass, not tarmac, meandering alongside the moat) and studied the situation. There was a single gentleman, about sixty, wearing a flat cap and jacket, attending the barrier, which was down. There was nobody else in sight. We looked at him and he at us. He must have wondered what the devil we were doing parked where, essentially, there was nowhere to park. I started daydreaming of the countless times I had played this long, impressive hole of golf with tall trees bordering the left side of the fairway and a row of firs standing guard over the green, which was protected first by a deep valley and then by a wide, treacherous bunker directly in front.

"Are we going in?" Catherine was obliged to ask as my reverie continued unabated. Now that the family connection had, regrettably, been allowed to fade, I was unsure as to what form of welcome we would receive.

"Indeed we are," I responded, crossing the road, pulling up to the barrier, and lowering my window all the way down: "Good afternoon."

"Good afternoon." He was a well-built man with a country-man's unself-conscious demeanour. The look on his wide, weathered face was neutral.

"My name's Anthony Russell. I'm Mrs. Remington-Hobbs's son, Lady Baillie's grandson. I was wondering if it might be possible for us to come in and have a look around. I haven't been back since my mother died."

His reaction took me by surprise. He came up to the car, leaned down, and shook my hand with a firm grip that didn't let go, and with his other hand he took my arm and held it, too. It was as if he could not believe it was me, and that my being there could be confirmed only by physical contact. No words were exchanged for a moment. He then released my arm but, still holding my hand, began to speak of my mother and of my stepfather, Col. Teddy Remington-Hobbs.

"I remember your mother and the colonel. I've been at the castle for about sixteen years now, and I got to know them very well. They are truly missed by everyone who knew them. Sadly there are not many left that did." He stood, releasing my hand, and I saw the discreet pin with "Les Bray" written on it. "The things that stick in my mind are their daily walks around the estate when they would happily talk to everyone and sign their guidebooks for them, and the colonel driving through the grounds with his table-tennis bat held up with a large 'Thank you' on it if people moved out of the way. Your mother would pose for pictures with the visitors, usually with the castle in the background of course."

I remembered my mother and stepfather doing just as Les

was describing. Since the opening of the castle and grounds to the public in 1976 I had frequently witnessed them interacting with the ever-increasing number of visitors. Though her former home had been, with some haste due to my grandmother's failing health, established as a public charity (the Leeds Castle Foundation) in order to avoid stratospheric death duties my mother saw to it that all those she came into contact with were afforded her warm, personal welcome, as her mother would surely have wished.

"At Christmas," Les said, "we used to have a staff party held at the local hotel—sadly no more—and they were the guests of honour. They would join in with the dancing and have a great time giving out prizes to the staff. Your mother knew everyone's name. She was very special. I wish they were here now."

Our family connection to Leeds had lasted seventy-five years, one of the longest associations in the history of one of England's oldest and most romantic "stately homes."

"I'll radio up to the office to tell them you're here," Les said. "Would you mind driving up there to get your passes? It's where the old laundry used to be."

Ah! The laundry! It had been managed in the fifties and sixties by Mr. and Mrs. Love, with three female assistants. On my bicycle tours, when not engaged in high-speed downhill trials, ignoring the possibility of any estate worker in his car coming round a corner from the opposite direction, I'd sometimes stop to peer through the tall windows and watch the ladies skillfully manoeuvring sheets through the gigantic roller, or ironing linen napkins, power cords dangling from the ceiling like puppeteers' strings. A private laundry apparently was a must because all the sheets were custom made for the enormous four-poster castle beds, and all the linens were from Porthault, in Paris, and hand embroidered in Italy. To send these delicate items out to be washed and ironed every week Granny B had deemed hazardous for their survival.

"Okay, we'll do that, thanks very much. It's been a pleasure meeting you."

"Likewise."

We set off for the estate office, and in my rearview mirror I saw Les bringing the barrier back down. His heartfelt words had touched me, and straightaway I regretted not telling him so. If I could kick myself for all the times I might have said something meaningful to someone when the situation had called for it, but failed to do so, held back by an invisible force that decreed, "Let's avoid sounding a little too dramatic, shall we?"—or, sometimes just by a simple lack of emotional dexterity—I would have a sorer bum than a constantly beaten nineteenth-century English public schoolboy.

Perhaps the most egregious missed opportunity of all was never telling Nanny how much she'd meant to me. At the very least she had deserved a resounding affirmation of my love for her, and it would have been so natural, so easy, during one of my visits to the cosy retirement apartment in Wimbledon my parents had bought for her, close to the famous tennis courts, to finally say the words. But they didn't come, and after she died in 1976 I felt ashamed of my weakness.

Les had reminded me not just of my mother and grandmother's lifelong connection to the castle and its people, but also of my own long-buried, deeply affecting ties, which rose to the surface as we drove slowly down the avenue of lime and sweet chestnut trees and the vision that is Leeds Castle, surrounded by her moat, golf course, and parkland, came once more into view.

"He was so pleased to meet you and talk about your family," Catherine told me. "It's clear he has fond memories of the way things used to be."

Forking left up the gentle hill towards the offices and what used to be called the stable yard, I easily succumbed to the nostalgia of the moment, aided and abetted by the afternoon's soft warmth and utter stillness.

"Me too."

Acknowledgments

I am incredibly grateful to a small number of people who made it possible for me write and publish *Outrageous Fortune: Growing Up at Leeds Castle*. Jennifer Repo, Gerald Sindell, and Bevis Hillier all lent their individual perspective and expertise in helping me to rework, restructure, and rebuild my earlier drafts. Thank you for giving me so much of your time and very special guidance. Also, thanks, Bevis, for outing some nasty clichés which (inexplicably) put in an appearance earlier on! Huge thanks to my editor at St. Martin's Press, Hope Dellon, for doing such a wonderful job on the book and, also, to her assistant editor, Silissa Kenney, who has been so kind and thoughtful to me throughout the lengthy process of "seeing into print." Thank you, Susan Llewellyn, for your copyediting; thanks to Chris Scheina for handling subsidiary rights; and thanks to the Art Department for a wonderful cover. My thanks to the Leeds Castle Foundation for permission to use photographs from their archives, and, especially, to Nic Fulcher, the former Heritage Manager at the castle, who assisted me greatly during my visits over the past two years. I look forward to meeting and working with everyone at the Leeds Castle Foundation in the future. To my friend and agent, Charlotte Gusay, I offer the biggest thank-you of all. You nurtured this project through every one of its stages and never gave up on me, even when a little hand-wringing entered the fray and a satisfactory end was still no-where in sight. Your enthusiasm for the book was infectious and provided me with extraordinary support. Thank you so much, Patt Morrison, for the introduction to Charlotte. Deepest, deepest thanks to my darling wife, Catherine. Everything good in life is due to you. You are also a fine and unflinching critic! Odo, what a son! I am truly proud of you. KBO.

Without you all there would be no *Outrageous Fortune*. Thanks again.

Anthony Russell
Los Angeles, June 2013